778.5
Kar
c.2   Kardish, Laurence

Reel Plastic Magic

778.5
Kar
c.2   Kardish, Laurence

20261

        Reel Plastic Magic

Siskiyou County Schools Library
Yreka, California

Reel Plastic Magic

Reel Plastic Magic

A History of Films and Filmmaking in America

LAURENCE KARDISH

Little, Brown and Company
BOSTON   TORONTO

To Sam and Tillie Kardish

COPYRIGHT © 1972 BY LAURENCE KARDISH

ALL RIGHTS RESERVED. NO PART OF THIS BOOK MAY BE REPRODUCED IN ANY FORM OR BY ANY ELECTRONIC OR MECHANICAL MEANS INCLUDING INFORMATION STORAGE AND RETRIEVAL SYSTEMS WITHOUT PERMISSION IN WRITING FROM THE PUBLISHER, EXCEPT BY A REVIEWER WHO MAY QUOTE BRIEF PASSAGES IN A REVIEW.

LIBRARY OF CONGRESS CATALOG CARD NO. 71-154965

FIRST EDITION

T 06/72

Published simultaneously in Canada
by Little, Brown & Company (Canada) Limited

PRINTED IN THE UNITED STATES OF AMERICA

Contents

1 Nitty-Gritty   3

2 On the Way to the White House   27

3 From Czar to Czar   81

4 Some Talents in and around Hollywood   106

5 Big Breaks   177

6 Another Cinema   212

7 Future Promise   248

A Highly Selective Bibliography   254

One Hundred Programs Illustrating the Growth and Scope of the American Film   258

Index of Films   281

General Index   287

Acknowledgments

Although there is some original material in the text, this book is not meant to be an original history. Rather it hopes to be a brief but comprehensive introduction to American filmmakers and filmmaking. The audience to which this book is addressed is young, curious about film, and without the background information to ponder more academic texts. This author hopes not only to satisfy the reader's curiosity but to further whet his appetite and send him to the films themselves. To this end I have used some information that has been collected by others, and to these other authors I would like to express my gratitude.

Many of the photographs in the book come from the still collection within the Museum of Modern Art, and I am most indebted to Mary Yushak Corliss, Stills Archivist, for her cooperation in the selection of these stills.

Reel Plastic Magic

1 Nitty-Gritty

More than a third of the time an audience spends watching a film, it spends in total darkness. It watches a blank screen. It must. Why?

To answer that, we must explain just what film is. What is its physical nature and why must it be as it is? When a reader picks up a book he picks up the actual material — ink on bound paper — from which he will derive his education and/or enjoyment. All the reader need bring to the book are his eyes and his mind. When a moviegoer picks up a piece of film, his eyes and mind won't do much for him. Until the film is projected, it has no meaning, force or power. The whole motion picture experience results from a combination of factors of which film is only one, inanimate part. At present it is a substantial one, but in the past there were motion pictures without film. Most certainly in the future, film will play a less important role in motion pictures than it does today. Indeed, it might disappear altogether.

The factors which combine to make the motion picture experience possible date back to observations made thousands of years ago, but it was not until the middle of the 1800's that many of these observations were translated into material terms. At the end of that century technology and scientific interest saw that these bits of material were integrated in a certain way, and this certain way gave the world the kind of motion picture it has known for seventy-five years.

It was the ancient Greek philosopher, Aristotle, who noted something wonderfully peculiar about a dark room. If there were a small hole in the wall, the sun outside would cast a circular spot of light onto the facing wall. So what?

3

At the original Olympics, it was also noted that when a discus hurler threw his stone his rapid arm movement seemed to describe a continuous arc in the air. His arm seemed to be in many places at once. So what? So, in these two observations, the origins of the contemporary motion picture experience were noted.

In Renaissance Italy Leonardo da Vinci took the dark-room observation and pursued it further. Not only did Leonardo see an area of light cast upon the facing wall, he also recognized that in the light there was an image of the area immediately outside the hole on the wall! The image was upside down, but it was learned that it could be righted with the use of mirrors. The image was fuzzy, yet it could be sharpened or "focused" with a lens. But the image was not permanent. It did not stay still on the wall. It disappeared when the sun went down, when the room brightened, or, in the natural course of events, it changed with the street outside. On Monday, a tree might be growing just outside the wall. At noon the image of that tree might appear on the wall opposite the hole. On Monday evening the tree might have been cut down to make way for a new church. If so, then on Tuesday noon an image of the church's first bricks would appear on the wall. The image of the Monday tree would be lost, only remaining as a memory in the viewer's mind.

The image in the viewer's mind has much to do with the second observation the ancients made. Instead of a discus hurler, watch a pitcher as he warms up. His pitching arm seems to be in several positions at once, describing a continuous line in the air. Wave a flashlight about, and a blur of light seems still to exist in those spaces where the flashlight has been waved a moment earlier.

Why? — because of a strange condition of human vision. This condition has often been described as a flaw in the human makeup. If so, then it is a glorious flaw. Without it there would be no motion picture experience.

When anything — any scene, any object — is observed, the image of that object remains in the mind for a short while. The viewer may turn away or close his eyes, but the image of whatever he has perceived stays with him for a very short time. This phenomenon of the afterimage is sometimes referred to as persistence of vision because one can see something for a split second even after the thing one was perceiving is removed. It now may be clear why the flashlight seems

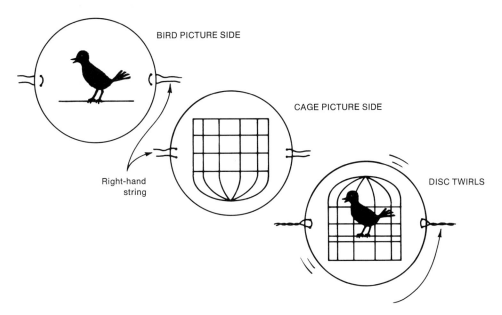

BIRD PICTURE SIDE

CAGE PICTURE SIDE

Right-hand
string

DISC TWIRLS

11. *The Thaumatrope, marketed under several names, including Wonder Disc.*

to draw one steady line of light. The viewer sees the fast-moving object not only where it is now but also where it was a split second ago.

A fine Christmas present given to children in the 1820's was a little flat disc called the Thaumatrope or "Wonder Wheel" (see Figure 11). Both sides of the disc were painted with different pictures. One side might have been painted with the image of a bird, the other of a cage. Strings were attached to the edges of the disc so that it could be twirled. When the disc was twirled the image of the bird and that of the cage merged. The two separate pictures became one image of a bird in a cage.

Later in the century a more sophisticated amusement received much popularity — the Zoëtrope or "Wheel of Life." There were many variations of this toy and each was given a name as formidable and fancy as Zoëtrope. Each of these names derived from Greek or Latin words, and when translated, many of them meant "illusion" or "motion." Indeed, motion is how the "Wheel of Life" improved upon the Thaumatrope.

The Thaumatrope merely used the basic idea of the afterimage; the "Wheel of Life" developed this idea. It used the afterimage to make its pictures move. How did this contraption work?

5

12. *The Zoötrope or Zoëtrope (Wheel of Life). By revolving the cylinder and peeking into the slot, one would see the jester juggling the balls.* (Museum of Modern Art/Film Stills Archive)

It was a cylinder, opened at the top, mounted on a stand. The cylinder could spin, and narrow slits were cut at regular intervals in its upper half. Along its bottom a cardboard strip was placed. On this strip were drawn a series of figures doing some activity (see Figure 12). One strip might depict a stick figure in various stages of jumping, another a face alternately smiling and frowning. The strip

6

was placed in the cylinder and the cylinder rotated. A spectator put his eyes to the slits. The slits would revolve rapidly and quickly. What would the viewer truly see? He would see a drawing and then, as the cylinder revolved from slit to slit, nothing, and then another drawing, and then nothing and so on. The slight pause between the separate images was necessary, because while the afterimage was making an impression on the viewer's mind, his sight had to be cleared to see the second picture. If there were no split-second pause between pictures, they would all merge in the viewer's mind, and he would see nothing more than a formless blur.

The viewer, however, would not be conscious of this process. So quickly would the cylinder revolve that the afterimage of the first drawing was still fresh in the mind when the second appeared. The two images fused and the stick figure would appear to be actually jumping, and the face really moving from a smile to a frown. Suddenly the inanimate hand drawings seemed to take on a mobile life of their own. Sounds incredible? If it does, try flipping the bottom corners of the first few pages of this book (Figures 1 – 10).

The "Wheel of Life" might have become a more popular novelty had it not been for the fact that all the figures it used had to be hand-drawn. This was an exacting and time-consuming task. What was needed and what was wanted was a system whereby hand-drawings could be eliminated. Some more economical method of "capturing reality" was desired. This method would have to be both more reliable and quicker than the artist's hand.

A Frenchman, Louis Jacques Mandé Daguerre, was a distinguished set designer, who had the pedestrian ambition to produce landscapes for the Opéra that were so real one would think that Mother Nature herself was the artist. In 1829 Daguerre entered into partnership with Joseph Nicéphore Niepce, an inventor, who may have taken the first photograph as early as 1816. Out of the partnership of Daguerre and Niepce came permanent photographic records of still life, which were burnt into metal. These copper plates were known as daguerrotypes, and they were named after the co-inventor, who survived his partner. Meanwhile, quite independently of the Frenchman, an English linguist, mathematician and scientist was pursuing his own investigations into a means of capturing an image

7

of nature and indefinitely preserving it. But, while Daguerre used a metal base, William Henry Fox Talbot was experimenting with paper and calling his discoveries "photogenic drawings." Although film had yet to be invented, it was the work of these men with metal, paper, and even glass that gave birth to the modern art and science of photography.

Today, "atomic" cameras can snap a photograph in a millionth of a second. When photography was in its earliest development, a quarter hour was still too short a time for an image to be captured. Why?

The example of the darkened room will help us once more. A literal translation into Latin of the words "dark room" is *camera obscura,* and the camera obscura is what that Renaissance man, Leonardo, called the dark-room phenomenon. A photographic camera is little more than a camera obscura, that is, a dark room. The dark room is the black chamber inside the camera behind the shutter. The shutter keeps out all light. When the shutter is moved an aperture, a pinhole opening to the outside world, is revealed. The aperture is like the hole in the wall of the dark room. As the light rays enter the camera into the dark room, they pass through a lens where they are focused. They are focused so that when they "hit" the "back wall" the images which they carry will be clear and sharp. (See Figures 13–16.)

In the camera obscura the back wall was nothing more than an ordinary wall. In the photographic camera, this wall is much more. It is a physical substance coated with certain chemicals which "capture" or "fix" the image. The chemical solution which does the entrapment is known as the emulsion, and the physical substance (metal, glass, paper, celluloid) to which the emulsion adheres is known as the base. Once the image is captured on the "back wall," it is removed from the camera and treated to further chemical processes. Eventually the image can be transferred or printed onto other substances.

For thirty years images could not be captured quickly. Emulsions reacted slowly to light rays. The image carried into the camera by the rays had to remain steady and constant for several minutes at a time. For the image to remain clear, the subject of the picture had to

8

remain stationary. This is why the first photographs taken tended to be of deserted studios and empty farmyards. People sitting for portrait photographers had the hard task of remaining immobile for up to a quarter of an hour. In the last century there was a joke that the only person to whom a Congressman would listen was his photographer — the Congressman had no choice; he couldn't move! The important thing to note is that early photographic methods could not adequately record any form of motion.

In 1861, a Philadelphia merchant, Coleman Sellers, took a series of photographs of a figure posed in various phases of a simple motion. He fitted this series onto a variation of the "Wheel of Life." Playing the Greek and Latin word game, in order to give his apparatus the same prestige the European contraptions enjoyed, he dubbed his creation the Kinematoscope. What is interesting about this name is that it is one of the first times a film historian encounters the word "kinema." From *kinema*, the Greek word for motion, comes "cinema" and "cinema" is a word that has come to mean the motion picture experience.

The Kinematoscope was a wheel of life fitted not with hand-drawings but with still photographs. Thanks to the phenomenon of the afterimage, one still photograph of a man jumping would merge into the next, of the man a little further along into this activity. The fusion of one still photograph into the afterimage of the last created in the viewer's mind the illusion of motion.

The Kinematoscope had a lot to do with motion pictures, but because its photographs were printed on glass plates and each was separate from the other, the Kinematoscope had little to do with film.

By 1872 with the help of fast-acting emulsions, the camera's vision began to outclass that of the human eye. Can you tell, just by looking at a horse in motion, whether he lifts all his legs off the ground at any one time during a gallop? For thousands of years artists could not; thus all paintings of a galloping horse were to some extent imaginary. The artists' perception was not discerning enough to catch this detail of animal locomotion. In 1872 Governor Leland Stanford of California, a breeder of horses and a noted sportsman, made a twenty-five-thousand-dollar bet. He was certain that a horse in gal-

9

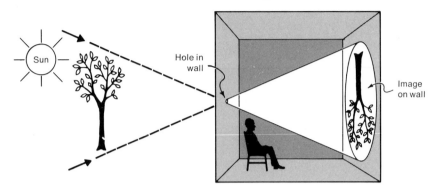

13.   *Let's say you are in a room. On the wall behind you there's a hole. Outside the room there is a tree standing in the sunshine. The light rays from outside come in through the hole and bring with them the image of the tree. This image appears on the wall opposite the hole. Although the image of the tree is upside down and fuzzy, it can be focused if you outfit the hole with a mirror and lens system.*

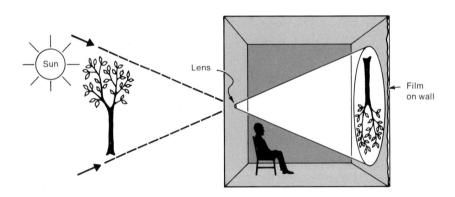

14.   *The image, however, is transitory, and disappears when the sun sets. If you want to "keep" it even after the sun has set or the tree has been chopped down, you can coat the wall with chemicals that "fix" the image permanently onto a special substance which retains that image for a long time. What have you done? You have turned the dark room or chamber (camera obscura) into a primitive camera. The back wall is no longer just a wall but becomes in effect a cover of photographic film. The hole in the wall can now be outfitted with both a shutter to control how much light is let in and a lens to focus the image clearly.*

10

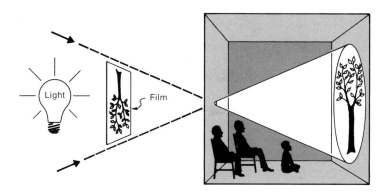

15.   *Now that you have captured the image of the tree, you decide one night to share it with a group of friends. How? By working backwards. You don't have the sun, but you do have an electric light. You don't have the tree but you do have its image, and you certainly have the dark room with a hole in it. So, if you go outside in the dark and take your light and shine it through the semitransparent "Wall/film" image of the tree, the light rays will carry the image of the tree to the dark room where your friends are sitting.*

Box with light, image of tree, hole in box with lens

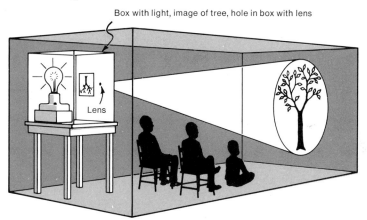

16.   *Now let's say it's cold outside and you want to present your friends with the image while you stay inside. You can build a little box in which the electric light shines past the tree image and through a small hole so that the light rays escape into the room. There is a lens fitted near the hole so that the image-bearing light rays will be in focus when they hit the far wall. What have you made? A primitive projector,* very primitive.

11

17. *Although this is not the sequence that won Governor Stanford his bet, this series of photographs illustrates the work for which Muybridge was famous.* (Museum of Modern Art/Film Stills Archive)

lop did raise its four legs off the ground. How could Stanford prove his point? Simple observation was not good enough; the horse's legs moved faster than the human eye could see, so Stanford came up with an excellent solution.

Stanford called upon a photographer based in California, Eadweard Muybridge (born Edward James Muggeridge), to help him win his bet. In solving Stanford's problem Muybridge, after many experiments, devised an interesting idea. He developed a high-speed camera which was in fact not one camera but a whole battery of them. Each was lined up close to the next, and to each shutter a cord was attached. The cords ran onto the raceway. As the horse

12

galloped past each camera, the cord was tripped and a picture snapped. Each picture was taken a fraction of a second after the last. After the pictures were developed and printed, they were laid side by side (see Figure 17). The movement of the horse was revealed. It was shown that during a gallop the horse *did* raise all its feet from the ground at once, and Stanford won his bet.

Muybridge went on to increase zoological knowledge by recording various types of human and animal locomotion, and his works attracted the attention of a French physiologist, Dr. J. E. Marey, who had been engaged in similar research activities.

Marey was interested in motion, and in attempting to study various methods of photographing animated states, the doctor hit upon an ingenious plan. Instead of using many cameras to photograph one image quickly after another, Marey mounted his photographic plates within a revolving cartridge on the barrel of a gun. In fact, Marey used a type of photographic revolver that had been developed in 1874 by an astronomer. His pictures were indeed snapped *shots*. Perhaps this is how the term "shooting films" entered our vocabulary. With one pull of the trigger, the cartridge, loaded not with bullets but with negatives on one glass plate, spun around the barrel, stopping not to fire a weapon, but to take a picture. (Shoot pictures, not people!)

All the images photographed were shot through the same lens. This is the essential difference between Marey's and Muybridge's machines. Marey's peaceful gun is considered to be an early, if primitive, motion picture camera.

An adequate base had to be found to which the picture would adhere. Glass was too inflexible, cumbersome, fragile, and expensive. Storage was a problem. With new chemical developments, paper was substituted for glass, but paper proved to be too susceptible to wear. Transparent celluloid, invented by the British and named by the Americans, was then tried as a base and discarded quickly because it proved to be even more inflexible than glass. However, by 1889, in the George Eastman photographic laboratories in Rochester, New York, a celluloid derivative, treated with fuel and banana oils, was produced which was transparent, strong and flexible. It became the base of photographic film.

13

This base was not developed specifically for taking motion pictures. Eastman had another idea. The Kodak snapshot camera had been designed for use by the American public. However, the original Kodaks came ready-loaded with a gelatinous base that could take twelve pictures. When those twelve shots were snapped, the whole camera had to be sent back to Rochester so that the negatives could be properly removed, processed, and at a cost of ten dollars (!) the camera reloaded. With the introduction of rolls of photographic film, the picture-taker could remove the film himself without having to send the bulky camera back to Rochester.

A customer request soon came to Rochester for a roll of film to be sent "with thanks." The request came from the laboratory of Thomas Alva Edison in New Jersey. Edison had been hoping to find some economical way of aligning motion pictures with his new and popular talking-machine, the Phonograph. Since his mind was occupied with a dozen other projects as well, the "wizard" had enlisted the services of young William Kennedy Laurie Dickson, to cogitate the problem with him.

Like so much film history, the following story of how Dickson came to work for Edison is an appealing legend. Because it was an attractive tale it became popular, and has often been mistaken for history. The tale reads that Dickson had wanted to work with Edison for many years. His youthful imagination had been fired by reports in the British press of the achievements of the American "magician." He wrote to Edison offering his services at a very small wage. Dickson admitted that he knew very little of what Edison was doing but that he would learn quickly. Edison sent back a somber note thanking Dickson for his interest and saying that he was not about to hire any more staff. He advised the young man to stay home. The young man didn't; he came to America and went, rejection slip in hand, straight to Edison. Edison hired him. So well did Dickson work out that within a short while he was entrusted with major research.

Actually, Dickson was born in France and moved to Virginia with his parents while still a young man. His interest in mechanical devices earned him a job with Edison. Apparently Dickson did not come to motion pictures through his work with the Phonograph; he had been intrigued with them for a while.

14

Dickson soon forgot his employer's concerns. He ceased to care about motion pictures as an adjunct to the Phonograph, and began to explore the possibilities of motion pictures themselves. Although he originally contacted Rochester in 1889, requesting a supply of the new photographic film for research not connected with motion pictures, by 1891 he had made the important connection. When Dickson began to have his pictures printed on the new nitrocellulose base, it marked the first days of a marriage between the movies and film. The marriage was to be so happy that the two terms became synonymous for almost three quarters of a century.

Out of Edison's laboratory and Dickson's investigations came the fabulous Kinetoscope of 1891, the machine to which most contemporary film equipment relates. The Kinetoscope was really a peep show. Only one person could see a film at a time. A penny deposited in a slot triggered a set of mechanisms which in turn enabled a viewer to peer into a slit at the top of the machine and see a motion picture. Some Kinetoscopes were outfitted with earphones so that a viewer could hear a somewhat synchronized recording. But it was not the earphone that caught the fancy of the public; it was the moving pictures.

Even though the patent for the Kinetoscope was registered in 1891, the first machines were not pressed into regular commercial service until April of 1894, when a whole battalion of Kinetoscopes opened to the public in a parlor on Lower Broadway in New York City.

How can these machines be described? Only by first understanding what Edison and Dickson did to the film they received from Eastman. The film of 1890 was not dissimilar to the material we know today. It was transparent, strong and flexible. It was and still is manufactured in long strips like a ribbon. The photographs were printed directly onto the cellulose. Hundreds, thousands of photographs, each taken a fraction of a second after the last, were all printed successively onto the one ribbon of film. Around each image a black border defined one photograph from the next. Since the black borders frame the photograph or image, a "frame" is what each separate photograph came to be called.

Unlike today's projectors in which film is wound onto a spool or

15

reel, in the Kinetoscope it was unwound, all forty feet, onto a complex system of rollers (see Figure 18). The rollers were activated when a nickel was deposited, and, moving, they would roll each frame up by the peephole slot. The glass in the peep slot was constructed with magnification powers. The image thus appeared bigger than the frame actually was. A rotating shutter by the slot shut out all light to the spectator when the border between frames came into view. This allowed a fraction of a second for a viewer's aftersight to take effect. Looking into a Kinetoscope a viewer saw forty different frames or photographs each second. He also did *not* see anything

18. *An inside view of the Edison-Dickson Kinetoscope. The film unwound on the rollers and was propelled by a viewer near a peephole in the machine's top.* (Museum of Modern Art/Film Stills Archive)

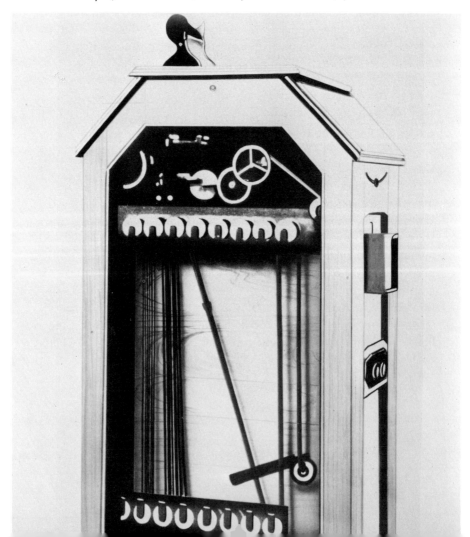

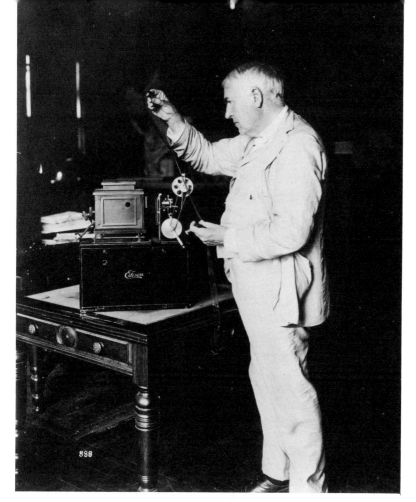

19.   *Thomas Alva Edison.* (Museum of Modern Art/Film Stills Archive)

forty times a second, but thought he was seeing one uninterrupted record of motion.

Reading about the history of film invites one to take another and more critical look at a favorite American hero, Mr. Thomas Alva Edison (Figure 19). Putting his contribution to motion pictures in perspective, Edison emerges as neither particularly original nor kind. Certainly he was not modest. After all, he claimed motion pictures to be his invention. Were they?

Edison's biography is the classic rags-to-riches story. What is remarkable about his life is that although he received less than three

17

months of formal education, he took out over a thousand patents for new contraptions. How was he able to do this? Edison was a "collective inventor." He borrowed and refined other people's ideas, and was more a spectacularly successful organizer of already established ideas than a dreamer out of whose fiery imagination sprang the basic inventions of mankind. In fact, there are very few of these dreamers, most inventors are of the collective sort.

Edison and his staff were all trained to keep abreast of international developments in the various sciences. His laboratory can be thought of as a forerunner to those divisions of today's large corporations engaged in applied research. Edison was aware of the needs of the American public, and to meet these needs economically, he sought ways of harnessing the new powers science had discovered. His triumphs did not come out of idle curiosity but rather out of practical considerations. What can be patented that people need? What can be mass-produced and sold at a profit? Invention in the Edison factory was a commercial thing. Historians today doubt Edison's self-professed humanitarian motives; his laboratory was business, pure and simple. It was based on capital, not charity.

Edison's experience with motion pictures speaks for itself. As we have seen, there was and is nothing new about the principles on which motion pictures are based. Photography came from France and England, and film from the Eastman laboratory in Rochester. Dickson, working in the Edison laboratory, was the man who integrated both these elements in the production of the Kinetoscope. True, it was Edison who initiated the research in New Jersey. But it must be remembered how he first considered the idea of motion pictures — as an adjunct to the already successful talking machine. It was Dickson who began to study motion pictures for their own sake. Indeed, so little did Edison think of this Kinetoscope novelty that it was not until three years after registration that the first Kinetoscope parlor was opened.

In registering the Kinetoscope patent in 1891, Edison made a serious miscalculation. He had the option of spending another $150 to protect his invention from foreign copy. Inventors, tinkerers and scientists in France, England, Germany, and Scandinavia were all toying with the idea of motion pictures during the last two decades

20. *One of the very earliest film studios, the Black Maria, designed by Dickson, in West Orange, New Jersey.* (Museum of Modern Art/Film Stills Archive)

of the nineteenth century, but Edison saw little reason for protecting his patent overseas. He thought the Kinetoscope would be an amusement of little value in history. He did not take out foreign registration, and so others were left free to copy the basic design of the machine. We are getting ahead of ourselves a bit, but this neglect came back to haunt Edison when he attempted to gain complete control over the making of movies in America.

Once Edison decided to manufacture the Kinetoscope he recognized that he would also have to manufacture film to be shown in it. In other words, a film studio had to be built. A big shack made of tar paper, the Black Maria (see Figure 20), was one of the world's first film studios. It was built in 1893 for the sum of $637.67.

The camera that shot film for the Kinetoscope was large and unwieldy. It could not be shifted with ease. It had to be housed where it could be permanently used and yet stored away from the vagaries of New Jersey weather. To accommodate the stationary camera,

19

the Black Maria was built on a circular track so that the whole construction could revolve. The ceiling of the Maria was built on hinges so it could be lifted. Once it was lifted, the sun's rays would light the studio, and as the sun traveled from east to west the whole building rotated, so that for every hour of daylight the sun would remain overhead above the stationary camera.

The first actors were Edison employees. Fred Ott, a mechanic, became famous for a close-up of his sneeze which was photographed for a pre-Kinetoscope (1888) experiment in motion pictures. A sneeze is hardly the most entertaining novelty, and when the Kinetoscope became popular, Edison and Dickson had to look elsewhere for their material. At first, vaudeville performers were pressed into service. They were asked to stage their most successful routines for the Kinetoscope camera. *The Butterfly Dance* (1894) performed by Annabelle Moore "in endless yards of silken draperies" was one, as

21. *The interior of a San Francisco Kinetoscope parlor in 1894.* (Museum of Modern Art/Film Stills Archive)

THE MUTOSCOPE.

rnal view, without the image cylinder. 2. Internal view with the cylinder in place. 3. Details of the mechanism seen from th front. 4. Details of the mechanism seen from behind.

22. *The Biograph Mutoscope.* (Museum of Modern Art/Film Stills Archive)

was *Fun In a Chinese Laundry* (1894). In this routine Hop Lee of the Heap Fun Laundry gets into trouble with a nutty policeman, and a small but frantic chase ensues.

The popularity of the Kinetoscope was astounding. Not only did hundreds of Kinetoscope parlors (see Figure 21) open up across the country within the next three years, but, as in all true business stories, success invited competition. The Mutoscope, although constructed in 1894, probably by Dickson himself, did not really become popular until 1897 when another machine from the Edison factory was laying the Kinetoscope to rest.

The Mutoscope (Figure 22) did not use film to provide the spectator with the illusion of motion. Within the body of the machine,

21

still photographs were mounted on individual cards in succession on one cylinder. When a penny or nickel (the price fluctuated) was deposited in the slot, each card in turn was flipped by the peephole and the illusion of motion was obtained. Slight variations of this machine still exist in penny arcades and at community fairs. Although the Mutoscope has had a longer life than its competitor, it is the Kinetoscope that is the more important in the growth of motion pictures because it used film.

The Mutoscope and the Kinetoscope shared one large problem. Each was a peep show, and only one person could be an audience at a time. Dickson was aware of the problem. How could many people see the same film at the same time? Dickson began to worry about how he could project a film.

In 1671, a Jesuit, Father Athanasius Kircher, who is now thought of as a charlatan (film history is full of them), wrote that someone had stolen his Magic Lantern idea. That someone, a Danish mathematician, he continued, was earning a healthy living by this plagiarism. Apparently, a quarter century earlier, the good Father had written a book in which various optical tricks were described. In this book, there was supposed to be a description of a machine designed to throw onto a far wall images painted on glass.

According to the cleric, the Danish mathematician read the book and copied the idea. In his second book, Father Kircher made a drawing of the plagiarized machine. It could not have done the job; it had no lens. Whether or not it was the Jesuit, the Danish mathematician or someone else who "discovered" the Magic Lantern is really not of interest to us. What is important to note is that projection devices must have existed at the time of Kircher's book, yet it took another two hundred and twenty years before this device was modified to meet the demands of handling motion pictures.

Today's projector does not vary much in basic principle from Kircher's supposed invention. And Kircher's Magic Lantern comes from the very same place as Leonardo's camera obscura, and that was the dark room Aristotle wrote about. Remember the hole in one wall of the dark room? Light rays streaming in from outside carry with them an image of the world immediately behind that hole. The images appear on the opposite wall. When a projector is in use, the audience sits in a darkened room. The only light in the room is the light that comes not from the outside but from the projector itself. This time the light does not bring into the room an image of the outside world, but an image of that which stands between its source and the opposite wall.

Think of it this way. The projector's light is analogous to the sun's light, the lens through which the light travels is the hole in the wall, and the transparent slide onto which an image is painted (or now, photographed) can be thought of as the world outside. The lens focuses the image, and the slides are submitted to the projector in an upside-down fashion so that the final image may be right side up.

In 1895 slides no longer needed to be projected. Film was the new material, the same material that ran through Dickson's Kinetoscope. Could a machine be perfected that would project up to forty-eight different frames every second? The problem was this: When a frame was presented, it had to remain stationary on the screen for a fraction of a second. Then, while the next frame was moving into position, the light source had to be cut off so that the audience would not be aware of the transition. Each frame was to be presented as distinct from the next. The audience had to be presented with a faster-than-the-eye-can-discern succession of photographs that would convince them that they were watching one continuous record of a motion or activity.

To help achieve this effect the film was perforated. Sprocket holes were punched at regular intervals along the edges of the film. The holes were fitted over tiny cogs which, when moving, propelled the ribbon of film along. But the cogs were not always moving. Based on a "Swiss" design (the Maltese cross) the cogs behaved in such a fashion that they would stop for the tiniest fraction of a moment in order to present a stationary frame to the audience. (See Figure 23.)

In Paris, two French brothers, Auguste and Louis Lumière, devised a projection machine called the Cinématographe, and invited the public to a café for one of the earliest commercial screenings of motion pictures. On the twenty-eighth of December, 1895, the public greeted the innovation with caution, but within a week so many people had come to witness this new marvel, that the café was turned into a cinema (movie theatre) that today still stands!

London was the next capital to be visited by this wonder, and New York's turn came a month later, in April of 1896. We know that

23

23. *A close view of four frames of a strip of 35mm film. A black border "frames" each image, and the sprocket holes running along the film's edges fit over cogs that move the film along in the camera, the developer, the printer and the projector. The images shown here are from D. W. Griffith's* The Lonely Villa. (Museum of Modern Art/Film Stills Archive)

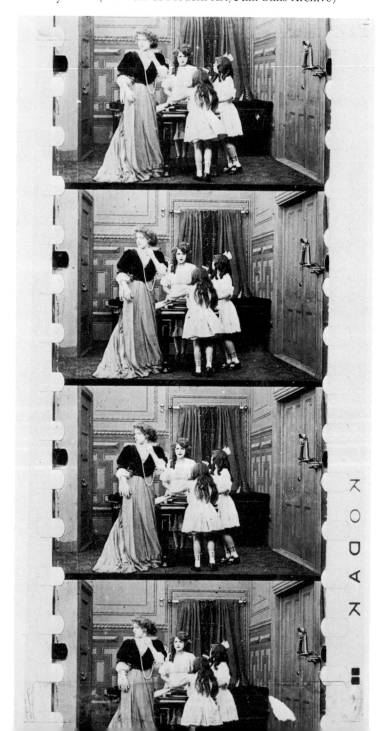

primitive projectors at least as capable as that of the Lumières existed in the States as early as 1895. A number were given trial demonstrations at several trade fairs. Why was there a pause of more than a year before motion pictures were projected commercially in the States?

Why? Because Edison, the man who best possessed the means to manufacture the projector, was hesitant to do so. So hesitant was he, in fact, that Dickson, impressed by the future of the projected motion picture, had to leave Edison's research factory, and continue his investigations elsewhere. We often hear of Edison's farsighted genius, but nothing betrays his shortsighted conservative sense more than the reason he gave for not pursuing investigations of projected motion pictures. "No . . . it will spoil everything. We are making these peep show machines [the Kinetoscopes] and selling a lot of them at a good profit. . . . Let's not kill the goose that lays the golden egg." Apparently Edison thought that if he built a projection machine only a dozen or so would be sold across the country, and they would be used to attract the contemporary audience of the Kinetoscope. In exchange for the manufacture of thousands of Kinetoscopes, Edison figured that he would build and sell only twenty projectors. It would be bad business. However, in 1896, when the business for the Kinetoscope began to fail, and when news of the French success made an impression on Edison, he decided to invest in projection devices.

The Edison Vitascope appeared in 1896. Actually, the designers of the Vitascope were Thomas Armat and a man who conducted some pioneer experiments in television, C. Francis Jenkins. Edison saw the Jenkins-Armat projector on display in Washington, and, impressed, purchased the rights to manufacture and distribute it. But why was the machine christened the Edison Vitascope and not the Jenkins-Armat Vitascope? The answer is simple. Edison had a marketable name, and in the words of his lawyers, "to secure the largest profit in the shortest time, it is necessary that we attach Mr. Edison's name in some prominent capacity to this machine." As it turned out, Edison's name could hardly have been more prominently displayed, but then again, to use it was good business sense; and more than anything else, that is what film was—a business.

25

Edison's lawyers assured Armat that they did not want to misrepresent the facts about the machine's origin and were more than willing to inscribe on the Edison Vitascope "Armat Design." They explained that after sales were "fully established" they would gladly release Armat's name as the inventor of the machine.

Edison had, as an economy measure, adopted the Lumière film speed of shooting and projecting at sixteen frames every second. He now had camera, film and a studio. All that was needed next was an audience that would sit together.

Where Macy's Department Store now stands, in New York's Herald Square, there was in 1896 a grand vaudeville theatre, Koster & Bial's Music Hall. On the night of April 23, with much fanfare in the press, Edison presented a public projection of his Vitascope. Although this was not the first public exhibition, it is from this date that the history of commercial theatrical film projection in America begins. The program of films was only one part of the whole evening's entertainment. A group of films shot by Edison in the Black Maria and in Europe by other pioneers made up the motion picture segment of the bill.

The films shown that first night included such attention-grabbers as *Kaiser Wilhelm Reviewing His Troops; Venice — Showing Gondolas,* and *Sea Waves.* They may not sound too scintillating to our modern tastes, but the audience that night was at first flabbergasted and then overwhelmed. Indeed, when a film showing waves washing the shore was screened, there were screams in the front rows. The ladies and gentlemen all thought they were about to be splashed!

Within a few months, the Kinetoscope rivals, the Mutoscope people, using a new projector modeled on the experiments of ex-Edison-employee Dickson and Dickson's new associate, Herman Casler, began commercial screenings at another impressive vaudeville house in New York. The new projector was named the Biograph. The Mutoscope company came to be known as the American Mutoscope and Biograph Company, and as Biograph, it soon became one of Edison's chief competitors. With the advent of competition the field of motion pictures became set for battle. In the combat an industry pieced itself together, and out of the scrambles of a hundred fortune seekers a new art was born in America.

2 On the Way to the White House

Edison, as we have learned, projected his films at one vaudeville house, Biograph at another. In addition to those being exhibited in the vaudeville theatres, films were still being manufactured for the Kinetoscope peep-show parlors. Film was also used, rather ingeniously, in 1904, when George C. Hale, the former chief of the Kansas City Fire Department, exhibited Hale's Tours at the St. Louis Exposition. Instead of sitting in an auditorium, the audience — who bought what looked like a railway ticket, sometimes with a destination printed on the card — usually sat in a small simulated railroad coach. Once "passengers" were in the compartment, the lights in the "train" would dim, and onto the front of the coach, or its sides where the "windows" were, the view would be projected. Since what was shown had been photographed from a moving train, it appeared that the stationary coach was indeed moving past rivers, mountains and whistle-stop towns. This display was a great success, and for the next several years Hale's Tours were franchised and exhibited across the country. Variations of the spectacle became integral features of later World Fairs.

There was at this time a great demand for material, a demand which could not be met by Edison and Biograph alone. However, Edison and Biograph both wanted to maintain a monopoly in the production of motion pictures. They would not sell their cameras to other producers. To do this would invite competition, and they preferred to be the only American producers. Edison, in fact, didn't even want Biograph to exist. He maintained that all other producers of motion pictures were operating under the patent that he had reg-

27

istered for the Kinetoscope in 1891. Edison argued that every other filmmaker was infringing on his designs and profiting thereby. Biograph denied this and cited certain modifications in its machine.

Edison's claim would not be satisfied for the next several years. In the meantime he waged a losing battle with motion picture producers, men so shrewd that they effectively outmaneuvered the letter of the law.

These producers, called outlaws and culprits by Edison, would not give up the goose that they believed would soon be laying golden eggs. With so many legal suits pending, the courts needed time to straighten out the maze of charges. Meanwhile the audience grew and so did the producers' profits from motion pictures. Biograph, which started producing films on a loan of two hundred thousand dollars in 1896, turned a *profit* ten years later of one-quarter million dollars. Producers decided that they would try to earn a fortune at once, even if later they faced the courts. So widespread was the practice of bootlegging machinery and importing cameras that no one really suspected Edison would be able to collect from all the "slippery eels." The risk was worthwhile, and it was taken. If it had not been, the history of the American film would be very different today.

Edison finally decided that if the law could not stop this "unauthorized" competition, he would try. Turning into a vigilante, he employed a corps of "detectives" and, to assist them, a host of "accomplices." Working secretly, a sleuth would learn of a setup operating without the approval of Edison, and one night the setup might be dismantled, its negatives exposed and its vital machinery returned to its "rightful" source.

It has been estimated that an independent producer between 1896 and 1909 spent only a quarter of his time in the making of motion pictures and the rest in avoiding Edison and the henchmen of one organization or another. Doubtless this is an exaggeration, but it does indicate that a state of constant combat existed. Most film making was centered in the New York City area. If a filmmaker could extricate himself from that hotbed of intrigue, he might be better able to devote his energy to the making of both films and money. It was a bit of this line of thinking that sent the first filmmakers out West. But there were other and better reasons as well.

On the Way to the White House

In 1907 one independent, Colonel Selig, was busy producing his film version of *The Count of Monte Cristo* in Chicago. Just after some outdoor shooting had been completed it began to snow. Prohibited by the weather from further "location" shooting, Selig sent his director and cameraman to California to finish the film, but he didn't send the cast. Overlooking this slight omission, the two-man crew was charged with finishing the film. In Los Angeles the crew met a starving hypnotist. Although this haggard person had never seen a motion picture, he was quite willing to earn an honest dollar by wearing a wig (as the Count) and by emerging from the sea. After the camera was set up and the hypnotist was dramatically engaged in emerging from the sea, a wave came and carried the poor man back into the ocean. Realizing that a ten-dollar wig was being carried away, the crew jumped in to rescue the property. As a secondary thought they saved the hypnotist. This story is probably apocryphal, but it describes well the hectic and impromptu atmosphere in which many of the earliest films were created. It is also indicative of an attitude that film producers historically were to maintain toward employees. Employees were considered not so much as human beings but as pieces of material with a market value. Employees were negotiable property.

After their first California success, Selig's men set up a rooftop studio on Main Street in Los Angeles in 1908, and the Golden Days of Hollywood were literally around the corner.

California's weather was sublime. In pre-smog days Los Angeles was the home of perpetual sunshine, and there was no need of cumbersome and expensive lamps in lighting film sets. Sunshine was not all that California offered. It had space. The topography of California embraced almost all conceivable landscapes — mountains, valleys, deserts, islands, forests, meadows and, of course, seacoast. The architecture was both Prairie America and Spanish Colonial. Almost any script could be photographed on a natural location in this state.

Compared to New York prices, land was inexpensive. In a rather quiet and respectable residential area, Hollywood, just outside central Los Angeles, real estate was being sold. Large pieces of land were being offered at less than a thousand dollars for a tract of several acres.

29

But why did the film industry settle in Los Angeles and not to the immediate north in San Francisco? By the turn of the century San Francisco was already a metropolitan area. By comparison, Los Angeles was a sprawling town of little merit. San Francisco had a number of theatres, restaurants, and the makings of a comprehensive public transportation system. The atmosphere of the Golden Gate City was tolerant, easygoing, relaxed, cheerful; Los Angeles tended to be more solemn, serious, God-fearing and puritanical. It would have seemed as if the eccentric personalities working with motion pictures would certainly find San Francisco more conducive to work and less suffocating to the mind than the smaller city to the south.

Los Angeles, however, was but a hop, step and jump from the Mexican border. If the marshals of the law were ever summoned by Edison, filmmakers could easily take their cameras, rush into their motor cars (another new device), and scramble over the border to where the marshals had no authority. There they would stay until Edison's men were called back East.

Motion pictures needed to move from music halls because in vaudeville houses they never really had a life of their own. Film was always consigned to the lowest parts of the bill, and used as a chaser either to clear the house between shows or to kill time between acts. But in 1900, when the White Rats, a union of vaudeville performers, went on strike, many theatre owners, in order to keep their houses open, were forced to rely on film. Films finally had a complete evening to themselves. Motion pictures were still very short, and long programs of one-minute films soon bored an audience. When the White Rats returned, some theatres dispensed with film altogether.

The idea of the motion picture theatre, the cinema, did not evolve from the vaudeville experience, but rather from the small Kinetoscope parlor. The proprietors of these temporary establishments realized that there would be less of an overhead and more of a market in projecting motion pictures to many customers at one time rather than peep-showing them one at a time. They began to rent Vitascopes, Biographs, Vitagraphs (another early formidable Edison competitor), and projection machines from Europe. One of these machines could reach an audience of hundreds at any one showing, and the "admission" price would remain the same.

The proprietor, now an exhibitor, faced a serious problem in this transition from peep show to public projection. The audience preferred the peep show. Why? In a projection room one had to sit among strangers. The room was small and the emissions from the projector made the atmosphere hot and heavy. The wooden benches that were used for seats were uncomfortable, and frequently there was no back support. Smoke from the projector sometimes blurred vision. Added to these inconveniences were many rumors of sundry crimes committed in these dark chambers.

As if the inconveniences and the rumors were not enough to make any prospective audience wary, there was the very real threat of disaster. Until the end of the Second World War, film was a highly

24. *Deteriorations of 35mm nitrate film.* (Museum of Modern Art/Film Stills Archive)

combustible material. It could burst into flames when subjected to a sudden rise in temperature. It was not uncommon for a smoking projectionist to effect a minor explosion by carelessly dropping a match. Until an acetate base replaced that of nitrate in the manufacture of film, noxious and unpleasant gases were released when the material began to decompose, and film decomposed easily with both age and use (see Figure 24). Even under the most ideal storage conditions, film had a relatively short life-span.

One of the most notorious catastrophes in film history happened in Paris in the spring of 1897. A certain charity bazaar that dated back to the court of Marie Antoinette was considered to be the social event of every Parisian's spring. On the afternoon of May 4, the dignitaries of France seemed to be congregated within the huge temporary structure that housed the celebration. There was a display of the wondrous new Lumière Cinématographe. The lamp in the projector was burning low. The projectionist, about to fuel the lamp with ether, lit a match to see better what he was doing. Although it was the ether vapors that caught the flame, and the paper decorations that spread the fire, the rolls of film exploded when attacked by the flames and contributed largely to the horror that immediately followed. Ventilation was poor; a holocaust ensued. There were few exits. Panic. The fancy costumes and the awesome reputations of those in flight could not fight the flames. The fire lasted one hour; it took Paris a whole day to count her dead. One hundred and eighty people lost their lives that sunny day. Among the dead were some of the most prominent figures in French politics, arts and society. The country went into mourning, and no one of any social standing in France, England and America would go near those "fire traps" where films were projected. Places where films were shown became known as dangerous, and perhaps even more damaging, as unfashionable. Nevertheless, this did not stop the new medium from attracting an audience, at least not in America.

There has always been a public for films in this country, and the first public for American films was distinctive. It was part of a social phenomenon unique in the twentieth century. Many of the first fervent filmgoers were the new Americans, the immigrants. During the last years of the nineteenth century and the early decades of the twentieth, America experienced a wave of immigration unparalleled in modern history, and the fact that the language of film is visual and universal was well appreciated by the foreign-language-speaking arrivals.

Film was also inexpensive to see. It cost from a penny to a nickel a show. Cheapness and comprehensibility made motion pictures attractive as an amusement. Consider the alternatives. To read books, the immigrants had to read English. Radio was not yet available. Gambling could be expensive. The saloon, although it functioned as a meeting place, could be costly and provoke unpleasant reactions the following morning. Indeed, when the Kinetoscope parlors began experimenting with public projections, the number of saloons in the nation diminished sharply.

It was not only the new Americans who attended this form of entertainment. The underprivileged members of American society who were without the finances and leisure to be able either to afford or appreciate the more socially acceptable forms of amusement, like the opera or even the theatre, flocked to the Kinetoscope shows. Such were the first regular filmgoers. And they numbered in the millions.

To prove to wary customers that no sins were being committed in the dark back rooms where films were projected, exhibitors would often cut a hole in the curtain that separated the projection room from the rest of the Kinetoscope parlor. The customer would be invited to look into the hole for a second or two. This was long enough to assure him that there were no illicit activities going on and to interest him in the day's program. As exhibitors tempted more and more of the Kinetoscope's audience into the back rooms, whole parlors were turned over to the projection of films. The parlors were scarcely more comfortable than the back rooms the audience once occupied, but the cleaner ones and the ones manned with a polite staff attracted a thriving business.

Exhibiting films became a family business. Vacant stores, at first turned into Kinetoscope parlors, were now used solely for projecting films. Brother could be the projectionist and Mother could sell the tickets. Father could act as a barker, attracting customers from the passing pedestrian parade, and he would occasionally explain this or that aspect of the film to the audience. After school, Sister could

33

clean the theatre. A projector could be bought for between seventy-five and a hundred and twenty-five dollars. A ticket booth had to be constructed and a permanent sign erected. Everything else — the store, the film — could be rented. The investment need not be large, but the return probably would be.

In 1905 the Nickelodeon appeared. This theatre was more than just a storefront operation, it was one of the first regular cinemas. The Nickelodeon (see Figure 25), also known as the Nickelette, was the idea of a Kinetoscope parlor proprietor, John P. Harris of Mc-Keesport, Pennsylvania. Going into partnership with his brother-in-law, Harris did not merely occupy a vacant store. He completely remodeled the hall with the intention of exhibiting films in a com-

25. *A Nickelodeon. Note the proclamation posted at the box office. It seems to be in contrast with the day's program,* The Artful Husband in Distress. (Museum of Modern Art/Film Stills Archive)

26. *Examples of slides projected at Nickelodeons.* (Museum of Modern Art/ Film Stills Archive)

fortable situation. His thoughts were of the audience. He saw that films would appear to be more attractive, would win some social approval, if they could be exhibited in less squalid surroundings.

Harris soon offered an extra refinement. The films he showed were not run in silence. They had a pianist to accompany them. After the first weeks the programs ran continuously from eight in the morning to midnight. The front of the theatre was enlarged and it stood recessed off the street so that its façade, garnished with bright colors, would look more imposing. A lobby was added so that an audience could wait out the end of the preceding program. Once the audience was seated, slides (see Figure 26) were shown that requested ladies

35

to remove their hats, gentlemen not to spit, and children not to annoy their parents. All this cost a customer a mere nickel.

Harris's original Nickelodeon had ninety-six seats, and they were continuously occupied. Harris soon began to construct a formidable chain of theatres. Word of the Pennsylvania success spread, and storefront operations were completely remodeled almost overnight. Motion pictures had finally found a permanent respectable showcase in the Nickelodeon. In 1908, three years after the original Nickelodeon, a survey estimated that there were close to eight thousand of these establishments across the country.

We have spoken of the filmmakers, the exhibitors, the theatres, and of the audience. What of the films themselves? At first, film was unwound in forty-to-fifty-foot lengths onto a series of rollers. Within a few years film was manufactured in one-hundred-foot lengths and rolled onto a spool or reel. Films of this length lasted about a minute and a half. The whole of an early motion picture was the length of only one shot. In those days a shot was defined as a single camera setup. Naturally, the length of these films and the fact that they were only one shot severely limited the themes that could be photographed. It is little wonder that the first films were little more than novelties, glimpses of famous personages in costume, brief snippets of sports events such as prize fights and races, tiny travelogues, vaudeville acts, and short excerpts from stage plays. One of the latter caused a rather loud scandal in 1896. Called *The Kiss*, it was the climactic scene. Although it recorded no more than a peck on the cheek, nonetheless it shocked many in its audience.

About four years after film's first public appearance, manufacturers of raw stock began to produce film in lengths of two hundred and fifty feet. In 1900 producers began to shift their attention to the making of longer films of about four minutes' duration. This increased length permitted a little more leeway in the choice of material. Expanded situations began to be shot (see Figure 27). A dandy, out for a constitutional, walks past a tenement. A washerwoman on a top floor inadvertently (maybe) dumps a pail of water onto the sidewalk and drenches the fop. Furious, the dandy looks up and makes an angry gesture in the air. A bricklayer, working on the building's façade, drops a brick. The brick lands on the passerby and that puts a definite end to his silent harangue.

27. *An Edison studio, 1912–1913. Since films were silent, several directors could work within one confined area.* (Museum of Modern Art/Film Stills Archive)

Films also were made that explored the potential of the camera to create sophisticated illusions. The films of the French filmmakers, Georges Méliès and Ferdinand Zecca excelled in creating these effects. In Méliès's pre-1902 hand-colored film *The Flower Fairy,* a winged woman with a wand appears at a window and coaxes flowers to grow right before the eyes of the astonished audience. This "growth" is accomplished through trick photography.

If the principles of motion pictures are understood, it is not actually much of a trick to create many special effects. Motion pictures are photographed at the rate of so many frames per second. The

37

camera shoots an action. Both the action and the camera can be suddenly stopped. Something may be added or taken away from the scene being shot. With almost every aspect of the action the same as when the camera stopped, the camera then can begin to photograph again. But there is a difference. There has been a change. Although there is nothing surreptitious about the change, the audience does not see the process; it only sees the effect. The scene on the screen appears as if the action were never broken. The flower fairy raises her wand. The camera stops. The fairy keeps holding up her arm. A flower is brought onto the set. As the fairy brings her arm down the camera begins shooting again. The wand action seems continuous, and the flower suddenly appears. This is the magic of film.

Indeed, this "stop-motion" form of photography is the basis for the animated film of which the cartoon is the commonest example. Inanimate objects and drawings are "made to move" by photographing them from a fixed position for a couple of frames at a time, then stopping the camera, moving the object or changing the drawing a bit, then resuming shooting. In a full-length animated film this laborious process may be repeated many thousand times. The results may very well be worth the effort. Suddenly, the laws of gravity, cause-and-effect, and natural science seem to be suspended, and not only do chairs and tables begin to move, but pumpkins begin to chase people uphill (*The Pumpkin Race*, 1907), it begins to snow on the moon (*A Trip to the Moon*, 1902), and a convict becomes so thin that he escapes through the bars of his cell (*Slippery Jim*, 1905). All these films are French (see Figure 28), but as we shall see, European films did influence American filmmakers.

Other favorite "tricks" that still remain popular involve the speed at which film is shot. Film is now always projected at a constant speed. So long as the film is photographed at the same speed at which it will be projected, the activity photographed appears normal. Someone may be photographed walking across the street. The camera may work very, very fast and take a hundred photographs every second. If the projector could project at a rate of a hundred frames per second, then the activity would seem normal, the walker would move at a usual pace. However, no standard projector goes this fast. Thus it takes a greater length of time for this sequence to go

28. *A striking tableau from one of Georges Méliès' many excursions into the fantastic,* An Impossible Voyage *(1905)*. (Museum of Modern Art/ Film Stills Archive)

through the projector than it did to go through the camera. As a result the walker appears to be walking very slowly, and his motions are languid and heavy. There is much more observable detail to his gait. This technique is known as slow motion. Slow motion is often used to create a certain sad or melancholic atmosphere. It is also used for the study of locomotion.

Fast motion, however, is almost always used either as a comic device or to punctuate a violent action. Indeed, in chase farces where people fall off ladders, cars are split in half by fire engines, and everyone gets thrown into the swimming pool, the action is often "speeded up" to "fake" the act. Speeding up really means that fewer

39

29. *A double exposure from Edwin S. Porter's* Uncle Tom's Cabin. *The dead body and the soul/ghost were photographed separately on the same strip of film.* (Museum of Modern Art/Film Stills Archive)

pictures per second are taken of any activity than will be projected. When projected, the action appears jerky and goes by more quickly than usual.

Double exposures also were common in early "trick" films. At first used to give characters and scenes a ghostly appearance (see Figure 29), the double exposure was later used as a bridge between shots in which one scene would "dissolve" into another. One shot would be taken, and then the film in the camera would be rolled back to a certain determined point. Another scene would be shot over the first. When the film was developed, printed and projected, both scenes would appear together. One would appear more solid than the other, which would have a transparent, specter-like quality.

40

While all these effects can be accomplished with relative ease today in the laboratory, they were first discovered by experimenting with the camera itself. Film history is peppered with legends of how this or that special effect was discovered by accident.

On his discharge from the American Navy, Edwin S. Porter billed himself as Mr. Thomas Edison, Jr. With a projection machine he headed for Costa Rica. Going straight to the Royal Court as Edison, Jr., Porter soon found that the impersonation got him into trouble and a court of law. He quickly returned to New York, and soon after projecting advertising films on a billboard in Herald Square, went to work for his adopted namesake. When he became a production head at Edison's Twenty-first Street Studio in 1900, Porter had the opportunity of seeing many of the latest films from France and England. Many of them used effects described above. Porter examined the films, and deriving ideas from them, introduced new methods in American filmmaking.

Both *The Great Train Robbery* and *The Life of an American Fireman* appeared in 1903 and were directed by Edwin S. Porter for the Edison Company. Several film historians think that these were the first story or narrative films to appear in this country. In regard to story, it is silly to make a distinction between the early comedy situations (the tenement example) and the films of Porter. All told stories. Porter's films are of historical interest not so much because they told stories but because of the ways in which the tales were told. That is, the way in which their action was developed "cinematically."

Both these films were long, longer than the standard two- to four-minute reels that were being produced in 1902 and 1903. Each film lasted somewhat under ten minutes and helped push the length of a reel up to a length of about a thousand feet (a quarter hour), which was established to last for the next ten years.

With the advantage of increased length, situations could be expanded and stories told in greater detail. Porter took advantage of this new length to begin the development of new techniques.

Parallel editing was one of these techniques. In *The Great Train Robbery*, a train robbery is staged. Meanwhile, back at the ranch, a dance is going on. In *The Life of an American Fireman*, a fireman

41

30–31. *Criminals stage a holdup while . . . the community enjoys a boisterous shindig. An early example of parallel editing from* The Great Train Robbery. *(These two stills, taken from frames of the actual film, show its worn condition. Usually stills from films are not taken directly from the print itself but are photographed on the set while the motion picture is in production. Such photographs are known as "production stills" and are used for purposes of publicity and display.)* (Museum of Modern Art/Film Stills Archive)

has a dream. Meanwhile, a fire has broken out. Up to this point film stories were told in such a way that the action in one scene would cause the action in a second which would cause the action of a third, and so forth. However, the robbery does not cause the dance and the dream does not cause the fire. Why bother to show the dance or the dream? These scenes, while they do not propel the action of the film, contribute to its effect in other ways. Filmmakers were beginning to learn that every shot (camera setup) need not merely advance the action. Suspense and irony are two qualities that could be added to a film narrative by juxtaposing different shots or scenes. It is ironic that while the fireman dreams, a fire has started or that while people are enjoying themselves at a dance, a robbery has taken place (see Figures 30, 31). These shots also add a modicum of suspense. Will the dancers be able to form a posse in time to catch the robbers? As the fire gets worse and worse Porter shifts (cuts) from the fire to the firemen on their way to the rescue. Will they get to the fire in time? "Parallel editing" is a rather formal, academic term which simply describes a way of putting scenes or shots together.

Speaking of scenes or shots, an attempt should be made to distinguish between these two terms. In the days of Porter a shot was defined as a camera setup. For most purposes a shot can still be defined in the same way today. A scene is usually composed of many shots. If you consider film as a language, a shot is a sentence and a scene is a paragraph. Just as there are guidelines but no ironclad rules in grammar as to where one paragraph ends and another begins, so there is no ironclad definition for a scene. We know that the paragraph is a unity, perhaps the expression of one thought. And this is also true of a film scene. Coming from the vocabulary of the American theatre, where a scene was usually defined by the raising and lowering of a curtain, the term in film is usually applied to a shot or combination of shots photographed in one particular place and covering one particular unbroken time sequence.

Up until Porter's day, American films were photographed much like stage plays. The filmmakers supposed the camera to be a privileged theatregoer who always sat in the center seat of the middle of an auditorium. But the camera did not have the mobility of the theatregoer; it did not shift position. There it would stand in one

32. *The shooting bandit, close-up from the beginning or the end of* The Great Train Robbery. (Museum of Modern Art/Film Stills Archive)

place as the cameraman cranked away. The set was the stage and the actors were always seen in full view, top of head to bottom of feet. Porter made some little change in this regard. In *The Life of an American Fireman,* Porter photographed a fire-alarm box in close-up. A hand pulled down the alarm, and the fireman awoke from his reverie. Some people complained that to see an object "divorced" from its surroundings (that is, not in full stage view) would confuse the audience. However, this close-up did not confuse the audience; what it did was to add a dramatic punch by emphasizing the urgency of the situation. In *The Great Train Robbery,* Porter added a close-up that became one of the most famous in the history of film. An outlaw lifts his gun, aims it at the audience, and shoots. Although this close-up (see Figure 32) did nothing to the story of the film itself, and was quite extraneous, it caused a commotion wherever the film was played. In the catalogue of Edison's films, it is noted that this scene could be placed at the beginning or at the end of the film.

The Great Train Robbery was the sensation of the Kinetoscope parlors and vaudeville theatres of 1903. So popular was the film that two years later when the first Nickelodeons began to appear across the country, they inevitably chose *The Great Train Robbery* as their première attraction.

Although it is not safe to claim that *The Great Train Robbery* was the first, it certainly helped to establish a genre (type) of film that would remain popular to the present day: the Western. While the concerns of the Westerns have changed (for instance, just who are the villains?) as the nation alters its moral perspective (the cavalry used to rescue harried white settlers; now in *Soldier Blue* and *Little Big Man* [both 1970] it ruthlessly slaughters Indians who are protecting their land from mercenary intruders), the Western remains as current as ever. However, the Western is no longer indigenous to America. Although the films are still set west of the Mississippi, the Italians, in the mid-sixties, began making Westerns as interesting as any shot in California.

In 1905, the year the first Nickelodeon appeared, Porter completed two more films noted for their extended use of parallel editing — *The Kleptomaniac* and *The Ex-Convict*. Porter had continued to make films after *The Great Train Robbery*, but these two should be singled out for discussion. They are interesting because both are also early examples of explicit social criticism in American "entertainment" films. It must be remembered that the early audiences of film were not comprised of the intelligentsia (university students and amateur critics) that attend much film today. It is only a recent phenomenon that the intellectuals of the community have become a bulk of the moviegoing population. In Porter's day, films were still "on the wrong side of the tracks," and Nickelodeons, even though they were an improvement on the peep-show parlors, still tended to attract the poor, the uneducated, and the new Americans. Porter realized what subjects would interest his audience, and told of situations in which the rights of the poor were violated in favor of the patronage of the wealthy. *The Kleptomaniac* is the story of two women who steal. One is a rich woman who is apprehended by the law. When tried in court she is freed. The indigent woman who steals only to eat is sentenced by the same judge to go to jail. The closing scene of the film reveals the blindfolded figure of justice holding a scale on which a bag of gold outweighs a loaf of bread. The situations of the two women are made manifest through the use of parallel editing. Here the cinematic device is used for contrast, and the contrast makes its critical point. Similarly, in *The Ex-Convict,* the meager life-style of the title character (he cannot find a job) is compared to the pretentious demeanor of a prospective employer.

In 1906 Porter completed a film which the Edison Company advertised as containing scenes of "photographic stunts that have never been attempted before." *The Dream of a Rarebit Fiend* is certainly a delightful semianimated film that depicts the incredible nightmare of an inebriated gentleman. However, it did not introduce anything to the American public which it had not seen in the French films of Méliès. Porter was more of an adapter of techniques than an innovator.

Porter's films had a rhythm and texture that other American films of the period lacked. By today's standards these films seem quite primitive, but seen in the perspective of film history, they were not only sophisticated, but daring in their construction. Although historians suspect that Porter was not fully aware of the techniques he introduced (otherwise why do they not appear in his other films of the period?), he did advance the film art in America. Porter was to remain active in film production until 1915, but few of his films after 1907 are of as much interest as those produced during the period 1903–1907.

By virtue of his films' popularity and financial success, Porter was considered the leading American filmmaker between 1903 and 1907. His crew, however, regarded him as little more than a "mechanic." Indeed, Porter had been a mechanic but those who called him that in relation to his films believed that the filmmaker was working more by experienced formulas and prescriptions than by imagination.

It was in 1907 that Porter supervised the production of a film with the thrilling title *Rescued from an Eagle's Nest.* It was not the film itself that has earned posterity's attention, but rather one of the performers in it. While Porter may have been called a mechanic with some justification, no one could possibly say this of one of the gentlemen who did a bit of the rescuing in *Rescued from an Eagle's Nest.* When this actor, D. W. Griffith, turned to the making of films in the following year, the magnificent happened.

The year 1908 would have been one of the most important years in the history of film as an art had it been only the year in which D. W. Griffith began to make films. However, it was also crucial to film as an industry. It was in this year that copyright problems involving films began to appear in the courts, censorship raised its noxious head, and a powerful monopoly of film producers was established. When the motion picture in America turned twelve, it reached puberty, and its maturity as both an art and industry began in earnest.

The year 1908 began modestly with the humble announcement that a production company, Kalem, had just completed what was described as "positively the most superb motion picture spectacle ever made in America." *Ben Hur,* shot on a New York beach, was composed in "sixteen magnificent scenes." Films were still only one reel, so the large action-packed book from which the film was adapted was neatly condensed into an experience of about fifteen minutes. (William Wyler's 1959 adaptation of the book ran well over three hours.) Kalem was wise in adapting *Ben-Hur.* Lew Wallace's book was not particularly well written, but as a religious adventure story it did capture the sentiments of many pious people who longed for real and spirited excitement. If the cinema could adapt novels of this magnitude, then surely it deserved the attention of those who had previously shunned it: after all, would a film of this colossal book not prove that film could be a true social art with moral significance?

Not only was the book's scope breathtaking but its action was continuous. An international best-seller, its name alone was thought to be enough to attract thousands of people into the cinema. It had attracted this number to the legitimate theatre where it played successfully on stages across the nation. But the stage was limited by its very physical borders, the proscenium. The camera, however, could photograph out-of-doors, and locations might appear more authentic.

However, Kalem neglected one point. *Ben-Hur* was still in copyright, and the film producers did not contact the lawyers of the author's estate to negotiate a fee for the film's adaptation. The author's lawyers did not know of Kalem's project until it was completed. Prior to 1908, filmmakers assumed that motion pictures were not susceptible to the laws of copyright. They thought they had com-

47

plete license to adapt whatever they wished from any medium. It cost Kalem much more than the original production cost of *Ben Hur* to find out just how wrong they were. Once the film was released, the author's attorneys filed notice on Kalem for copyright infringement, and although the courts did not reach a decision until 1911, when they did, it was the U.S. Supreme Court that made Kalem settle with the Wallace estate to the tune of $25,000. Meanwhile, other producers took note and began to negotiate for materials or properties (books, plays and even poems) the copyright for which was still in effect. Most narrative films, even the ones produced today, find their original ideas in literary forms. Few have been based on original ideas.

It seems that the development of the American film industry has always been intimately linked with court decisions. After years of litigation, the courts in 1907 ruled in favor of Edison in a dispute with another major film producer. It was late, but Edison finally got his satisfaction. The other film producers ran frightened. At last their game was declared illegal, and they understood that it would only be a matter of time before Edison would make the rounds claiming damages on patent infringements. A truce had to be effected, and in 1908, after months of negotiations, ten groups formed the Motion Picture Patents Company. Each party claimed that whatever equipment it presently possessed for the manufacture of motion pictures did indeed date back to the Edison Kinetoscope. Each agreed to pay Edison a royalty for the privilege of operating under his patent. In turn, Edison recognized the refinements and the modifications that each of the parties had effected in its particular apparatus. Furthermore, every member of the Patents Company agreed to form an information pool in which notices would be circulated concerning this or that member's technical accomplishments. Each member was free to borrow an idea of his fellow member. To this effect the Patents Company issued ten licenses, one to each member, "to manufacture movies under all the patents." This was fine for the members of Patents Company. But there were more film producers than there were members of the Patents Company. What of them? They would have to go out of business. The Patents Company decided that it would issue no more than the ten original licenses and that was that. All the other producers would be bought up.

The Motion Picture Patents Company was a monopoly. Among its ten members it effectively controlled all the registered patents on motion picture equipment and processes in America. Granted, the ten parties of the company represented the largest producers of motion pictures, including Edison, Biograph, Selig, Kalem, and even the American representative of Méliès. Yet there were many smaller producers who could not guarantee as consistent an output of films but who were determined not to go out of business. In their way these independents were to prove as stubborn and as wily as did Biograph, Selig and Kalem in the days when they avoided Edison's detectives. With Nickelodeons raising their price to a dime and the volume of business rising by several million admissions, these independents were not going to let a major catastrophe like the formation of a trust stop them. They knew they could operate until the courts ruled on the legality of the Patents Company. Was it not a trust, a monopoly designed to restrict competition? If so, then would this cartel not be declared illegal?

The Patents Company was more ruthless in applying strong-arm tactics than Edison ever was. One independent production scheduled a mob scene of twenty people in which one-half of this vast number were supposed to attack the other half. However, instead of attacking the other actors the aggressors attacked the camera. A donnybrook ensued and five of the gladiators ended up in the hospital. An investigation afterward showed that some mysterious organization had commissioned a group of hoodlums to infiltrate this production and sabotage it. If the independents meant business, so did the Patents Company. To escape the wrath and scrutiny of the Patents Company, the independents headed straightaway and lickety-split for California, and it was in 1909 that the westward trek began in earnest.

Feuds between the Patents Company and the independents involved equipment. The best foreign-made equipment was based on designs Edison had registered in the U.S. Since Edison did not protect his investment from foreign patenting, such equipment was within the bounds of legality so long as it was kept out of the country. However, some poor cameras were based on designs that did not date back to Edison's patents, and these could be safely imported into America. They did not do a good job, and their built-in faults often ruined the film. To overcome both the faults of these cameras and the watchful eye of the Patents Company, it was a practice for the independent producers to purchase two of these defective cameras. The ill-working insides would be completely removed from one, and mechanism based on Edison's patents would be substituted. The other model would be left as it was. This model would not be used except when an agent from the Patents Company would come searching for infringements. The independent would gladly show the agent the ill-working but never-used model, and then continue to shoot with the renovated machine.

The independents also infuriated the Patents Company by hiring the Patents Company's best men at wages considerably higher than those offered by the Patents Company. Although the independents were not as wealthy as any individual member of the trust, they did not have the overhead of the members of the trust. The independents felt that they could afford to buy talent expensively in the knowledge that it was quality and experience for which they were paying.

The Patents Company attempted to monopolize not only film production, but film projection as well. The design of projection machines derived from the patents of one or another member of the trust. The Patents Company decided it had the right to enforce a weekly two-dollar licensing fee from every exhibitor. Moreover, they threatened to remove the projector from theatres screening films of the independents. The exhibitors felt as if they were being treated in a manner similar to that of the Massachusetts colonialists who were taxed for tea, but they had little choice but to pay and complain. They did both. They continually referred to the fee as a LICEense charge.

In a burst of self-righteousness that certainly put shame to the Christmas spirit of 1908, the mayor of New York, before he departed for the quiet of his country home, left an order for his chief of police. The order read that every motion picture theatre in New York City was to be closed at midnight Christmas Eve. The Nickelodeons, Mayor George McClellan preached, were unclean and immoral places of amusement. Of course, this action was illegal, and even though the theatres were closed, the courts saw to it that within a few days the Nickelodeons were opened once more.

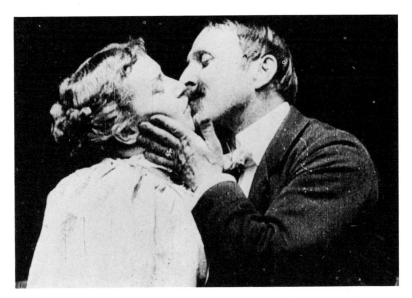

33. *Scandal! The 1896 May Irwin–John C. Rice kiss.* (Museum of Modern Art/Film Stills Archive)

The mayor would never have acted in the way he did unless he knew his act would be in concert with public sympathy. By 1908 moral indignation against Nickelodeons, "this new and terrible form of vice," had been fanned through the press to such a degree that constitutional rights were being jeopardized by such hasty and thoughtless acts as those of the mayor of New York.

The cries for film censorship began in earnest in 1907, only two years after the opening of the Nickelodeon. A Chicago newspaper editorial of that year wrote that films had no redeeming features to warrant their existence and that they catered to the low passions of childhood (see Figure 33). Since motion pictures were "hopelessly bad," they obviously could "not be defended." This simple nonargument seemed persuasive to many. The movies were the danger of which all educated people spoke; they were a chief corrupter of youth and, at times, seen as more evil and insidious than liquor and opium! To "prove" the point that motion pictures were degenerate and harmful, a group of concerned citizens "exposed films . . . for what they were." What the group did was to scour the bulletins in the press listing titles of films, and it came up with the following

51

horrors: *Beware My Husband Comes, Paris Slums, College Boy's First Love* and *The Gaieties of Divorce*. The group neglected to mention such other supposedly evil films as *Quaint Holland, The Wonders of Canada* and *Cinderella*.

The outcry against the new form of amusement quickly spread. In Providence, Rhode Island, it took a humorous turn when members of the Murphy clan of Pawtucket turned out in force to suppress a screening of *Murphy's Wake*. Why? In the film, Murphy, although dead and gone, wants to join into the festivities surrounding his funeral. Every so often, when the attention of the guests is diverted from his corpse, Murphy sits up and takes a swig from the nearest bottle. Then he falls back, content. The clan thought the film would be insulting and demeaning. When it was invited into the theatre to witness the "offense" it was seen that the film was done in jest. It is reported that "a pleasant time was had by all."

The story of film censorship in America does not end as cheerfully as the story of Murphy and the clan. Chicago was one of the first cities to inaugurate film censorship (1907). The police department privately previewed every film before it was allowed to be publicly exhibited in a theatre. The police department deemed whether or not the film was fit to be screened. The film could be deemed unfit for several reasons (morality, religion, politics). If the film was deemed unfit, offending passages were cited and these had to be removed. Only then would the department grant a license for public exhibition. Sometimes a film would be banned in toto. More and more communities established the precedent for licensing film through *prior* (to public exhibition) *restraint*. It was not always the police department that previewed the film. Some cities and states formed their own film licensing boards to review films. This process of review always cost money, and although the community insisted that this process of review was necessary to protect the integrity of its citizens, it was not prepared to pay for it. The cost was passed on to the producers and exhibitors. Unfortunately, it was not so much prior restraint that upset the filmmakers as it was the threat to their profits. If every community in America formed its own board of review to grant licenses, a filmmaker would have to pay thousands of dollars just for the right to exhibit his work across the country.

The Patents Company decided to combat the threat of community censorship. Court decisions took a long time, and the trust knew it had to work quickly. In 1909, with the help of a charitable organization, the Patents Company founded the National Board of Censorship. This was the industry's first attempt at self-review. This self-censorship has existed in modified form up to the present day. The National Board of Censorship did not raise the question of the legality of the censorship. (Why should films be censored before they are shown and not books before they are published? Shouldn't films enjoy the same freedoms as that of the press?) What it did try to do was to stem the threatened tide of thousands of community review boards. Parties participating in the trust agreed to submit some of their more controversial films to the National Board of Censorship. They also agreed to abide by the Board's decisions as to the suitability of certain scenes. The National Board of Censorship was created by the industry and not by the government.

While those community boards that were established before the National Board were not put out of operation, the industry did succeed in holding back the threatened wave of community and state censorship. Nonetheless, Pennsylvania, in 1911, established its board and it was followed by those in Kansas and Ohio two years later. Although the name of the National Board of Censorship was changed to the more melodious National Board of Review to stop making censorship sound like such a worthy activity, censorship boards sporadically continued to spring up. The Maryland Board of Review, which is one of the few still in existence as of 1971, was legislated into being in 1916, and the New York board, which isn't, arrived in 1921.

While the questions of censorship, the Patents Company and copyrights surely must have appeared formidable to the industry in 1908, a quieter, more profound and important event was happening. One man began to turn a frenetic industry into an art. On 11 East Fourteenth Street, on the northernmost edge of New York's Greenwich Village, D. W. Griffith, the actor in *Rescued from an Eagle's Nest,* became a director for Biograph.

"Lawrence" (a theatrical pseudonym for David Wark Griffith) was born into a poor and proud Kentucky family in 1875. His father

53

had been a colonel in the Confederate army. The colonel's men called him "Thunder Jake" because his voice roared with authority, and no one could escape paying attention when he gave orders and told stories. Young Griffith was no exception. He listened while his father spoke about the glorious exploits of the Confederate army and how genteel life in the South had been before the Civil War. Through these tales Griffith began to admire Southern Victorian virtues and sentiments. The antiquated attitudes and prejudices which the colonel instilled in his son may never have appeared prominently in Griffith's personal life, but they eventually caused considerable controversy about his art.

At one time or another in his early career Griffith was employed as a store clerk, a shoe salesman, a hop picker, a newspaper reporter, and a slightly successful playwright. Hating inactivity, Griffith tinkered with ideas for get-rich-quick inventions such as nonpuncturable tires. All this took place while Griffith was an actor appearing in companies that toured the country and presented melodramas. In 1906, after his play was produced and ran outside New York for two weeks, Griffith, in need of money, reluctantly decided to become involved with film, and found work at the Edison studio. Griffith had come with a script, but was invited to act instead. At that time, film was regarded as little more than a novelty. Although there was money in performing in films, theatrical actors scorned the new medium. They believed that appearances in motion pictures would ruin their prestige as artists.

Their beliefs were well founded, for at the time actors in film were no more than performers of exaggerated motion. The art of film acting had not yet been developed. All that seemed to be required was gesticulating, wild and exorbitant movement. As gesticulators, actors were granted anonymity. Aside from the name of the production group and the title of the film, companies tended to shy away from giving any further credits. They feared that if any actor became popular, and known by name, the public might ask to see more and more of him. The popular figure would then be in a position to bargain for a contract, and his name would become negotiable. Even the first film financiers realized that the appearance of film stars would skyrocket production costs.

On the Way to the White House

The actors in the early films were just as happy not to be identified for fear their careers in the theatre might be damaged. Unfortunately, these performers were obligated to serve in capacities other than those of actors. They were expected to nail down the set, sew costumes, help with makeup, and run errands. One film might find them playing a lead role, while another might find them in a bit role. The actors resented such casual treatment, and rightfully felt insulted when ordered to do jobs for which they were not trained.

After his acting experience at the Edison studio Griffith approached Biograph as an author. He was invited both to act in films and to write for them. For his acting he made five dollars a day, and was paid three times that for any scenario used. Finally, he was given the opportunity to direct. He hesitated, confiding to his wife that he was anxious about concealing his occupation from family and friends. When a Biograph executive assured Griffith that his acting job would still be waiting should he fail as a director, Griffith took the plunge. Motion pictures were never the same.

Griffith worked at Biograph from 1908 to 1913. He not only continued to write, but he also supervised the production of many films and personally directed an estimated four hundred and fifty others!

To understand Griffith's achievements in the development of film art, a look must be taken at the films of the period. In 1908 almost all films were made in one reel. Basically there were only two types of films, both narrative, and each involved much action — the adventure and the comic. For the most part, the films told simple stories simply, with each scene developing the narrative a step forward. For its material the cinema was tied to literary forms, but in its construction, film was tied very much to conventional ideas of the theatre. Scenes were often no more than one shot which began when someone entered the set, and ended with an exit. As mentioned before, the camera remained stationary as if it were a wooden spectator sitting in the center of an auditorium. The head and feet of the performer were always shown. The trust insisted that if you paid for an actor, then you had to use all of him, and all of him was inevitably shown.

Griffith changed all this (see Figure 34). He began to place his camera at various angles in order to add drama and tension to a scene. When Griffith made *Ramona* not only did he pay the unheard-

55

34.   *Griffith directing Mae Marsh, one of the director's favorite actresses, in* The White Rose (1923). (Museum of Modern Art/Film Stills Archive)

of sum of one hundred dollars for adaptation rights, but he placed his camera so far back from the focal object that a whole panoramic landscape was revealed. This may appear common now, but to give such space a dramatic vision was revolutionary in 1910.

Griffith had to fight with Biograph for this right, but this was not the first fight he had with his bosses. As early as his first year as director Griffith had to struggle with Biograph executives so that he could use close-ups for more than just shock effect. When he first approached Biograph to film Alfred, Lord Tennyson's, poem *Enoch Arden,* the studio balked because such a project could not have been described either as an adventure or comedy film. Griffith's will prevailed. He was allowed to adapt the poem into a film, titled *After Many Years.* He also fought to shoot a sequence of this film in which a wife waits for her husband. To emphasize her inner torment Griffith shot the wife in close-up. The executives insisted that the audience would lose its orientation if not permitted to see the whole body of the actor. To the executives' minds Griffith compounded this confusion by cutting away from this close-up shot to that of the object of her thoughts, her husband stranded on a desert isle. The executives argued that the audience would not be able to make the connection between these two shots. Previously, to convey the idea of a thought, a device similar to the balloons used in comic strips was

56

employed. Above the shot of the person thinking, another shot in double exposure revealed the object of that person's thoughts. Both the thinker and the thought appeared in the same frame. Griffith separated these two elements and was accused of trying to dumbfound the audience. The audience may very well have had to make some sort of mental adjustment in establishing the connection between the two shots, but it was moved by the close-up and understood the desert island scene. When *After Many Years* was released, it was popular with the audiences, who learned to "read" film in a new way. It was hailed as a masterpiece by the few critics of film at the time, and was one of the earliest American narrative films considered worthy of importation into other countries.

Griffith soon began to shoot scenes which were comprised of more than one shot. He also mobilized the camera, so that from shot to shot within a scene it was placed at the point of greatest dramatic intensity. Close-ups, medium and long shots abounded in his films. Griffith also broke up the theatrical unities which so stultified film's growth. He began shots in the middle of an action, and ended shots before the action was completed. He so fractured the photographed action that he would cut away from an incomplete action only to come back to it somewhat later.

Under Griffith's direction, film acting became an art. While Griffith strove to break film construction away from moribund theatrical conventions, he attempted to lure some Broadway actors to the screen. When ten dollars a day proved insufficient to attract the talent of the Great White Way, Griffith offered twenty.

Although his actions seemed exorbitant at the time, critics and audience showed their preference for Biograph films by attending them in great numbers. Since his films excelled at the box office, Biograph allowed Griffith his eccentricity.

Biograph's films enjoyed a superior reputation. They were more realistic, natural and subdued than those of rival production companies. This was not only due to the presence of Broadway players, but also due to the attention Griffith gave them. Prior to Griffith, films were made in one take; that is, the action was photographed once and once only. Some films were never even rehearsed before they were photographed. Rehearsals seemed a waste of time (after

57

all, actors needed only to gesticulate wildly). Shooting more than one take was absolutely out of the financial question. Before Griffith, few had heard about shooting for mood or atmosphere. Executives would recoil in horror at such profligate expenditure of time and stock. Griffith proved it was not a waste. The great and sensitive care that Griffith exercised in making his films showed on the screen.

Griffith not only went to Broadway in search of acting talent, he also preferred to work with newcomers whose only recommendations might be a pleasing appearance and an attractive personality. Actors were still required to do odd jobs around the Biograph studio, but they respected the director's attention. He had the uncanny ability of coaxing the most natural appearances from the most callow of actors.

In a short time Griffith had established a troupe of players who kept appearing in similar roles from film to film. To find actors for his "repertory" company Griffith might meet friends of friends, and was even known to ask a passerby with an interesting demeanor if he or she would consider appearing in a film. Indeed, there is a story that Arthur Johnson, the lead in the first film directed by Griffith, *The Adventures of Dollie* (1908), was chosen in just this way. Johnson was strolling down a New York street just when Griffith, dissatisfied with the looks of the present Biograph performers, was intent on finding a new face.

Griffith worked closely with his cameramen. Indeed, it was his first cameraman, Arthur Marvin, who helped get Griffith to direct at Biograph. With his sense of daring Griffith earned the cooperation of another of his cameramen, Gottfried Wilhelm ("Billy") Bitzer, who was to become one of the cinema's most celebrated cinematographers and the director's closest collaborator (see Figure 35). It happened this way.

Sets had been lit directly from above. The mercury-vapor lights, powered by electrical current, were cumbersome to move and emitted a harsh glare. It was difficult to photograph shadows, and impossible to create any sort of quiet, reflective atmosphere. When Griffith tried to subdue the lighting, his assistant complained that any decrease in light intensity would prevent an image from being registered on the slow-working emulsion. Nothing would appear on the

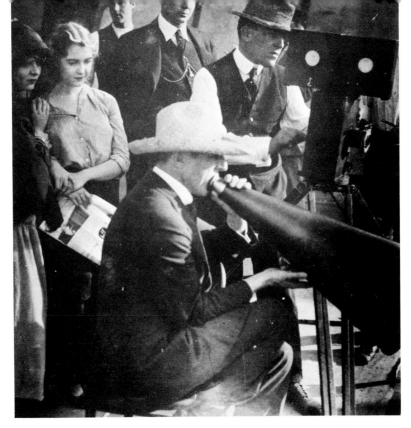

35. *David Wark Griffith with megaphone. Billy Bitzer, Griffith's frequent cameraman and one of America's leading cinematographers, stands by the camera. Behind Griffith, the sisters Lillian and Dorothy Gish wait for further orders.* (Museum of Modern Art/Film Stills Archive)

film, they said. Griffith insisted on establishing new precedents and began experimenting in lighting sets differently. He bathed his characters in fireside glows, with soft shadows, in twilight and with halos of light originating behind the head of the player. Eventually Billy Bitzer was won over.

As Griffith used lighting to enhance atmosphere, he also used shots that did not develop the story line. When Griffith went to California on a temporary scouting visit in 1910 he shot a religious film, *The Thread of Destiny*, in the San Gabriel Mission. Griffith is said to have photographed much footage of the mission even before he began rehearsing the story, and the building itself became a character in the film. In the film there are many shots of dim corridors, worn walls, cells for meditation, and the surrounding terrain. In fact, the story itself seems subordinated to the shots of the mission.

The Thread of Destiny was also notable in that it featured Mary Pickford, the young actress who soon was to define the star system that would dominate Hollywood until the mid-sixties.

One of Miss Pickford's earliest films was *The Lonely Villa*, made in 1909. Mack Sennett was also associated with this picture. It was one of the very few films for which Sennett supplied the idea, which he had picked up from a newspaper story. The plot of *The Lonely Villa* came out of a bull session with the staff of Biograph. (Most scenarios of the time were modified during thinking sessions in which the executives, directors, actors and technicians sat around chatting and swapping ideas.) Mack Sennett was a young Canadian working at Biograph, who tried to impress Griffith with his ideas. He would "accidentally" meet Griffith while the director was out walking and chat with the captive director until Griffith arrived home. At any talk session it was regarded as inevitable that Sennett would put forward the same idea, and he was continually frustrated in getting it accepted. This idea was his "cop" picture, in which a crime would be committed and a group of cops would engage in an extended and elaborate chase with the criminals.

After acting, writing and even directing some memorable comedies at Biograph, Sennett left Griffith and headed west. In 1912, after a fortuitous conversation with a couple of gamblers turned producers, Sennett found himself the head of a small and makeshift studio — Keystone. The name was taken from a line on the Pennsylvania Railway. At Keystone Sennett was to direct some and supervise the directing of all the lunatic comedies in which order was wrecked in an explosion of frantic destruction. More often than not the Keystone comedies, which became world famous, involved the Keystone Cops (see Figure 36), a bizarre collection of incompetents in hot pursuit of a party that frequently turned out to be innocent. The Keystone Cops' car rammed into buildings which collapsed, was continually being split into two by mammoth vehicles, flew over caverns and between mountains, and swam over bodies of water. Logic was thrown out the window, and so were many of his performers. Maidens were tied to railroad tracks, pies were continually being thrown

36.   *Alert and ever ready — Mack Sennett's Keystone Cops!* (Museum of Modern Art/Film Stills Archives)

in the actors' faces, and water was poured all over their clothes. As a foil to the Keystone Cops, the Bathing Beauties appeared. The Beauties were a host of shapely females dressed in the bathing fashions of the period. They were usually found cavorting by the seashore until interrupted by the Cops; then they too would become inexorably involved in the chase. Several fine comic and even dramatic stars of the twenties appeared first in Sennett's films. Indeed, it was Keystone that first hired one of the most popular "comic" stars of the screen, Charlie Chaplin.

The fact that Sennett contributed to the idea of *The Lonely Villa* does not alone make the film exciting to an audience. And yet it was — very. Parallel-shot construction was hinted at in Porter's *The Great Train Robbery,* and developed with a measure of sophistica-

61

tion in *The Ex-Convict* and *The Kleptomaniac*. With Griffith this construction becomes a conscious, fully expanded cinematic device. In *The Lonely Villa* (1909) and more so in *The Lonedale Operator* (1911), the story of which also owes its origins to the Sennett idea, Griffith developed a tension which grew through the judicious use of editing. In these works, a party of innocents, women and children, are being held at bay by a group of criminals. Meanwhile, the man or men in the family rush to the rescue. Since good always triumphed, the outcome was almost certain, but it was in the getting to the outcome that the excitement was generated. Not only did Griffith crosscut from the bad men to the victims to the good men to the victims to the bad men to the good men and back and forth once more, but (as each party got closer to the other) the length of the shots became progressively shorter. Shots of a few seconds gave way to shots that lasted a split second, and eventually the shots became so short that they almost flashed by subliminally as the climax was reached. The images were cut so quickly that an afterimage of one scene would blend into the image of the next. Finally, as the parties collided into one another, the pace broke into one longer sequence, in which the innocents faced the outlaws who were apprehended by the rescuers.

Griffith was not content to create excitement only through crosscutting. As the climax approached, the shots tended to be close-ups, emphasizing the terror and anxiety of the principals. As if this were not enough, he also had his camera move, following the actors within the shot. This is particularly true in *The Lonedale Operator*, where the camera rode along a train to the rescue.

There are four *basic* types of camera movement. Griffith explored than all. When a camera *tracks* or *trucks* (see Figure 37), it moves on a straight horizontal line back or forth; when it *dollies*, it moves in a straight line (not necessarily perpendicular) up or down. Some people use the words "track" and "dolly" synonymously but "dolly" usually does refer to a vertical movement. The word "tracking" comes from the tracks on which a wheeled platform could be fitted. Since early filmmakers wanted to avoid jerkiness of image, the camera was placed on this platform so that it would photograph smoothly as it traveled. A dolly was a cranelike device designed to lift the camera on a vertical plane.

37.　An intrepid cameraman preparing a tracking or trucking (perhaps "training" would be a better word) shot. (Museum of Modern Art/Film Stills Archive)

Tilting or panning refers to the movement of the camera on its own axis. The tripod on which the camera sits does not move from its fixed position, but by swiveling the camera on its axis, the camera's lens can be moved horizontally (pans) or vertically (tilts). A complete pan or tilt (the latter very rare) describes a circle, a rotation of 360 degrees.

Griffith began as a director making forty-five dollars a week plus a royalty of one mill on every foot of film sold. Within twenty months the director, from royalties alone, was earning close to a thousand dollars a month. Griffith's films had become enormously popular, and although the audience knew that Biograph's films were more interesting than the films of other production companies, they did not know who was responsible for them, for Griffith's name did not appear on the Biograph films. The films themselves were distinguished by an AB trademark impressed onto the sets. This was done not so much to identify Griffith's films as Griffith's but as Biograph's. This method was used to prevent copyright thievery by any of Biograph's competitors. With an AB appearing in the body of a film, no one

63

could remove the opening title of an already made film and claim the film as his own. Although by 1911 other media were protected from filmmakers infringing on their copyrights, it was another year before copyrights extended to motion pictures and distributors and exhibitors were prevented from pirating work. Until this time only the photographs that constituted the work could be protected, and so single frames, printed onto sheets of paper or cards, had to be submitted to the Library of Congress! It is a sad fact that Méliès died penniless because he was not able to realize profits from the films he financed. The films he made were often "pirated" and "duped" (copied) so that the profits from their exhibition went into another's pockets.

In 1909 critics were rhapsodizing about the quality of the Biograph product. They claimed that the company had got to the core of making films, had passed that primitive stage of merely taking photographs of puppet-like figures moving about a stage, and that Biograph pictures actually "thought." They commented on the fact that Biograph moved its cameras close to the actors so that an audience could better get "into the minds" of the characters. In other words, people not only noticed that Biograph's films were different, but they began to analyze the differences, and with this analysis true film criticism was born.

By the time Griffith's 1911 contract came to be signed, the director finally divested himself of the name he had taken as an actor and signed his own name.

He was the top creative man in the Biograph studio, but he was restless. He had business executives with whom to contend continually, and Biograph, being a prominent member of the conservative Patents Company, gave Griffith conservative and cautious financial bosses.

The fields of film production, distribution and exhibition were continually growing and new approaches were constantly being demanded, but the trust would not budge from tried business practices which no longer were valid. By 1912 the Motion Picture Patents Company had become positively foolish.

One particular source of irritation to Griffith was the trust's refusal to consider films as anything more than a one-reel product.

Because the trust was successful in distributing films that lasted up to a quarter hour in length in 1908, it felt that no audience would sit for more than fifteen minutes watching a narrative unfold in 1911. Longer films — up to two and a half hours — were being produced in Europe, and some American exhibitors were pleading with the trust to supply them with films of up to three reels. The Patents Company was adamant in its one-reel stance. However, Griffith's vision and maturity needed longer films. His talent demanded a broader scope in which to develop, and in 1911, the year of *The Lonedale Operator*, Griffith remade his 1908 "poem" film, *Enoch Arden*. This time it was completed in two reels. Biograph was horrified. The company was determined not to break distribution precedents, so it went against Griffith's wishes and distributed the film to theatres, one reel at a time, over a two-week period. Nonetheless, many of the film's exhibitors behaved shrewdly, and simply held up the first reel until the second arrived, then played both together.

When independent producers outside the trust began to cut into the Patents Company's territory by supplying the demand for longer films, the trust began begrudgingly to acknowledge the inevitability of two- or three-reel films. But when Griffith completed the four-reel *Judith of Bethulia* secretly in California, it was just too much for Biograph to handle.

In 1913 Griffith had moved away from Los Angeles to a small town so that he might work on his new film in privacy without interference. Longer foreign films, such as Italian biblical epics and recordings of famous theatrical players in famous works, had begun to play in independent New York theatres by 1912. Griffith may not have had the chance of seeing these five-reels-and-up films, but his imagination was fired with reports of their existence, their success and their potential. He longed to have the freedom that others had.

When his biblical adaptation was finally completed, it was one of the longest films (around fifty minutes) ever made in America. It was also the most sophisticated and complex. The scenario was a quite liberal rewrite of the Old Testament tale of the Jewess who beheads the captor of her people.

Biograph did not regard *Judith of Bethulia* as an accomplishment.

It would be an understatement to suggest that it behaved foolishly when a copy of the film was received from the West Coast. The company thought it would teach Griffith a lesson, and in doing so Biograph did nothing less than to commit suicide. It shelved the film. Biograph let the film sit in its vaults and when it attempted to release the film, in the following year, the gargantuan and ploddy Italian religious spectacle *Quo Vadis?* (1912), with its two-hour-plus running time, made *Judith* seem like a dwarf.

When Griffith returned to New York he found Biograph caught up in that syndrome from which he had tried to break away. Biograph was once again photographing stage plays. While Griffith was out in California, an enterprising, independent producer, Adolph Zukor, had bought the American rights to the world-famous French actress Sarah Bernhardt's filmed performance of *Queen Elizabeth* (1912). The film was little more than a series of animated tableaux, static and retrogressive in style compared to the vibrant works of Griffith. But Bernhardt was a popular and hailed cultural phenomenon. Her appearance gave such prestige to the new medium that legitimate theatres became frightened at the growing fame of films. Unfortunately for Miss Bernhardt, who thought that film would immortalize her, her performance was better suited for the stage. She did not understand what film could do. Nothing more was immortalized than a series of gesticulations. Without a voice and without close-ups of her expressive face, Miss Bernhardt was reduced to something much less than her usual magnitude. Indeed, almost any one of Griffith's film actors showed more sensitivity than either Miss Bernhardt or many of the "famous players" who followed. Griffith's actors expressed emotion through the lifting of an eye, the slight shift of the body, the turn of a head, the wringing of hands or the shedding of a simple tear. Griffith also knew where to place the camera to capture these dramatic movements.

Biograph, however, exasperated at what it considered Griffith's reckless behavior in turning out such an unmarketable fiasco as *Judith of Bethulia,* demoted him on his return to the East. He was told that he would no longer direct: he would supervise productions, and that was all. Griffith was frustrated once more. Biograph not only had misread the trend of the times, but it misunderstood all that

Griffith accomplished. And what Griffith had accomplished were the films that made the studio possibly the most popular in America.

In 1913 Griffith broke with Biograph. In a highly publicized announcement he stated his new relationship with another production company. Within several months and for a thousand dollars a week, Griffith produced nine films and personally directed four long (about an hour) films for his new associates. Although at least two of these four films, *Home, Sweet Home* and *The Avenging Conscience* (both 1914), were considered major achievements of their day, they did not particularly interest Griffith. His mind was on his next film, which, when completed, made every film before and almost every one since look minor.

Indeed, it was Griffith's next two films that caused one critic to say that they "earned for the screen its right to the status of an art, and demonstrated with finality that the movie was one of the most potent social agencies in America." *Birth of a Nation* hit America with the force of a hurricane. *Intolerance* soon followed.

For some time Griffith had been looking for a property that, when adapted, could make use of all that he had learned during his five years at Biograph, and the self-taught Griffith had learned a considerable amount. Such a property would have to have tremendous scope and invite creative embellishments.

A popular book called *The Clansman* had been made into a play that successfully toured the South, and it was as a dramatic piece that Griffith first came to know of the work. *The Clansman* was a naïve, ugly, racist work written with a prejudice that had been unquestioned in the South. The author, Thomas Dixon, Jr., considered his book to be a "saga of the South." It told of the honorable way of life among the wealthy white property owners (that is, land- and slave-owners) and how their idyllic existence was disturbed by the Civil War, which was caused by a radical group of lunatic abolitionists. The evils of the Reconstruction (black suffrage!) were told luridly in mawkish and sentimental prose. (See Figure 38.) Only the defeated gallant white men could restore the South to her former honor. How did they do this? Through the formation of the "nightriders," who were to become the Ku Klux Klan (see Figure 39). In fact, the book was little more than popular praise for this "noble

67

38.   The Birth of a Nation *views black suffrage as a carpetbaggers' ploy in the rape of the South during Reconstruction. In this sequence white Southerners are denied the right to vote.* (Museum of Modern Art/Film Stills Archive)

institution." It was a work calculated to excite anyone convinced of Dixie's righteousness. And, to an extent, Griffith was.

A child's mind is influenced by his parents' convictions, and Griffith, as a child, had been susceptible to his father's tales and prejudices. All that seemed romantic in America's past seemed to him to lie in the Old South. *The Clansman* caught his imagination. Moreover, its flowery style also appealed to the literary ambitions of the director.

This is not to say that Griffith was consciously vicious. He probably did believe that the white man was superior to a man of any other color, and his films betrayed their creator as a man who had fallen prey to that diseased ideal which equates whiteness with purity, innocence, virtue, beauty and chastity. An obvious example of Griffith's vision was his choice of heroines. They were almost all

68

young, delicate, under twenty, with long, blond hair and with skin the texture of peaches and cream. They were almost always caught in circumstances beyond their control. If they were in trouble, the fault did not lie in them; they were victimized.

The titles for Griffith's films which "explained" the action also told of the director's sentimentality. His characters were called "the Dear One" or "the Precious One." While this might sound sickly sweet in the hard-boiled no-decoration world of today, these terms had a dramatic significance to Griffith, and to much of his audience.

Griffith expanded the scope of *The Clansman* by incorporating into the film other writings by Dixon. An entire county was rumored to have been rented for the panoramic battle scenes, and Griffith hired thousands of extras. (Many, but not all, of the blacks in the film were played by whites, as was the custom, in black makeup.) There were six weeks of rehearsals: the film was shot in four months. Few, if any, shooting schedules in America had ever approximated this length. During shooting Griffith did not consult any detailed

39. *The "noble" Klan, out to restore the honor of the South, terrorizes a newly enfranchised black in* The Birth of a Nation. (Museum of Modern Art/Film Stills Archive)

script. While he did have scraps of paper with jotted notations, the whole complex film was plotted in his head, and the whole film was photographed with one three hundred dollar camera!

When Griffith's investors became restless and frightened by Griffith's tactics, he threatened to use his own money to buy them out. Griffith wanted to maintain his creative freedom at any price.

The Clansman was completed early in 1915 at the unparalleled cost of $110,000. It originally ran the staggering length of thirteen reels (three hours); it was soon cut a bit to twelve and a half. The trust, which could have been helpful, was appalled and called the film monstrous. Griffith, who was only too familiar with this reaction, decided that since he had helped finance the film himself, he and his partners would also release it. Their organization, Epoch Film Company, set itself to distribute "the monster."

The film opened in Los Angeles on February 8, 1915. On February 20 it was privately screened in New York. At the end of the screening, the Reverend Thomas Dixon, Jr., not known for his modesty, is said to have shouted to Griffith, "*The Clansman* is too tame. Let's call it *The Birth of a Nation*." Assigning the Revolutionary War to the back pages of history, it was agreed that this biased and formidable drama of the Civil War be called *The Birth of a Nation.*

It was as *The Birth of a Nation* that the film opened on March 3 at the Liberty Theatre, which still stands on Forty-second Street in New York. At that time the theatre had been the home of live performances. It was made into a motion picture theatre for the run of this spectacular film. The admission of two dollars a seat placed the film on a price level with the legitimate theatre.

Whether *The Birth of a Nation* is still the most profitable film ever made is questionable. Another Civil War drama, *Gone with the Wind* (1939), re-released every so often, claims that honor. So does *The Sound of Music* (1965) and so will *Love Story* (1970). Because bookkeeping methods have changed since the initial release of *The Birth of a Nation,* it is difficult, if not impossible, to verify the financial figures. That is not what is important. *The Birth of a Nation* is certainly the most controversial American film ever produced. Fifty-five years have done little to reduce the response the film elicits.

People are forever getting angry with the film; others are forever apologizing.

In spite of the fact that earlier films like *Slavery Days* and *Coon Town Suffragettes* were more blatantly racist, it was *The Birth of a Nation* that gathered about it a notorious reputation that invited clashes and near-riots in communities where it played. It was not unusual for a battery of police to attend its premiere in various cities. Fear of the black community's response delayed the premiere of the film. The Klan attended the spectacle and made it a cause for celebration. In the North the film was roundly denounced wherever it was exhibited, but wherever it was exhibited it also broke attendance records and continued to do so year after year whenever it was re-released.

On February 22, 1915, the newspapers reported that "the East Room of the White House looked like a miniature moving picture theatre when President Woodrow Wilson and a few members of the Cabinet saw *The Birth of a Nation*. . . . The President evinced a desire to see the show after he had heard it praised. . . . The pictures were thrown onto the panels of the East Room wall." The President, moved by the film, is quoted as saying that the film "was like writing history with lightning." The motion picture had at last come to the Executive Mansion.

Although many film historians write that there was little that was new in Griffith's techniques in *The Birth of a Nation*, everything Griffith developed in terms of cinematic expression in his years making short films at Biograph was perfectly integrated into this one film (see Figure 40). If film historians think that nothing new appeared in *The Birth of a Nation*, they must also admit that little new has appeared since. All the elements of cinema are to be found in the film: camera placement, camera movement, crosscutting, editing and lighting for mood and atmosphere, impromptu scenes and highly stylized sequences, intimate shots and panoramic vistas, superb performances ranging from the quiet to the hysterical. Even the size of frame changed shape according to what Griffith wished to emphasize. The film was, of course, silent. A compelling score of original melodies and old Dixie tunes was composed for its presentation. The score, played in first runs by a full symphony orchestra, not only

71

40. *Lillian Gish as Elsie Stoneham in* The Birth of a Nation. *Griffith "frames" his actress in a close "iris" shot that gradually opens in a circular fashion to reveal the face of the heroine.* (Museum of Modern Art/Film Stills Archive)

evinced memories of the Civil War and the Reconstruction period, but was perfectly synchronous with the action. In assessing the power the film must have had on its original audiences, the effect of the music should not be underestimated. It was an integral part of the film.

Fortunately the nation has matured somewhat since the film first appeared and its theme is now greeted more with embarrassment than joy. The film no longer evokes the same strong emotions, and students of film can finally begin to appreciate it for the passionate, personal film and work of art it is. It is passionate for the wrong reasons, and what it reveals about some of the filmmakers' ethical standards may be unfortunate, but it is an honest film, and that is no mean commendation.

Many censors have got hold of *The Birth of a Nation* throughout its long exhibition history and cut scenes and titles from this and that part. This is a pity, because such excisions destroy the unity of the film and the vision of its gifted creator. A racist tone runs through every foot of the film, and the only way to get rid of this tone is not to cut out bits and pieces but to ban the entire film. The censors did not want the film to offend anyone, but they could not hide what was intrinsically there. *The Birth of a Nation* is so uncompromising in its philosophy that its racist theme cannot be concealed by deletions.

After *The Birth of a Nation* opened, the National Association of Colored People immediately issued a document denouncing the film, and the president of Harvard University spoke out against the film as "a perversion of white ideals." Griffith denied that he disliked blacks, and placed the blame for the woes of the Reconstruction on the carpetbagger. Implicit in this denial, however, was the feeling that the North did enfranchise a people not suited for public office. There is no record of Griffith's ever having an unhappy experience with blacks, or blacks being treated poorly by Griffith. Griffith was probably not conscious of his racism, and if made conscious, would probably have been horrified with himself. However, that conjecture is hypothetical. He never really understood the root of the adverse criticism of the film. He never could see that to look longingly back to the Old South was to subscribe to a morally reprehensible ethic.

The controversy generated by the film caused Griffith himself to become a crusader. He went so far as to publish a pamphlet denouncing intolerance. Griffith felt himself the victim of intolerance when liberal groups agitated for the removal of his film from the screens of the nation. In the pamphlet the filmmaker did not so much answer his critics as launch on a diatribe against intolerance. In his pamphlet, *The Rise and Fall of Free Speech in America,* he wrote: "Intolerance is the root of all censorship . . . [it] smashed the first printing press. . . ." All that is quite true, but it is ironic that Griffith pointed it out in defense of *The Birth of a Nation.*

It may not seem possible, but Griffith's next film, made with the considerable profits of *The Birth of a Nation,* excelled the Civil War film in terms of size, scope, and perhaps even artistry. Addressing himself to the theme of his recently published pamphlet, Griffith made the incredible *Intolerance.* For sheer complexity this 1916 masterwork has still not met its match in American film history. Made in fourteen reels with a running time of about three and a half hours, *Intolerance* was a giant. Some of its sets were three hundred feet high (Figure 41). Its grandiose banquet scene alone is reputed to have cost close to the total of *The Birth of a Nation* alone. A whole city had to be erected to accommodate the extras, and by the time the original negative was completed, nearly a half million dollars had been spent on the production. Judging by the 1916 financial perspective, this sum was astronomical, and seen in the perspective of contemporary financing, it has seldom been equaled.

It was not the money spent on *Intolerance* that made it remarkable, but its structure. *Intolerance* told four separate stories. Each story was complete in itself, and the whole structure was framed with an elaborate prologue and epilogue. The stories were not about four different people in the same location at the same time; each was independent of the others and each was concerned with a different historical period. Even more amazing was that Griffith was not con-

41. *When the sets for* Intolerance *were constructed they towered over all the buildings in the immediate area. After the shooting, they were termed a fire hazard and ordered dismantled.* (Museum of Modern Art/Film Stills Archive)

tent to tell one story first and let another follow. All four narratives were told simultaneously. With one cut the audience witnessed the Fall of Babylon, the next would take the audience to medieval France for the St. Bartholomew's Day Massacre, the next to the Palestine of Christ and the next into a contemporary milieu (Figures 42–45). Actually the contemporary story was a complete feature film about the harm that reformers could do. *The Mother and the Law* was completed just as *Intolerance — A Drama of Comparisons* began to grow in Griffith's mind; it was released as part of the longer film.

Neither location nor time was the unifying factor of four stories in the film; its unity arose from the abstract theme of intolerance. This thematic approach was new. Taking the crosscutting technique to an extreme, Griffith moved fluidly and easily about the scope of history as the evils of intolerance were vividly revealed in each of the four stories. Images cascaded one upon the other. By the film's climax the results of intolerance throughout the ages met in one tremendous visual crescendo.

Much has been written about this tremendous original work, but like *The Birth of a Nation* it really must be seen before it can be discussed in detail (see Figure 46). It can be said, however, that the film exerted a profound influence on filmmakers all over the world. Lenin, one of the leaders of the Russian Revolution, was so impressed with the film he said that of all media of communication, film could be best put to the service of the State. Indeed, prints of the film became the bible, the training manual, for a whole generation of gifted filmmakers in the newly founded republic.

Unfortunately, the time was not propitious for *Intolerance*. In 1916 not only did it confuse its audiences, but it hit the American public as it was finally and reluctantly shedding its isolationist spirit and preparing to fight the Germans in the First World War. When the bellows of war begin to blow, tolerance is one of the first virtues to go up in smoke. Because the film preached compassion and understanding rather than physical confrontation, *Intolerance* was barred from some communities.

Not only did the audience shun the film, but the critics, while generally admiring the film, simply could not become ecstatic over it. It

42–45. *Scenes from the four stories of* Intolerance: *"The Fall of Babylon," "The Palestine of Christ," "The Saint Bartholomew's Massacre of the Huguenots in France, 1572," and the modern episode with Mae Marsh. Like the Fall of Babylon, this sequence, entitled "The Mother and the Law," was released as a separate feature-length film after the initial release of In-tolerance.* (Museum of Modern Art/Film Stills Archive)

46. *To emphasize certain motions, objects or vistas, Griffith altered the shape of the frame by masking part of the lens. The shape of the frame in this still anticipates the wide screen that came to popularity after 1952.* (Museum of Modern Art/Film Stills Archive)

was too complex. Too much work was involved in "reading" it, in deciphering the images, in getting the stories straight. Nonetheless, the stature of *Intolerance* has grown with time. As audiences become more fluent in film, Griffith's accomplishments become clearer. To an audience in the seventies which has grown up with a heritage of cinematic expression, the film is certainly easier to comprehend than it was to its audience in 1916. But concentration is still needed; the film demands both attention and work from the audience. In 1916, when films caught the immediate emotions and passions of an audience, *Intolerance* was regarded as an oddity, a rare bird, an intriguing departure, and a blind alley. When the format of *Intolerance* annoyed audiences and the film failed, Griffith tried to recapture some of his investment by releasing the Fall of Babylon story and the modern sequence as two separate full-length films. However, he never recouped his losses.

With the financial failure of *Intolerance*, Griffith had to sacrifice his new-won independence for a while. Up until the time that the filmmakers of the "underground" began to emerge after the Second World War, it was assumed that creative filmmakers would have to modify their own visions to suit their studios' concern for the box office. In the sense that Griffith struggled for his independence and, for a while, answered to no other taste except that of his own sensibility, he may have been the first "avant-garde" American filmmaker.

Although two films made after *Intolerance*, *Way Down East* (1920) and *Orphans of the Storm* (1922), were tremendously popular, Griffith made no other films of the scope of his four-piece masterwork. All of his films are of interest today; one in particular — a quiet, atmospheric and muted love story of a tragic relationship, *Broken Blossoms* (1919) — is a classic. Although he experimented with sound (on discs separate from the film) as early as 1921 with *Dream Street*, the experiment was regarded as a failure. His first all-talking film, *Abraham Lincoln* (1930), won much praise but his second such film, the last film he ever directed, *The Struggle* (1931), received such adverse criticism that it was actually withdrawn from theatrical distribution. Lonely and neglected by a community that owed so much to him, Griffith died in Los Angeles in 1948.

Griffith was film's great genius. The Homer of the screen described his objective simply: "The task I'm trying to achieve is above all to make you see." He did make us see, and in the process revolutionized the medium.

3 From Czar to Czar

No one knows whether Nicholas II, the czar of Russia, actually received the following telegram during the chaotic days of the Russian Revolution, but the legend persists that it was sent. Addressed to "N. Romanoff" in St. Petersburg, it read something like this: "When I was a poor boy some of your police were not kind to me and my people. I came to America and did well. Now I hear that you are out of a job over there. Since I hold no ill will for you, you can come to New York and I will give you a job acting in my films. Salary is no object. Please reply at my expense." The telegram was charitably signed by Lewis J. Selznick. Although some dispossessed Russian noblemen did find themselves working as bit players in Hollywood, there is no indication that the czar ever considered this kind offer.

In the last years of the 1910's Selznick was also a czar. He was not one of the kind being overthrown from power in Europe, but a new sort whose money and influence grew as the twentieth century progressed. Although Selznick's power was not as great as that of those who inherited his work, it did extend over millions of people, across many national boundaries, and into the minds of moviegoers in many parts of the globe.

Early in the century, France, Sweden and Germany had exciting motion picture industries, but during the First World War, European theatres were closed and the nitrate used in the making of raw stock was diverted to munitions. During the war American films played in bombed-out cinemas and, after the war, American capital built new theatres. Since an American film usually earned back its

81

investment at home, its release on the continent brought a clear profit. Many European countries tried to reestablish their national industries after the war, but most were not successful in producing great numbers of films. American films which had already recouped their investments could be distributed more cheaply than any European ventures. Just as the studios saw to it that there was no competition at home, so the czars of the American motion picture industry determined there was to be little abroad. Who were these czars? They were heads of motion picture studios. And what were the studios?

Two men, each first an actor, did much to define the course of the motion picture in America. David Wark Griffith helped determine it as an art and Thomas A. Ince as an industry.

Ince, born into a theatrical family, spent many of his boyhood years performing in plays, writing, and being an agent for vaudeville troupes. In 1910, Ince, like Griffith, was in need of money and condescended to appear in the new medium of the motion picture. He then reluctantly graduated to direction. In 1911, after meeting with the same two men who would send Sennett to California, Ince was sent to Los Angeles to direct a number of cowboy films.

When Ince first reached the West Coast, he discovered that no proper facilities for shooting films existed. Since he had no equipment, Ince began to acquire sophisticated apparatus. As his melodramatic Westerns became more and more popular, Ince's motion picture factory became increasingly complex. Within two years Ince was established as his own boss, and he purchased eighteen thousand acres of land. On an area of land larger than Manhattan Island, Ince established Inceville, the first of the huge motion picture production plants which were to punctuate the landscape of southern California. There were offices, sets, places in which to make and spaces in which to store costumes and props, cutting rooms and projection rooms, where Ince and his directors could look at what had been photographed each day (the rushes). On Inceville's land there were installed a tribe of Sioux Indians lent by the United States itself (!), a traveling Wild West show, several herds of cattle, and the cowboys who were to become the famous heroes of the early Westerns.

With the construction of Inceville in 1913, Ince stopped directing, but this does not mean that he ceased being involved in the production of his films. Quite the contrary. Ince freed himself from directing so that he might oversee the complete activities of his vast organization. It was in this managerial and administrative capacity that Ince excelled. Ince's studio was the paradigm of organization, because in order to produce his films economically, he wanted to insure that everything was systematized and disciplined.

Although it was said that he never read a book from cover to cover, Ince had the greatest respect for stories. It was the story, he maintained, that caught and held the audience's attention. His employees dubbed him "the doctor of the sick film" because he acted like a surgeon and cut films ruthlessly when their stories wandered from the original ideas.

Not content to limit his stories to Westerns, Ince prided himself on building elaborate sets to make foreign locations appear authentic, and he created one of the first special-effects departments capable of "re-creating" tropical storms, hurricanes, typhoons and earthquakes.

Although Ince did little, if any, actual direction after 1913, the films he produced are considered to belong more to him than to any of the men he named as directors. Ince managed to stamp each production with his character, to infuse each film with his personality and he was very much *the* filmmaker in his studio (see Figure 47).

47.   *Part of the Ince studio.* (Museum of Modern Art/Film Stills Archive)

Not only was the decision to turn this or that idea into a film solely his, but he played an integral part in adapting the stories for the screen. His scenarios and shooting scripts were extraordinarily detailed. They listed camera angles, camera placements, the duration of each shot, the reactions of the actors, and precisely how the footage was to be edited. To all this information was appended a schedule. Directors were instructed how long they were allowed to shoot a sequence, when to move from one site to another, and how to proceed with the editing. In Inceville, that model of productivity, the schedule was equal in importance to the script. Whereas Griffith is said never to have used a script in shooting any of his many films, Ince always required strict adherence to one. The entire film was photographed, edited and completed in his mind before someone else shot the first frame.

One Ince director who had more freedom than most was William S. Hart. Hart, also an actor, was one of the first cowboy heroes. He was predated by Gilbert M. Anderson (really Max Aronson), known to fans as "Broncho Billy" (Figure 48), who appeared in about

48.   *Broncho Billy. Here he is seen in a publicity shot to be used in conjunction with one of his films.* (Museum of Modern Art/Film Stills Archive)

four hundred one-reelers and had a small, anonymous part in *The Great Train Robbery* (1903). Another popular cowboy star was Tom Mix, a real deputy U.S. marshal, who before he made his first film in 1910 brought in actual bandits, both dead and alive.

Of all the American films that were popular overseas, the Westerns tended to be favorites. Indeed it was the Westerns that shaped many Europeans' notions about America. It was quite common to find a Frenchman or Italian who thought that outside New York City, outlaws and Indians roamed a nation of limitless prairies.

Although Broncho Billy's and Mix's early films were quite simple, William S. Hart attempted to bring a deeper drama and a sense of style to the Western (*Hell's Hinges*, 1916). He was determined to present a more accurate, if less thrilling, picture of the Old West. When he was asked to comment upon *The Covered Wagon* (1923), a popular spectacle depicting the pioneer trek westward, Hart cited scenes in which cattle, their necks yoked together, were herded across a river, and a scene in which a wagon train was settled in a blind canyon. Hart insisted that the pioneers would never have committed such follies. Nevertheless such scenes were dramatic, and that dramatic film directed by James Cruze made millions of dollars.

Ince moved from Inceville into an even more modern studio and produced *Civilization* (1916), an antiwar film whose scope was inspired by the successful *Birth of a Nation*. Completed before *Intolerance*, at a time when the United States was undecided about joining the conflict that would become the First World War, the film was credited with helping Woodrow Wilson win the 1916 presidential campaign on an isolationist platform.

Civilization (see Figure 49) tells of a ruler desperate for power whose ruthless ambition brings war into the lives of his subjects. The autocrat does not suffer the ensuing carnage — his subjects do. Starving and angry, the mothers of the dying soldiers form a secret organization which puts an end to the horrors wrought by the monarch's greed. Christ appears on earth, and civilization is resurrected. The film echoed the convictions of its audience. Many Americans, seeing European nations hopelessly involved in brutal hostilities and not wanting to become involved in that foreign war, believed that only some form of divine intervention, a miracle, could put an end to the slaughter.

49. *Ince's view of the inside of a submarine, from his "pacifist" production,* Civilization, *directed by Raymond B. West and Irvin Willat.* (Museum of Modern Art/Film Stills Archive)

Soon Griffith and Ince made a working agreement, and Triangle Productions was formed. Logically enough, there were three sides to Triangle Productions. While Mack Sennett produced short comedies, D. W. Griffith and Thomas Ince supplied the company with feature-length films. Working independently in his own studio, each man agreed to supervise or direct one film a week; Triangle released a long program weekly. Each program consisted of two long films and a short comedy. These programs were some of the earliest double features. The theatres chosen to present this sort of program were the most prestigious in a community. Up to this time theatres had screened shorter programs and changed their feature films at least once during the week. Once a film had finished one screening, it would immediately begin again. Triangle did not want to run their films continuously, and so scheduled them for screening only once each afternoon and evening for a full week. A full orchestra accompanied the film, and in certain cities the admission was as high as two dollars. These plans were too ambitious. There were not enough people who were able to afford the weekly admission. In the three months from September to November 1915, Triangle dropped its admission to a quarter and stopped its double-feature policy. Three years later, financially exhausted by the large salaries it had been offering to attract popular stage performers from Broadway, Triangle collapsed. Shortly thereafter Ince dropped out of production and in 1924, he died mysteriously either on a millionaire's yacht or in his home of a heart attack. There are rumors of foul play associated with Ince's death, and even though they have been persistent, they have never been substantiated.

What Happened to Mary, a continuing episodic story about an orphan, began production in 1912. Each installment was complete in itself, and every month a new chapter would appear in the nation's theatres. The series *What Happened to Mary* differed from the serial *The Adventures of Kathlyn* (1913) in that while each of Mary's episodes ended happily, Kathlyn found herself in the most perilous circumstance just as "To Be Continued" was flashed on the screen. How would Kathlyn extricate herself from what appeared to be a fatal situation? As the audience returned at regular intervals to find out, Kathlyn emerged victorious, only to be entangled five minutes later in another near calamity, and "To Be Announced" appeared on the screen once more. It has been estimated that between the time Kathlyn suffered her first hair-raising experience to the last serials produced for the nation's theatres around 1957, over four hundred of these installment films were released. Some had as few as three episodes, others as many as thirty; each chapter ran usually fifteen to thirty minutes. Unlike *Batman* (1943), *Superman* (1948), and the spacemen, *Flash Gordon* (1936) and *Buck Rogers* (1939), the earliest heroes of the serials tended to be heroines, pure and pretty, demure in the company of gentlemen, athletic in the clutches of villains. These innocents were dangled from cliffs, weighted down at the bottom of lakes, and tied to railroad tracks. The serials bore titles like *The Hazards of Helen* (1916), *The Exploits of Elaine* (1915) and *The Perils of Pauline* (1914). The last has become a legend, and the name of its star, Pearl White, became a common phrase denoting a virtuous person in distress. The mindlessness of the serials (very much like the adventure series on today's television) soon proved irritating, and by the mid-twenties the serials were relegated to neighborhood showcases, where they were reserved for afternoon performances and weekend children's programs.

In one respect the trust was right. If an audience could identify an actor by name it would request to see more of him. And that actor, made aware of his ability to attract an audience, would be able to negotiate for salaries that would become higher and higher. Eventually, when the production company was not able to afford the amount requested, the actor might turn to rivals who could. When no producer could meet an actor's price, the actor would become a producer himself. Fearing this kind of domination by stars, the trust was adamant in its refusal to credit actors. However, if the Patents Company was bound by its own decisions, the independents were not.

One of the most popular actresses of the day was an unnamed miss, known as "the Biograph Girl." Carl Laemmle, whose business was threatened by the Patents Company, wooed this actress away from Biograph with two promises. First he would raise her salary, and then, after much publicity, he would release her real name to the public. In 1910 "the Biograph Girl" disappeared. There was talk of kidnapping, and a St. Louis newspaper carried a story that the missing actress, Florence Lawrence (Figure 50), was fatally injured in a

50. *Florence Lawrence.* (Museum of Modern Art/Film Stills Archive)

streetcar accident. The Biograph Girl was dead! Laemmle was quick to respond, saying that the shocking report was a silly and cowardly lie disseminated by Biograph and that Florence Lawrence was not only alive but the star of his next film. To prove the rumor false, Florence Lawrence made an appearance at the St. Louis première of her film. Laemmle "stole" an actress and created a star. He also had pulled one of the industry's earliest publicity stunts.

Exhibitors and distributors, recognizing the drawing power of the popular and *named* performer, rushed to use Laemmle's films. Other independent producers took up the practice of identifying actors, and after much hesitation the members of the Patents Company followed suit. But Biograph held out, insisting that it was the name of the studio and not that of the performer nor director that built a corporate reputation.

When Biograph belatedly (1913) began to credit individuals for their part in the productions, appropriately it was Griffith's name that appeared first.

One of the very early production companies, Vitagraph, in 1911 began issuing a house organ that contained news of interest to its employees and exhibitors of its films. Although circulated among its staff only, the magazine found its way into outside hands. The public was fascinated by it. There had always been a great deal of curiosity about what leading performers of the company were doing and saying, and, visualizing a new potential, the publication changed its scope, expanded its format, and went on sale to the public. It no longer concerned itself with parochial matters but became a colorful journal of gossip and fact dealing with the professional and private lives of the stars. Rechristened *Motion Picture Story Magazine,* the magazine had grown by 1912 into one of America's first film fan magazines. In the next fifteen years such publications as this and *Photoplay Magazine* would become some of the most popular reading matter in the country.

By the end of the second decade, the studios grew into complex organizations. They came to encompass the real estate on which the production plant was built, the plant itself, the costumes, the sets, the books waiting to be turned into films, the writers who turned books and stories into films, the makeup, the lights, the raw stock, the animal livestock, the carpenters and the carpentry shops, the canteens, the cameras, the laboratories in which the film was processed, the advertising and publicity men, the printing presses, the posters, the catalogues in which films were listed, the performers, the stars, the cans in which the reels of film were transported, the theatres, the carpets in the theatres, the usherettes, the ticket takers, and the popcorn sold in the theatre lobbies. They unified systems of distribution and exhibition, and in short, the studios aspired to be self-contained universes which controlled every aspect of the commercial cinema.

It was not unusual for one or two men to be in charge of this universe. These men were the studio heads. Sometimes the power was shared by others, but the head was known by those around and under him as a czar. And the only aspects of the business not directly controlled by the czar were the two found at the opposite ends of the whole filmmaking process — the audience and the chemical manufacture of the raw film stock.

In the first years of movies, exhibitors bought films outright from production companies or producers. They exhibited the pictures several times during a period of one to three days. An exhibitor who owned several theatres might bicycle the print from a screening at one house to a second Nickelodeon for a later screening, but when the motion picture had finished its run it was of no further use. It had to be destroyed. Even though the film itself may have been in fair condition, it could no longer be shown; everyone in the community had seen it. This was wasteful, and because of the volatile and combustible nature of film, it was dangerous.

As the number of filmmakers grew, so did the number of sources from which films could be bought. As central depositories of films were established, exhibitors found it economical to go to this one source for the films of many producers. Exchanges were set up. The exchange was the office in which the exhibitor traded one film program for another. Distributing descriptive catalogues to exhibitors, the exchange also functioned as an advertising agency for the producers. No longer did the exhibitor have to buy the film only to throw it away after a short time of limited use. The exhibitor could now rent a print from the exchange, and after a set period return it

named
from a
pendent
d out of
on pro-
depend-
aemmle
theatres
theatres
der con-

offered
pany in-
with no
ed to be
ight into
re would
aemmle,
ful in it-
tury Pic-

film busi-
Nickelo-
with the
Loew. It
t wanting
o Studio,
(MGM).

Pickford,
ned with
n agency,
ne overall
roduction
pendence.
nts Com-

nother. The film would then be recycled
was shown until it became so worn that it
through a projector. As the print became
as the film was viewed more widely in
munity, the rental cost or leasing fee of

who made the film and who leased it to
r). The exchange rented the film to the
wed the film in his theatre and then re-
e exhibitor paid the distributor, and the
r for the film. Theoretically, to encour-
the competition on which the American
to survive, production, distribution and
e and independent of one another.
able to offer his work to a number of
om the works of many producers, would
t according to public interest and the
er thought that the payment was not
he had the freedom to look for another
as able to survey the catalogues of sev-
y, on the basis of quality and interest to
ty in his theatre. All this was true in
promise of quick capital and a steady
lustry away from free trade into restric-
s.

so did the Patents Company. The stu-
ploy against the threatened monopoly,
nts Company died — and it died very
os appeared — the studios themselves

ne gentleman who had so graciously
ffiliated his IMP production company
utors and exhibitors to form Universal
ly, which is today's Universal/MCA.
or, the man who had brought Sarah
e to America, associated himself with
ful group of distributors and theatres.

91

The company that was formed, Paramount Pictures, wa
after an apartment building, and its trademark was taker
sketch doodled on a blotter. Laemmle and Zukor, both ind
producers, formed their companies in order not to be lock
theatres. The Patents Company owned most of the design
jectors, and had warned that theatres booking the films of i
ent producers would find themselves without projectors.
and Zukor knew it was no use making films if there were nc
in which to show them. The producers, to be assured that
would be available, put a number of independent houses u
tract. Other houses were built or bought outright.

William Fox ran an exchange, which the Patents Compar
to buy. Fox was determined not to sell. The Patents Com
sisted that if he refused their offer he would find himsel
producers to rent from and no theatres to rent to. Fox wan
guaranteed that he would have films to distribute, so he bo
a production company. He also wanted assurance that the
be theatres that would play his films, and like Zukor and
he put a chain of houses under contract. Large and powe
self, the Fox Film Corporation merged with Twentieth Ce
tures to become, in 1935, the gigantic 20th Century-Fox.

Marcus Loew was so attracted by the razzmatazz of the
ness that he rented seats by the day so he could open hi
deon. His little theatre grew into a string of big theatres
consequence that the Patents Company soon threatened
also threatened two brothers, Jack and Harry Warner. N
to be at the mercy of the trust, Loew acquired the Met
which later was incorporated into Metro-Goldwyn-Mayer
The Warner brothers also went into production.

Even the stars got into the act. Charlie Chaplin, Mar
and Miss Pickford's husband, Douglas Fairbanks, Sr., j
Griffith to pool their resources and formed a distributi
United Artists. Founded in 1919, UA did not have just
production plant; each of the individual members had a
unit of his own, and this assured each founder of his ind

In 1913 William Fox brought the Motion Picture Pa

pany to court, charging it with being engaged in unfair business practices and maintaining that the organization was a monopoly operating in violation of existing legislation. Fox asked the court to curtail the Patents Company's activities. It took four years for the company to be legally declared a trust, but by that time it did not matter much. The trust, tied as it was to its old ways, and still distributing inconsequential short films, could not compete with the ingenious tactics of the independents, nor could it cope with the salaries most popular performers were demanding. Indeed, by the time of its demise the trust's last subsidiary was collaborating with its enemies, the independents, in order to exist.

Thus one giant monopoly was replaced by several of even more gargantuan proportions. From this time until the courts acted again in the late forties, American motion picture production, distribution and exhibition were controlled by a small number of large studios. These corporations were run by a small group of men whose power rivalled that of Oriental potentates.

The men of the "front office," the studio heads, the chief executives, the czars, all were — all had to be — shrewd and daring businessmen. While their capacity for financial dealings was never doubted, many did not seem psychologically prepared to handle the power that their immense wealth bought. Indeed, sometimes they behaved rather foolishly. Some resented not having the artistic abilities of their employees, the directors and writers, and while they tried not to allow their resentment to affect their business negotiations, their hostility was sometimes evident. One executive was so annoyed that a script writer had won an Academy Award for a screenplay, he ordered all the writer's phones disconnected and the poor man's potted plants unpotted as well. While this represents a bizarre example of executive behavior, there were cases of talented persons being demoted so that "success would not go to their heads."

The czars were either men who had come to America as immigrants or they were second-generation Americans. They had begun as merchants in other businesses (clothing, jewelry) and soon became attracted to the dazzling promise of the new medium. For the most part they entered the motion picture business as operators of Kinetoscope parlors or as proprietors of Nickelodeons. While some may not have been distinguished for their honesty, all were hardworking. By toiling as many as eighteen hours a day, they built their businesses and within a decade won huge success. They seemed to be a living proof of the American Dream.

What was the success that these men won? It must have been satisfying to have helped in the elimination of the trust. But once the Patents Company was destroyed and the studios established, the studios and their heads gave truth to the cliché that "power tends to corrupt and absolute power corrupts absolutely."

The studio, it was felt, had to be built up continually; its influence always had to be extended farther. Such men as Fox, the Warner brothers, and a little later, Louis B. Mayer of Metro and Harry Cohn at Columbia, could not resist the pressure to compete with, to impress and to outdo the others of their peer group.

With such power came financial rewards. It is no wonder that studio executives behaved as if they were members of royal courts. Intrigues and all manner of power plays were rampant behind studio walls.

The chief executive of each studio was the focus of the buzzing, jockeying and jousting for power. To maintain his supreme position he had to keep both his partners and his subordinates in equilibrium. The executives' fears seldom had to do with the world of political or social change outside the studio; they were concerned with holding on to personal power — keeping their status secure.

As the studio grew, so did responsibilities. After a while the studio head was not able to act as a super-Ince. There was too much activity. Some responsibility had to be delegated. Reluctantly, it was. When it was handed over it was delegated quite cautiously and usually only given to members of a studio head's family. To insure that the power not slip away, marriages often were made between the children of executives, and nepotism, the favoring of relatives, still prevails within the industry.

If the studio executive's mind was not particularly serene, what of the minds of his employees? As a studio grew vaster, there was a strong need to hold its component parts more closely together. The system became inhuman in its operation. People came to be considered pieces of property and to each a price was affixed. That price fluctuated with fame, and fame was really determined by the powers in command.

The contracts by which employees were bound to the studio were feudal in character. They usually ran for a period of seven years. Actors, writers, and often directors had to agree to be locked in for this long period of time or face unemployment. Contracts were standard from studio to studio and if an employee succeeded in doing the impossible by shortening the agreement, he found himself out of work; no one else would hire him. Studios also bargained for each other's talent and had the prerogative to rent out employees. The talent had nothing to say about it; indeed, they usually didn't even receive a raise in pay. The studio kept whatever profit there was from the transaction.

A contract usually stipulated weekly paychecks but did not promise actual work, and employees felt that this was demeaning. There were many more people under contract than there were studio jobs at any given time. A talent scout might sign an aspiring young actress fresh out of drama school to appear in a film. A young writer might be hired to work with five collaborators on one screenplay. But once the assignment was completed there was no guarantee that another job would follow. It was steady work that everyone wanted. Actors had to keep their names and faces before the public. Writers and directors needed to practice their respective talents. If any employee incurred the displeasure of an executive, he would find himself still collecting his salary, but, until his contract expired, he was relegated to anonymity and his professional career was irreparably damaged.

Many famous performers thought they could use their popularity as a basis for bargaining, but even those who achieved great celebrity found it no protection. Fame could be taken away so easily. Even a popular player could be kept idle or assigned unsuitable parts. A comedian might be given a serious role or an attractive young actress selected to play a grandmother. And if these roles were not accepted, a length of time equal to that film's production was often added on to the seven-year contract.

The stars found the contractual system particularly grueling. Directors, writers, technicians, theatre managers — none of them had their private lives so exposed to public scrutiny. The public had as great an interest in the off-screen lives of the stars as it did in the films in which they appeared. Stars had to wear personality "masks" at all times. Whenever they were in the public eye, they had to conform to the image that the studio's press corps had created for them. The image was as much a part of the star as was his talent. Since it was thought that it was the star's image which attracted the public, the studio carefully controlled what the public knew about each performer.

A performer was ordered to keep his real private life concealed. Another private life was invented, and when the star was in public he had to live out this fabricated life. Information about this fantasy life appeared in the fan magazines, many of which were edited by the studios. After their debuts, many magazines degenerated from information about new films to gossip about stars. Unfortunately, many performers found it difficult to maintain this charade and found themselves in psychological despair. Hollywood created dreams, and many people working there found themselves incapable of living them.

From the bit players to the flagship theatres, the czars were rulers of their own organizations, but towards the end of the twenties two factors complicated their authority: morals and sound. While the studios were acquiring more and more properties, America had entered that free and easy living period, the Roaring Twenties. Millions of people, despite Prohibition, pursued a fast and reckless life. Drugs were a national concern; drinks were consumed in a thousand illegal speakeasies; skirt hems went up; and for many, a Puritan morality went out the window. The roar of the twenties was reflected in both the life-style of the Hollywood stars and in the films they made.

A number of stars became the victims of morphine, cocaine and opium. Some died. Popular figures became involved in ugly scandals; others created resentment by the lavish and profligate way in which they spent their money. It was one thing to give a party; it was quite another thing to send all your guests flying in a dirigible and, no

96

longer on United States soil, to invite your guests to consume what Prohibition denied — champagne.

Hollywood pressmen were no longer in control of their clients' images. How could an All-American Boy like Wallace Reid die at thirty of complications stemming from morphine addiction? Someone was trying to sell the public a dirty bill of goods. The deceased had not been a proper, healthy, robust lad after all. Was this the example with which schoolboys identified? If so, then these examples had to be stopped.

Church and women's groups from all over the country threatened to march into Hollywood en masse, brooms in hand, to sweep out "studio sewers." The Hollywood studios were not really within marching distance of any place, but the agitating groups were committed. Not to be deflected from decency, they attacked what was closest to them — the motion pictures themselves.

The National Board of Review, which had been created with the trust, had in effect died with it. Since there were new powers in Hollywood, it was their responsibility to straighten out the morality of their subjects and their product — the stars and films. In 1922 twelve top executives formed the Motion Picture Producers and Distributors Association. The M.P.P.D.A., whose name was soon changed to The Motion Picture Association of America (MPAA), made a very smart move. It hired "the General," Will Hays, Postmaster General, a respected Presbyterian Church elder and a community leader.

His stature did much to calm the cries of the reformers and to assure the public that Hollywood wanted to do what was right. The Hays Office set about purifying the industry. At first it merely issued statements of high moral purpose. The industry leaders promised compliance, but they didn't comply. Hays followed his pronouncements with a list of sultry books and controversial plays which he requested the studios not to buy. The books were best sellers, and the plays Broadway successes. The industry realized that there was considerable cash value in these titles, and so it negotiated a deal with the Hays Office. The producers promised to use only the titles of controversial properties. They would buy the works and have their own writers rewrite the stories so that the final product, the film, would not be offensive. The stories were indeed rewritten. Sophisticated stories became simpleminded, yet offensive passages often were not excised. Once more Hays tried to do his job: in 1927 his office published a list of "Don't show this!" and "If you're going to show this, then be careful" in films. The descriptions tended to be very broad, and the studios and their exhibitors did not heed Hays' recommendations.

In 1929 the stock market crashed, and during the course of the depression which followed, the period of cavorting came to an end. People suddenly made poor became severe and intense. Life meant work. The morality of the twenties was no longer applicable in the somber thirties; there seemed to be a grass-roots reaction against lightheartedness and frivolity. This feeling manifested itself in an intense hostility toward the depression-proof film industry, in which men could still amass considerable wealth.

In the late twenties and early thirties a new type of genre of film appeared: the gangster film. The underworld had gained national prominence during the twenties, when criminals supplied Americans with illegal alcoholic beverages. The thirties brought misery, and the recent way of life seemed eons of years away. With the sense of remoteness came nostalgia. The gangster films functioned almost as historical documents. *Little Caesar* (1930), *The Public Enemy* (1931), and *Scarface* (1932) appear as classic films today, but when they were released many critics thought that they tended to romanticize hoodlums and made gangsterism attractive. It was bad enough that Hollywood made films that titillated audiences; now films seemed to sympathize with lawbreakers. *More* pressure was put on the Hays Office.

The controversy became particularly acute with the publication of *Our Movie Made Children* (1933), a book by Henry J. Forman, in which the author presented a study of the effect of popular films on mass audiences. It examined the power of the medium, and its ability to influence the minds of young people. Forman concluded that most films could have an adverse effect on children.

The Catholic Church began to organize boycotts of certain films, and it threw up picket lines around theatres in which these films were playing. Under such pressure the films were withdrawn. In 1934 a group of bishops organized the National Legion of Decency (later changed to the National Catholic Office for Motion Pictures). The Legion reviewed films prior to release and rated them for Catholics. The original ratings ran to four categories, which ranged from "morally unobjectionable for general patronage" to "positively bad." By 1936 two more categories were added. A "positively bad" film was a condemned film, and it was considered a sin for church members aware of the rating to see it. The ratings functioned not only as a guidepost for Catholics; they also exerted economic pressure on the studios. A producer wanted to avoid having his film condemned. The "C" rating would limit the size of an audience considerably. Meanwhile, the filmmaker was under pressure from an even more effective censorial organization, and one which made the Legion of Decency look like a haven of radicalism.

Before the Legion had been established, a multidenominational group of clerics and "morally concerned" laymen insisted that the Hays office compile a more definitive list than the General's collection of "Do not show this's." The group attacked the problem of sin in the cinema, and "solved" it with a vengeance. In 1930 the Production Code emerged. It was a listing of all that should not be shown nor even suggested on the screen, and functioned as an encyclopedia of what a "decent" community considered gross, tasteless, sacrilegious and obscene. The group maintained that strict adherence to their code would cure films' moral sickness and "raise the moral standard of the nation." If the industry had not been under such intense pressure to reform its moral standards, it probably would have told the code, which was censorious in the extreme, that it could not be serious in its severe approach, but the industry chose to demonstrate concern. If there was to be censoring it should be exercised not by the out-of-industry Legion of Decency, but from within the industry itself.

By 1934 each member of the MPAA (representing all the large studios) promised to submit its scripts and the films produced from these scripts to the code's office. The code would examine various film projects for their moral health and might demand that certain cuts be made. If its recommendations were not heeded, the offending producer could be fined twenty-five thousand dollars. It was not the twenty-five thousand dollars, however, that forced the studios to recognize and obey the code. It was a small sum compared to everyday film production costs. What forced compliance was that members of the MPAA controlled almost every first-run theatre in the nation. A film could be made without the seal of code approval, but without a theatre in which to exhibit the film there was no possibility of any financial return. Each studio promised that it would not allow any of its theatres to present a film that did not have the blessing of the sanctimonious code.

From 1934 until well into the 1960's Hollywood strictly adhered to the code and censored itself. This industrial self-censorship was probably harsher than any governmental form which would have been open to both public opinion and court tests. Although the code was designed "to recreate and rebuild human beings exhausted with the realities of living," it probably did more to distort man's image of himself than any other cultural limitation in the nation's history. It certainly did "rebuild" human beings; it rebuilt them into *in*human beings. The code's "brave new world" was one in which good was equated with conformity and/or sweetness, in which good was always rewarded, in which suicide was seldom contemplated, in which drugs simply did not exist, in which sex was never mentioned, in which marriages were mostly happy and any unhappiness was caused by one partner's incurable selfishness, in which children called their father "Sir," in which babies were never naked, in which no one ever went to the toilet, in which the pains of childbirth were seldom witnessed, in which profanity was never used (profanity being words such as "jerk," "lousy," and "ass"), in which unmarried people never kissed passionately, and when they were married were consigned to separate beds, and in which cows had no udders. Even Walt Disney was requested to remove a cow's teats from a drawing!

It is understandable that the code wanted to preserve the sanctity of the family structure, to encourage piety, and to discourage unsavory examples. But it attacked the problem in the wrong way. It

100

advocated ignorance, but ignorance solves nothing. The authors of the code were aware that people have passions and deep conflicts, but they upheld the policy that these aspects of the human makeup were not fit subjects either for public display or for discussion in motion pictures. It may be argued that there is validity to the idea that some matters should be aired only in the privacy of a doctor's office, but there certainly was no excuse for the absurd degree to which this idea was expanded and imposed. Many European films of the time excelled in probing the human character, but most American films sadly lacked this quality.

By the early twenties most Nickelodeons had closed their doors. They were replaced by fewer and larger motion picture theatres. Some of these structures were so extraordinarily elaborate they were rightly called "motion picture palaces." As early as 1914 a three-thousand-seat cinema, the Strand, had been built in New York City, and two thousand seats became the standard size for a first-class, first-run theatre. Some were decorated like French châteaux, others like mosques out of the Arabian Nights, and still others like the magnificent regal tombs of the Egyptian Pharaohs. The aisles were carpeted, the ceilings painted with stars, and the spacious lobbies filled with statuary.

The grandest palace of them all, the Roxy, took two years to complete; it opened in New York in 1927. Its seating capacity was six thousand two hundred and its lobby could accommodate another two thousand patrons. It contained a hospital with two nurses and a physician. Its orchestra pit could seat an orchestra of one hundred and ten musicians, for which three conductors had been hired. Like the program at Radio City Music Hall today, the several daily film showings were preceded by musical extravaganzas in which complex scenery was utilized, sets were changed frequently, versatile performers displayed a multitude of talents, vocal choruses sang, and ballet troupes danced (see Figure 51). For some years the Roxy even featured a full-scale ice-skating show on its stage. The Roxy was torn down in 1960, but Radio City Music Hall, constructed in

1932 as part of the Rockefeller Center complex, has survived its predecessor.

William Fox, owner of the Fox Studio, saw the Roxy while it was being completed and was greatly impressed with this spectacular monument to the motion picture. He felt compelled to contract for the palace as a "flagship" theatre. Flagship theatres were those selected by the studios to premiere their "A," or high-budget, high-quality, pictures. By the time the Roxy came under the aegis of the Fox Corporation, the studio system was complete and functioning well.

The decor and ambience of the theatres did much to disguise the commercial nature of the industry. The theatre acted as the attractive and seductive packaging of the merchandise. Surrounded by plush trappings as it viewed the picture, and knowing about films only from sitting in a theatre, the public associated the glamor of the theatre with the *making* of the film product. The theatre was a place of relaxation and comfort where the mind was soothed from the tensions of daily life. The theatre was a refuge. To the audience, film was magic, an exotic excursion into a silver dimension.

51. *A stage show at Radio City Music Hall.* (Museum of Modern Art/Film Stills Archive)

During the early twenties the studios had made such a tremendous investment in property that even with millions attending the theatres, motion pictures suffered a significant loss in profits. In 1926 the Warner studio was on the verge of bankruptcy, and in desperation, it made a gamble. On August 26, 1926, it presented its first "sound" film, *Don Juan,* publicly. Although various sound systems had been developed over the years, it was not until the American motion picture found itself in dire need of some new attraction that sound was explored seriously. Warners used a system called Vitaphone, in which the sound was recorded on separate discs, which were played in such a way that the sound was synchronized with the action of the film. *Don Juan* was essentially a silent film. Actors did not speak, and titles were still used to describe the action. The essential difference was in the way the music, formerly played live by an orchestra or pianist, was now presented.

With the exception of Fox, the studios resisted the conversion to sound. It was a period of tight money and, as usual, the studios behaved conservatively. If sound should be widely used, theatres would have to be rewired; this would be expensive. Elaborate recording equipment would be necessary; its purchase would be costly. Musical sound films would lead inevitably to talking sound films, but many stars had unsatisfactory voices. One famous handsome actor had a voice with a high-pitched squeal. A popular actress, born in Europe, had never bothered to learn English. Voices would have to be trained. New talent would have to be found. All things considered, sound seemed more bother than it was worth.

Warners, however, released a sentimental film in 1927 which was so tremendously popular that all hesitation was swept aside. In *The Jazz Singer,* a popular entertainer of the day, Al Jolson, first warned the audience, "Wait a minute, you ain't heard nothing yet!," and then proceeded to sing, "Toot, Toot, Tootsie, Good-bye." He was really singing good-bye to the silent film. Like *The Jazz Singer,* other first sound films were not so much "talkies" as silent films with a synchronized musical score and an occasional dialogue or song sequence. There were few conversations in these films. The studios cautiously geared themselves to sound production, and many of the early sound films were directed in such a way that they could be understood if

103

they were projected silently. Sound pictures might have disappeared after a short life as a novelty if the technique had remained that of the Warner Vitaphone system.

But with the development of the Fox-Case Movietone process, sound pictures took a new direction. Movietone was adapted from a process developed by a pioneer in technology, Dr. Lee de Forest, who in turn perfected Phonofilm from another process patented by another inventor. The Phonofilm, a sound-on-film process, was used as early as 1923, when a few prints of *The Covered Wagon* were released with the orchestration (the musical score) on the film itself. In the Movietone process, sound waves were translated by means of a photoelectric cell into stimuli of light, which were then recorded directly onto the film. Picture and sound shared the same ribbon of celluloid, and each was in constant synchronization with the other. Separate discs were not needed. The Movietone technique meant that sound and image would stay "married" and move together.

Since the studios did not have enough funds to finance the expensive shift to sound, loans had to be secured from investment houses and banks. At first Wall Street had been reluctant to establish itself in an unstable market where personal fortunes quickly fluctuated. However, when New York financiers recognized that about a billion and a quarter dollars had been paid in admissions in 1930, they had to acknowledge that here was a depression-proof industry. Although loans were made, the financial titans of the east, represented ultimately by the Morgan and Rockefeller groups, were more interested in acquiring the source of the sound films, the Vitaphone and Movietone patents. Through a complex series of legal maneuvers that would easily take a heavy volume to document, by 1935 all relevant patents were in the hands of these combines. Although the studio boss was still commander in his own organization, he needed Western Electric, a subsidiary of American Telephone and Telegraph, or RCA Photophone's cooperation, if he were to make sound films.

The shift to sound, as well as the attacks by censorship groups, had played havoc within the industry. There were new alliances, new affiliations and new parties with whom to deal. By 1936 few of the original film czars, the men who had outfoxed the Patents Com-

104

pany, were active in the companies they had established. Nevertheless, the companies that remained established were for the next fifteen years very well established.

4 Some Talents in and around Hollywood

During the reign of the large studios an exciting array of talent was bought by Hollywood. MGM advertised that it had more stars than there were in the heavens. If that were so, some of the stars shone more brightly than others. Nevertheless, the studios did play home to a number of remarkable talents. Although the scope of this book is not wide enough to allow a description of all the fine artists who were attracted by and to Hollywood, a mention of a few might indicate the breadth of talent that worked for the studios.

Florence Lawrence and Broncho Billy may have been the *first* film stars, but the one most popular and most loved was certainly "Little Mary" — Mary Pickford (Figure 52). Mary was born in Toronto as Gladys Smith; her father died when she was very young, and while she was still a small child she joined her mother onstage in a touring minor theatrical company. Her sweet appearance won her early popularity. In 1909, at the age of sixteen, she made her debut in films and was directed by Griffith for the next several years. It was Griffith who first popularized her in the appealing role of a Cinderella in distress. This was a part she was to play with great finesse (*The New York Hat*, 1912; *Tess of the Storm Country*, 1914 and 1922; *A Poor Little Rich Girl*, 1917; *Stella Maris*, 1918; even *Pollyanna*, 1920). She came to be known as "the child with the golden curls" and then, "America's Sweetheart." The public loved Mary's childlike ingenue image and would not allow her to mature in her films; it avoided the pictures where she was cast as a grown woman. Not wanting to play young roles while she was in her middle thirties, Mary Pickford retired in 1933 after the making of *Secrets*. She still lives in Hollywood and is one of that community's spectacular legends.

106

52. *Probably the most celebrated star of all, "little" Mary Pickford, "America's Sweetheart," in one of the many films in which she played "the girl with the golden curls."* (Museum of Modern Art/Film Stills Archive)

Miss Pickford's skill as a businesswoman was extraordinary. As her fame increased, so did her efforts for better wages, and her powers of bargaining were such that she drove not a few companies to the brink of bankruptcy. In 1920, in a wedding of the brightest stars, she married Douglas Fairbanks, but not before they, together with D. W. Griffith and Charlie Chaplin, had organized United Artists. They would make their own films, and each film was guaranteed distribution through their company.

Douglas Fairbanks had been a popular Broadway performer before he appeared in films. By 1915 he had been in a few films, displaying an abundance of zest and energy and remarkable physical skills. Gifted with an exceptional athletic ability and high spirits, Fairbanks created an image which made him as celebrated as Mary's sweetheart image made her. Cavalier, devil-may-care, with optimism and a buoyant sense of humor, Fairbanks jumped, leaped, dashed and somersaulted triumphantly over villains and out of tricky situations. His down-to-earth character cut through the affectations and pretensions of others. In a way, Fairbanks — brash, youthful, enthusiastic and successful — symbolized America of the post–World War I period. He became the idol of most American schoolboys (Figure 53), and an admirer went so far as to name a peak in Yosemite National Park after him.

53. *The buoyant Douglas Fairbanks, Sr., about to perform a spectacular leap in the exciting* Thief of Bagdad. (Museum of Modern Art/Film Stills Archive)

Fairbanks collaborated with directors, writers and designers on all aspects of the productions in which he starred. This collaborative spirit was found in the approach of many great film stars who were concerned that the total impression of a film be in concert with the characters they portrayed. After the founding of United Artists, Fairbanks moved from the making of contemporary action films (*The Mystery of the Leaping Fish,* 1916; *When the Clouds Roll By,* 1919) to the production of sumptuous and spectacular costume melodramas — swashbucklers such as *The Three Musketeers,* 1920; *Robin Hood,* 1922; *The Thief of Bagdad,* 1924; *The Iron Mask,* 1929.

Innocence was one of the great virtues of pre-depression America. Both Pickford and Fairbanks, who continually played characters facing life with an enthusiasm born of ingenuousness, made this quality an economic asset. As America matured, so did her celebrities.

108

Her idols became more complex, brooding, somewhat more sensitive, with deeper sources of emotional power.

Perhaps the only actress to rival Pickford in popularity was a mysterious and enigmatic Swede, Greta Gustafsson, who had come to America with a compatriot, Mauritz Stiller, a prominent director invited to Hollywood to make films. While Stiller's career faded, Gustafsson's blossomed. Her last name was changed to Garbo, and it was as Greta Garbo that she became celebrated. (See Figure 54).

Appearing in a number of mediocre films and a few classic ones (*Queen Christina,* 1933; *Camille,* 1937; *Ninotchka,* 1939), Garbo infused a whole work with her electric presence. Her image could not have been more unlike Pickford's. Garbo was a tragic heroine, a woman of the world, understanding of its ways and extraordinarily sensitive to its manners. Every gesture, every movement, no matter how small, had a significance, a psychological meaning of its own. Unlike other stars, she successfully resisted studio interference with her private life. Her off-screen life was shrouded in secrecy. A jealously guarded private life only made the public more curious. Garbo retired from motion pictures abruptly while she still was in the midst of her fame. She has not made a film since 1941.

Some popular actresses have been very accomplished performers; others merely have been images designed by studios. A few have been both. A personal and highly selective list of the latter would have to begin with a contemporary of Mary Pickford: Lillian Gish

54.   *Greta Garbo (center) and Robert Taylor in George Cukor's version of* Camille. (© 1936 — Metro-Goldwyn-Mayer, Inc.)

who, like Pickford, first appeared in Griffith films (*Broken Blossoms,* 1919; *Orphans of the Storm,* 1922).

Although there were a number of famous stars in the twenties, perhaps the only one to enjoy the celebrity of Garbo was a one-time Sennett Bathing Beauty. Gloria Swanson appeared in a number of dramatic films (*Zaza,* 1923; *Stage Struck,* 1925) and performed with admirable understanding and enthusiasm, but in those films where she was required to play gently comic roles, she excelled. Her timing was extraordinary and her grace remarkable. Directed by Allan Dwan in *Manhandled* (1924), she portrays a New York shopgirl who suddenly finds herself lifted from the crowded basement of a department store and the even more crowded subways to a world of fashion salons and private limousines (Figure 55).

55. *Gloria Swanson in Allan Dwan's* Manhandled. (Courtesy Universal M.C.A.)

In the thirties more actresses of stature appeared. While Bette Davis and Katharine Hepburn played well in intensely dramatic roles (respectively, *Jezebel*, 1938, and *Morning Glory*, 1933), they were also fluent in performing comedies (respectively, *It's Love I'm After*, 1937, and *Bringing Up Baby*, 1938). Continuing the tradition of the vamp seductively pictured by Theda Bara in the early 1915 film *A Fool There Was*, there was that supreme mancatcher, Mae West, a buxom lady with more elegance and style than beauty, and a wit so sharp that it brought forth not only laughs but loud cries for censorship (*She Done Him Wrong*, 1933). Jean Harlow, who died before the decade's end at twenty-six of a neglected disease, has been underrated. Perhaps her image of flamboyant sexuality obscured critical appraisal, but in films like *Dinner at Eight* (1933), she displayed a fine comic sense. Marlene Dietrich was pictured as such an irresistible force (*The Devil Is a Woman*, 1935) that even when she played a perfect wife and mother (*Blonde Venus*, 1932) men were still attracted by her fine beauty.

During the forties the phenomenon known as the "love goddess" captured the public imagination, but to the G.I.'s at first fighting and then stationed in both Europe and Asia, Betty Grable (*I Wake Up Screaming*, 1941), Jane Russell (*The Outlaw*, 1943), Lana Turner (*The Postman Always Rings Twice*, 1946) and most spectacularly, Rita Hayworth (*Cover Girl*, 1944 and *Gilda*, 1946) were exquisite "pinup" girls.

Often Hollywood even made stars of women whose athletic abilities already had earned them some measure of fame. Both Annette Kellerman (*Neptune's Daughter*, 1914) and Esther Williams (*Neptune's Daughter*, 1949) were champion swimmers. Norwegian Sonja Henie was a celebrated figure skater before she made such films as *Sun Valley Serenade* (1941). The fluffy plots of these entertainments were merely devices to showcase the stars' particular talents in elaborately staged routines.

While both Bette Davis and Katharine Hepburn continued their bravura performances into the forties and fifties (respectively, *All About Eve*, 1950, and *The African Queen*, 1951), another Swedish actress, Ingrid Bergman, both began and ended a highly successful career within the decade. A cool and exacting actress, she had played

111

roles of innocent, victimized women (*Gaslight,* 1944) or of exceptionally virtuous ones (*The Bells of St. Mary,* 1945). When she announced that she would have a child out of wedlock, the public was stunned and outraged: her films were boycotted. On her return to the American film (*Anastasia,* 1956, photographed in England), she won an Academy Award for her performance, but her subsequent popularity was not as wide as it had originally been. However, by that time the whole idea of the star was beginning to lose its halo of romanticism.

Just as Garbo's image was different from Pickford's, so was that of Rudolph Valentino different from Fairbanks'. Having failed to graduate from a military academy in Venice, Italy, the young man emigrated to the States, and before he found his way into films worked at many odd jobs. The first thing he did when he made his appearance in a film was to change his name. He had to, for who would be able to remember or cope with Rodolpho Alfonzo Rafaelo Pierre Filibert Gugliemi di Valentina d'Antonguolla? In his early films Valentino was cast as a bit player, often as a villain. He did not achieve fame until he was spotted by the casting director for a big-budget romantic film, *The Four Horsemen of the Apocalypse* (1921). When the film was released he became popular overnight. Whereas Fairbanks' attraction emanated from his good-naturedness and carefree attitude, Valentino's lay in his deep moodiness and languid sexuality. His passion compensated amply for his lack of humor. Women all over the world swooned when Valentino, dressed as a wild Arab (*The Sheik,* 1921), swept across the burning desert sands on his horse and carried away his beloved (Figure 56). After being operated upon for an inflamed appendix, Valentino suddenly died at thirty-one of peritonitis. His premature passing made such an impression on lovesick followers that it led a number of them to suicide.

It was difficult for American male contemporaries of Valentino to identify with him. Considering other leading men of the period, he was *not* exceptional in this regard, but his complexion was too soft, his manner too feline, and his demeanor too suave to be considered natural. John Gilbert, who came from the American theatre, in the early twenties had an image almost as exotic as Valentino's. Even

112

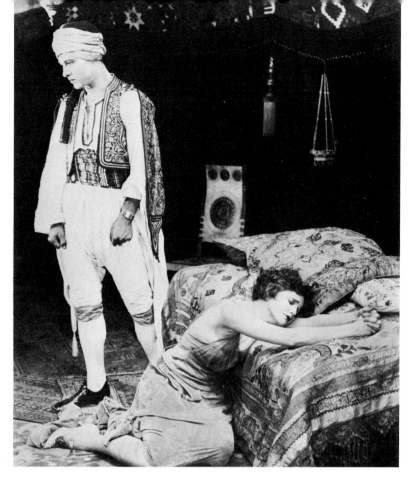

56.   *Rudolph Valentino as the exotic, romantic Arab in* The Sheik. *Women all over the world were as emotionally affected by Valentino as Agnes Ayres appears to be in this still.* (Museum of Modern Art/Film Stills Archive)

though he later adopted a quieter manner, when sound arrived, he found that his high-pitched voice was not suitable for the roles he had once played. Once Gilbert exited, Gary Cooper and Clark Gable appeared, to set the tone for actors not only of the thirties but of the forties and fifties and into the sixties as well. Clark Gable was "natural" and became a hero as Fairbanks had been in his time. Gary Cooper worked in a low key, demonstrating how a man could remain civilized while making good use of all aspects of his mental and physical possibilities (*The Virginian,* 1929; *Sergeant York,* 1941;

High Noon, 1952). (See Figures 57 and 58.) When in *It Happened One Night* (1934) Gable was revealed as not wearing an undershirt, the sales of undershirts was reported by worried manufacturers to have been cut by half. The swagger he demonstrated in *Gone With the Wind* (1939) was widely imitated by men who began to treat their girlfriends as Rhett Butler treated Scarlett O'Hara.

There is a subdued nature to the acting style of most male dramatic stars, the model for which may have been the performances of Gable and Cooper. Humphrey Bogart (*The Maltese Falcon,* 1941; *Casablanca,* 1942), Henry Fonda (*You Only Live Once,* 1937; *The Grapes of Wrath,* 1940), Cary Grant (*Only Angels Have Wings,* 1939; *North By Northwest,* 1959), Alan Ladd (*The Blue Dahlia,*

57. *Clark Gable and Claudette Colbert erect the "Walls of Jericho" in Frank Capra's sly comedy,* It Happened One Night. (Courtesy Columbia Pictures)

114

58. *Gary Cooper on the set of the 1929 version of Owen Wister's much-filmed novel,* The Virginian. (Museum of Modern Art/Film Stills Archive)

1946; *Shane*, 1953), Gregory Peck (*Spellbound*, 1945; *The Gunfighter*, 1950), James Stewart (*Mr. Smith Goes to Washington*, 1939; *Rear Window*, 1954), Spencer Tracy (*Boys' Town*, 1938; *Northwest Passage*, 1940), and John Wayne (*Reap the Wild Wind*, 1942; *Sands of Iwo Jima*, 1949) all portrayed the man of action who seemed to have an underlying philosophy that civilized restraint and rational thought need not hamper the ability to act forcefully. This is not to say that the above actors always played this type of role, nor is it to suggest that one's performance could be substituted for another's. After all, in 1938 both Bogart (*Treasure of the Sierra Madre*) and Wayne (*Red River*) played fanatic men who drove themselves to defeat, but the two desperate characters were played in different styles.

Not only were there actors and actresses who were stars. There were singer/comediennes like Jeanette MacDonald (*Love Me Tonight*, 1932), dancers like Ruby Keeler (*42nd Street*, 1933),

115

singer/dancers like Ginger Rogers (*Shall We Dance,* 1937) and Miss Rogers's 1933–39 dancing partner, the extraordinarily limber and durable Fred Astaire. Astaire, who was born in 1900, can still be found fit and dancing on television specials, and has an elegance of style rarely found. Not only is his dancing skill remarkable, but he also devised many of the ingeniously choreographed interludes in his films. In *Royal Wedding* (1951), directed by Stanley Donen, Astaire casually makes his way up a wall and dances, upside down, on the ceiling! Astaire's most recent film musical role was in *Finian's Rainbow* (1968).

There were also the children. Jackie Coogan appeared in *The Kid* when he was seven (1921), and Shirley Temple (*Wee Willie Winkie,* 1937) first appeared in films while she was still a baby. Deanna Durbin (*One Hundred Men and a Girl,* 1937), Judy Garland (*The Wizard of Oz,* 1939) and Elizabeth Taylor (*National Velvet,* 1944) all became popular while still in their early teens. The roles these young people played tended to be cute and both precious and precocious; most of the time the characters they portrayed were endowed with a moral sense finer than that of the adult characters with whom they associated.

There is one breed of performer that has not survived, and mention should be made of those character actors who, like Boris Karloff, the original and most famous Frankenstein monster (1931), and Bela Lugosi, the first Dracula in American cinema (1931), specialized in grotesque roles of the undead (werewolves, vampires and zombies) and of the deformed. The one actor whose remarkable talent actually created this special province was born of deaf and dumb parents. From a very early age young Lon Chaney had to use both his face and body in the most plastic manner to communicate better with his parents. Although he appeared in about one hundred films after his debut role in 1913, it was not until he was "cured" of a crippling disease by *The Miracle Man* (1919) that his singular talents were properly shown, and achieved fame (Figure 59). From that time until his death at forty-four in 1930, he was known for his exceptional ability not only to create the most macabre roles (often at great pain to himself; see the ghoulish prowler in *London after Midnight,* 1927), but also to bring feelings of tenderness and sympa-

116

59. *Lon Chaney, without and with makeup, in* The Miracle Man. (Museum of Modern Art/Film Stills Archive)

60. The Phantom of the Opera (*Lon Chaney*). (The Museum of Modern Art/Film Stills Archive)

thy to his most beastly looking creations (*The Hunchback of Notre Dame,* 1923: *The Phantom of the Opera,* 1925) (see Figure 60). His monsters were remarkable in that they were human and humane, even romantic! Chaney was expert in the use of makeup, but hesitated to use it if he could achieve a similar startling effect through facial contortion. His art was not limited to contortions of face; his body was as supple as that of any advanced yogi. In *The Unknown* (1927), Chaney plays an armless circus wonder who shoots rifles and smokes cigarettes with his feet, and in *The Penalty* (1920), Chaney is an ugly, mobile underworld leader whose legs had been amputated while he was a boy. (His girlfriend must sit under the piano when he plays so she can work the foot pedals with her hands.)

The star treatment, in which a whole studio geared itself to the fabricating of an image, succeeded in creating many exciting presences. A large number of films were especially designed as vehicles for the stars so they might be kept in the public's attention. These films served no other function than to emphasize the appearance of the star. In the fifties, however, the fundamental nature of the studios began to change and so did the nature of stardom. But this is material better suited to Chapter Five.

The comic was a special star, and the period of the twenties is remembered by many as the Golden Age of Comedy. Born in poverty, Charlie Chaplin (Figures 61, 62) left school for the stage and

61. *Charles Chaplin in the comic genius's first appearance in his famed costume:* Kid Auto Races at Venice (*known also as* Kid Auto at the Races). *Here he plays the brash, nasty and aggressive character of his earliest films.* (Museum of Modern Art/Film Stills Archive)

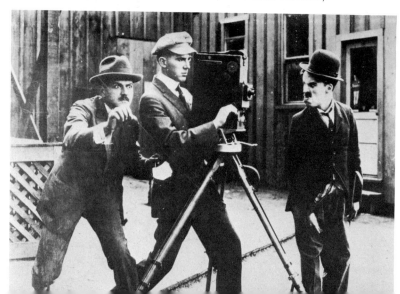

62. *And so, good deed accomplished, Chaplin, now the beloved tramp, winds his way out of one situation and into the next. This pose from* The Tramp *speaks eloquently of the performer's "persona," or character, which became world famous.* (Museum of Modern Art/Film Stills Archive)

was trained in acrobatics and mime. He came to America from England as part of an act in a pantomime show. Having toured the States for three years, Chaplin was spied by a Keystone talent scout, and was sent to California, where he made a number of films primarily distinguished by the frantic Sennett pace (*Laughing Gas*, 1914; *Tillie's Punctured Romance*, 1914).

Having achieved a degree of celebrity, Chaplin graduated from a salary of $150 a week to almost ten times that when he quit Keystone for work at Essanay, where the filmmaker began to develop his renowned character of the tramp (*The Tramp*, 1915). The over-assertive figure who disrupted the meet in *Kid Auto Races at Venice* (1914) matures into the resourceful little vagabond whose costume was to become the world's most famous. Continually oppressed, he

119

63. *Chaplin and the foundling (Jackie Coogan) are on the lookout for the law in* The Kid. (Museum of Modern Art/Film Stills Archive)

always neatly outfoxed his oppressor in ways that were both startling and funny. In 1916, at the age of twenty-seven, he joined the Mutual Film Corporation at a salary of $10,000 a week with a bonus of $150,000. His first films had been half-reelers; now, with the growing length of other films, Chaplin's next works were two-reelers, and although each can be considered excellent, special mention should be made of *One A.M., Behind the Screen, Easy Street,* and *The Immigrant.* By 1918, in his own studio, Chaplin began production of a series of eight films to be released through a major chain of theatres. As a derelict, he befriends a sorry canine in *A Dog's Life* (1918); *Shoulder Arms,* made the same year, is touched with some bitter-

120

ness in its story of a private who bumbles his way to heroism in the trenches of World War I.

In surely one of the most touching films ever made, *The Kid* (1921), Chaplin, penniless and living in squalor, finds an abandoned infant (Jackie Coogan). Despite his circumstances he raises the child himself. With a great capacity for love and remarkable resourcefulness at overcoming a lack of material comforts, he succeeds in inventing a sympathetic life-style (see Figure 63).

He and the kid go into the window-repair business. The kid breaks the windows; Chaplin appears nonchalantly on the spot to repair them.

The Gold Rush, which Chaplin directed in 1925, is a dark comedy. The tramp shows up in the barren Northwest. Man's reaction to deprivation may be a strange subject for comedy, but Chaplin takes this unlikely material and gives it a humorous, if grotesque, touch. At one point in the film a delirious starving prospector imagines that Chaplin is a plump chicken and chases our poor hero round and round an isolated cabin.

Chaplin the pantomimist behaved cautiously when pictures began to "talk" in the late twenties. He composed the musical scores for two films, *City Lights* (1931) and *Modern Times* (1936), but he himself did not utter a word in either of them. When he did speak as *The Great Dictator* (1940) he spoke gibberish, a gibberish that formed an intelligible language. Breaking away from the tramp character, Chaplin in this film played a dual role of the oppressor and the oppressed. Hitler's attitude to the world was neatly satirized when the dictator began to play with the globe as if it were no more than a colorful beach ball.

Chaplin was to make two more films in America. In the sardonic *Monsieur Verdoux* (1947), Chaplin played the debonair Bluebeard, a delightful man, but a murderer with no guilt. The film so disturbed and offended a public used to black-and-white issues that it elicited cries of moral indignation. It was a failure at the box office and Chaplin himself withdrew the film from circulation. *Limelight* (1952), a sentimental but touching tale of backstage life, was greeted with scarcely more enthusiasm.

The filmmaker grew increasingly bitter about his career in the

States. The press had made a scandal of his private life, the Internal Revenue Service claimed discrepancies in his tax statements, and government offices accused him of being sympathetic towards Communism. Chaplin exiled himself to Switzerland. He has refused to allow his satiric *A King in New York* (1957) to be shown in America. His last film to be seen here was the British-made *Countess from Hong Kong* (1966), starring Marlon Brando and Sophia Loren. As director of this quaint contemporary comedy, he cast himself only in a minor role.

Chaplin can be called the world's most renowned film comedian. His many films have been shown anywhere in the world that a movie house existed, and his antics have transcended time and place.

Like Chaplin, Buster Keaton was born into a theatrical family and made his debut in film after extensive gymnastic training and an apprenticeship in American vaudeville. Both men were strong, agile, graceful and boyish. Each created a specific personality that remained essentially the same from film to film and adventure to adventure; but each gave this character a remarkable dimension. Keaton's costumes changed, but the man in the costume remained a very particular person. He impersonated this character by maintaining a certain melancholy facial expression. Keaton was celebrated as the "Great Stone Face," and his relatively dour look did indeed make his face seem immobile. But he conveyed a host of emotions by subtle small actions, a quick alteration of expression, or a sudden halt. A wink of his eye was as revealing as a flood of happy tears.

64.   *Buster Keaton up front on a driverless train in* The General. (Museum of Modern Art/Film Stills Archive)

Unlike Chaplin, Keaton was not able to direct all his films. He did, however, work closely with the director; sometimes he took over from unsure hands. Keaton's timing was perfection itself, and the speed of his reactions was a source of constant amusement. The fluidity of his motions was as notable as his boundless athletic capacity. His comedy frequently had to do with recalcitrant mechanical contraptions (cannons, diving gear, motion picture cameras, boats, trains, and in the short film, *One Week*, 1920, even a do-it-yourself house) and his eventual mastery of them. In tackling unpleasantnesses, Chaplin was slick in his resourcefulness; Keaton usually fumbled his way to success. In *The Cameraman* (1928) Keaton forgets to turn off the mechanical action of his camera, and some valuable footage with which he wins his girl is shot. In *Seven Chances* (1925) he marries a girl and gains his inheritance in the nick of time (and one of the most exciting nicks of time in film!), due to the malfunctioning of a clock.

One of Keaton's most hilarious films, *The General* (1927), is said to have been based on an incident which occurred in Big Shanty, Georgia, during the Civil War. The hero is a locomotive train engineer (Figure 64). His occupation exempts him from army service. His plucky efforts at disguising himself in order to be able to enlist come to no avail. By getting the "General" (a famous train of its day) across the lines, our brave hero is able to prove his worth both to his girl and the army.

In *The Navigator* (1924) he is cast as an idle rich young man whose every whim is accommodated by servants, but who soon gets the opportunity to prove he is competent enough to overcome the greatest odds. Finding himself on an ocean liner without a crew, he succeeds in running the ship on a voyage solely with the help of his society girlfriend. *Sherlock Jr.* (1924) is one of the strangest of films. In it Keaton plays a motion picture projectionist who is studying to be a detective. Yet it is he who is falsely accused of a crime; although he does not solve this crime, while on the job he falls asleep and his dream self jumps from the auditorium into the screen. And it is in the movie that is being projected that Keaton solves the crime. Keaton's dream self is a master detective who, like all dream figures, has uncanny and supernatural abilities. Although there are sequences that are as funny as the funniest scenes in any of his films, one sits in amazement at both Keaton's and his talented cameraman Elgin Lessley's tremendous understanding of the film's potential to create the most effective illusions.

No less weird and unsettling is Keaton's short film, *The Playhouse* (1921), in which multiple exposures are perfectly used. Keaton plays every role in this film, each performer onstage, and every member of the audience (man, woman and child).

Keaton maintained his own independent production organization until 1927. Unwisely, he sold out to a large studio, for whom he then went to work. Keaton was used to working informally; he maintained congenial relations with his crew, whom he hired as much for their skill at playing baseball as for their technical competence. Casual sports were not allowed to be played on a no-nonsense studio lot; so

65.   *Harold Lloyd, a fine comic talent of the twenties, falls into a precarious position in* Safety Last! (Museum of Modern Art/Film Stills Archive)

Keaton and his studio boss soon had an altercation, and it was Keaton who suffered. Work that he wanted to do was taken from him and he was offered roles in only minor films. Although he appeared in over fifty films during this period, his reputation went into eclipse. He passed into relative obscurity until the very last few years of his life. Keaton died in 1966 just as a new audience was growing for his silent-film work.

Chaplin and Keaton were not the only comedians to distinguish the silent film. Other talents included the two "regular guys" Harold Lloyd (*High and Dizzy,* 1920; *The Freshman,* 1925) and Charley Chase (*Mighty Like a Moose,* 1925; *All Wet,* 1929), the underdog Harry Langdon (*The Strong Man,* 1926), and Raymond Griffith, whose *Hands Up!* (1926) bears an interesting resemblance to *The General.* Lloyd (Figure 65) retired from films at the height of his success; Chase continued to make short comedies (some of which he directed under his family name, Parrott); Langdon and Griffith never did adapt to the demands of the sound film.

The nature of filmed comedy changed when sound was introduced. While there has not been a period to match the intense comic activity of the days of the silents, there have been a number of creditable comics in "talkies." As the emphasis changed to spoken words, humor became something other than visual. Jokes were told and laughs were provoked by the way lines were delivered.

W. C. Fields, a master of the drawl (*The Fatal Glass of Beer,* 1933), was probably the only man who made a profession out of being cantankerous. His hatred of pets and children is amusingly shown in *It's a Gift* (1934) and *Never Give a Sucker an Even Break* (1941). Whenever Eddie Cantor got into the most improbable locations, such as ovens and vats of boiling oil (*Whoopee!,* 1930 and *Roman Scandals,* 1933), the tone of his voice was as comic as his continually dazed expression. Much of the humor in a Danny Kaye film (*Up In Arms,* 1944 and *The Inspector General,* 1949) derives from the speed of the comedian's delivery and, despite the breakneck verbal pace, from the careful articulation of each syllable. Bob Hope's hopeless womanizing got him into elaborate situations, which in his cowardice he wished he were out of. But his film character was not nearly as funny as his devastating wisecracks, one-line retorts as

66. *Stan Laurel was the thin and placid half, while Oliver Hardy was the chubby and bullying half of the great comic duo, Laurel and Hardy. Here they are pictured in a still from* Brats. (Museum of Modern Art/Film Stills Archive)

humorous in the telling as in their substance. While Hope played in some more serious films (*Beau James*, 1957), Jerry Lewis still plays the same zany incompetent he did when he first appeared in films with Dean Martin in 1949 (*My Friend Irma*).

It was not only the single comics who made the twenties so rich a time for comedy. There was the irrepressible team of Laurel and Hardy. Stan Laurel and Oliver Hardy worked for Hal Roach, a producer whose studio earned a considerable reputation for itself by making short comedies (close to two thousand from 1915 into the forties!). Both men began as separate comics (Laurel played in the same pantomime troupe that Chaplin had), and each worked alone for a good many years before they were teamed up in 1927 to become comedy's most famous twosome. They were perfect foils for each other. Ollie was fat, impatient, and incredibly pompous; Stan was thin, incredibly patient, and meek. On the screen, both were inexpressibly stupid. Whether they were doormen (*Double Whoopee*, 1929). Christmas-tree salesmen (*Big Business*, 1929), two sailors out on a jaunt with their girls (*Two Tars*, 1928), or piano delivery men (*The Music Box*, 1932), their adventures would start a chain reaction which would lead inevitably to a veritable orgy of

126

total destruction (Figure 66). Cars were stripped, houses demolished, whole areas filthied up by debris or paint, and swank hotels turned topsy-turvy.

When it came to lunatic behavior and insane whoop-de-doings, the Marx brothers, each acting a prize booby by himself, could not be equaled. If ever two films have to be seen to be understood or believed, they are *Duck Soup* (1933) and *A Night at the Opera* (1935).

The Marx Brothers gravitated from vaudeville to the Broadway stage, and from there, via their live production of *The Coconuts,* to films. Their costumes and manners were as flamboyant as their names — Groucho, Harpo, Chico and Zeppo. Groucho appeared with his lip moustache aquiver above a fine cigar and the coattails of his too large tuxedo trailing behind him. He walked in a suggestive, slouched position, and did not wander casually into situations; he propelled himself into them under such disguises as Rufus T. Firefly, Otis B. Driftwood, Wolf J. Flywheel and J. Cheever Loophole. He was always the con artist supreme, sharp of tongue and fast in wit. His public behavior, like that of Harpo and Chico, was crude and crass. Each was adept at turning any attempt at order or any logic completely inside out and upside down. They moved very quickly, darting from one situation to another, and polite society had to beware, for the brothers were each capable of the most outrageous antisocial behavior.

Harpo had a mop of curly blond hair and he wore outlandish suits and titanic ties. His harp usually appeared out of nowhere, and a hardware store supply was kept up his sleeves. Harpo never uttered a word, but he would punctuate his actions with the loud beep of a horn he always kept on him. Only in sound film comedy could Harpo's silence be used so effectively. His dumb act did not hamper him in getting the best of rivals; if anything, it only made matters worse for the others. As they raged at him, Harpo would suddenly sit down at his harp and play (he was self-taught) spontaneously and quite well. Chico was also an expert at the piano and was shown demonstrating intricate finger actions on the keyboard with much comic effect. Zeppo, the fourth brother, appeared in only five of the Marx Brothers' thirteen films.

Although their films were directed by others and their plots were really banal stories of romance and intrigue, the way the Marx Brothers played havoc with the narratives was quite deliberate. Their priceless and complicated routines were written and staged by both the brothers themselves and comic writers such as S. J. Perelman and George S. Kaufman; to attempt to describe these "narratives" would be to invite lunacy on the part of both author and reader.

Like the Marx Brothers before them, (Bud) Abbott and (Lou) Costello moved from vaudeville to films. Their first film was released in 1940, and they continued to appear together in an average of two a year until 1956. Perhaps a quick survey of some of their titles might supply a clue to why they have been ignored by most historians: *Abbott and Costello Meet Frankenstein* (1948), . . . *Meet Dr. Jekyll and Mr. Hyde* (1953), . . . *Meet the Mummy* (1955). The humor (both the jokes and the situations) was not original; the films were not distinguished in the making and looked cheap; and yet hilarity did flow from this team's reactions to the desperate situations into which they always landed. Levelheaded and usually cool Abbott would entice the short, chubby and hysterical Costello into daring schemes that the terrified Costello would ordinarily shun. In discussing matters, the conversation, not so funny in itself, took on a delightful tone as it shot back and forth from Abbott's authoritative, demanding voice to Costello's quick but querulous answers. Costello's slow scream to panic, "Aaabbottttt! Hey, Aaabbottt!," was an expertly timed bit of recurring business that always provoked mirth.

Each of the comics and other stars discussed here can be identified by a certain manner peculiarly his own: his style. But what of the films? Can a film have a style of its own?

Style is a difficult word to define, and many equate it with the idea of art. The problem of its definition today is especially complex. There are many acceptable approaches to film; the story is no longer the beginning and the end, as it was for Ince and the many who believed in a strong dramatic plot as essential. Although films have been built around performers and even around musical scores, the films of the studios were often tailored around certain conventional story lines. Style, until recently, was concerned with the way the story was shaped and the manner in which it was told.

What happens in a film may not be so important as how an audience sees what is happening. Although it is not a totally correct analogy, it might be useful in thinking about style to think of two different writers handling the same story. Suppose William Shakespeare and Ernest Hemingway retold the story of the murder of Abel by Cain. Shakespeare would probably speak of the crime in poetic images composed into eloquent constructions that would have a melodic tone. Hemingway's description would be more immediate and terse, and it would be given in brief and unadorned terms. The two completely different descriptions of the same event could be interesting because each might be rendered in such a way that at least it would indicate who its author was. The interpretations might not differ, but the *manners* in which both stories were related would. That difference is a clue, a rather simple clue as to what style is.

By the twenties the studios had grown into such complex conglomerates that it was impossible for the studio heads to worry about the production of any one film in particular. The studio head had to delegate responsibility. He appointed someone to take his place in the supervision of most production. Since the big studios often made more than one film a week, several such supervisors were needed. A familiar term was used to describe the function performed by these men. They were called producers. As producers, they acted as liaison between management (the front office) and personnel (the creative talent). In this way they were much the same as foremen.

A budget was compiled, a cast list made up, and a production schedule was composed in the main office. Most often a producer or the director was present and gave advice. The production schedule was a bulletin which detailed what scenes would be shot when, what materials were needed, how much they were to cost, how long a sequence should take to shoot, and how much that should cost. It was the producer's task to see that the production conformed to this schedule, and if it did not, he was authorized to set it right. Setting it right might mean a lot of things, not the least of these was removing the director whose temperament or exacting vision was causing a delay in production.

The director had to work under the economizing eye of the producer. The director might come to a production when it was half complete. The script was written, the cast assembled, the crew hired and the sets designed, constructed and waiting. Although he was responsible for shooting the film, the director could also really leave the production half-complete. Each sequence might be photographed several times before the director was satisfied with what was shot. Out of these "rushes" the producer, rather than the director, might be the one to select the shot that would finally appear in the film. An editor, handed a script of the film, could put the shots together in some prescribed order. A composer under contract to the studio would be asked to write a score which would be played by the studio orchestra, led by the studio conductor. Even when the musical track was recorded onto the film, the work was far from complete. The film still had to be tested before the public.

"Sneak" screenings would be arranged in southern California, where selected theatres would be chosen to preview a film, the title of which would remain unannounced. Unaware of what it would be viewing and not conditioned by advance advertising, the audience was supposed to react naturally to what appeared on the screen, and the film would be changed according to this popular reaction. If the film were a comedy, and the director, producer or front office felt that the audience was not laughing enough, slow scenes would be cut from the film and new sequences might even be added. Sneak previews radically altered the construction of some films. For example, narration was added to and many scenes cut from *The Red Badge of Courage* (1951) without the director's, John Huston's, participation. Depending on audience response, release dates could be postponed up to a year until the proper reaction was achieved.

The production of a film was blueprinted in the front office. Its construction was delegated to a host of skilled workers, each with his own specialty. The whole operation was coordinated by a producer-foreman. The film was extensively revised by a "sneak" audience. It should not seem strange that the studios have often been compared to factories functioning with assembly-line formality.

If most preshooting and postshooting aspects of production were completed by others, what creative function did the director perform? In some cases, very little. He was just another workman who ordered the materials about on the day of shooting. Perhaps this is why most directors of American films were regarded as technicians, while it was the stars that were hailed as the artists.

Like directors, screenwriters, some of whom were famous dramatists and novelists, were considered mere technicians as well. On not a few productions writing turned out to be as compartmentalized as anything else on the set. One writer might be hired to rethink a novel into a film. He might give his idea to another writer, who would put it into a screenplay and who, in turn, would pass it on to another, who would write the dialogue, who would pass it along to someone else to improve the dialogue, and this writer might pass it to another writer to add a few jokes, who would. . . .

Yet there were a number of fine directors who were able to make many distinctive films. Working within the rather rigid structure of the system, these men transcended the limitations imposed on them. They worked collaboratively with the casting office, with the art director who designed the sets, with the cameraman, with the editor, and of course, with the producer. Such a director conferred with the other professionals about the effect he wanted to achieve, on the tone he wanted the film to take. Even if his crew said that this or that was impossible, the director might insist on his way; and if he was on good terms with the technicians, they would cooperate with him in experimenting. If the experiment were successful, the director might have another hard time convincing the producer to leave whatever was unorthodox intact. The good director was not only a creative talent, he was also discreet and tactful, a superb politician. When he could not change front-office orders he knew enough not to keep trying. He did his best with the material at hand. If he had been given a poor actor, the director would see that the motion or placement of the camera would help convey whatever emotion the actor attempted. If the costumes were absurd or out of place, the director saw to it that the lighting played down any grotesque effect they made. He was also concerned with rhythm and pacing. The director would work with his cameraman in choosing certain angles and tracing certain moves; he worked with his editor in seeing that shots were the right length and that beginnings and endings of sequences were not disturbed. Film music has a tremendous, if subtle, emotional impact, and a bad musical score can drown out the mood of a scene or a whole film. The director had to see that a score consonant with the action was composed, and he helped record the music onto the track.

Being under a similar, though usually not as strict, contract as were the stars, the director could not dictate to the front office. He could be insistent but he always had to be polite and, worse, obliging. Although he worked cooperatively with the whole crew, he was not allowed a most important prerogative, the right of final cut. The way the film was finally assembled was always left to the discretion of the producer; and this privilege was usually surrendered by the producer to the front office and the preview audience. The best the director could do was to argue and plead that the film remain as it was originally shot. It almost never was. Practically every film was a compromise between a vision, artistic or not, and the hand of the front office. This is not so much a condemnation as a description of the way in which films were produced. Even though the studio system has changed, it is still very true that financial considerations interfere with original plans. Although it is not as true now as in the past, the reality of Hollywood dictated that even the most creative director — or anybody, for that matter — had difficulty in calling a completed film his own.

It was in France that the *auteur* ("author") viewpoint about film was most clearly enunciated. While in America critics and audience tended to identify films more by their stars and by production companies, several French writers tended to credit films to directors as well, and although there are many accepted ways of looking at film today, the *auteur* theory has become one of the most popular. People now tend to identify the director as the author or singular creative force of the film.

There have been some notable examples of directors who worked within the confines of the Hollywood studio system and still managed to make personal contributions to the art of the film. Creating their own distinct styles of storytelling, they expanded the ability of film to communicate. While some of these directors' films have become timeless, all stand as a testimony to man's talent for improvising within structured situations.

It is impossible to describe the career of Cecil B. DeMille in a few words. A whole book is needed. Generations of film scholars have been waiting for this book; they probably will have to wait another generation. Copies of DeMille's early films must be found, widely circulated, and seen. Perhaps these early works may shed some light on the controversy surrounding his reputation. Everyone seems to agree that Cecil Blount DeMille was a shrewd and expert showman; but many will argue that the man lacked a creative genius.

Whoever writes the definitive book about DeMille should also have a fair knowledge of sociology and American history, for it seems that no other director had such an uncanny feeling for the national pulse. DeMille anticipated public taste. When America moved away from her severe temper of the World War One years, DeMille had a number of sophisticated, even naughty, social dramas and comedies (*Old Wives for New*, 1918; *Don't Change Your Husband*, 1919; *Male and Female*, 1919), waiting for the moral relaxation that was to characterize the twenties. Sounding like the R-rated films of today, the films were advertised in the same way — "wild youth at its wildest." They were, however, so full of observed social detail concerning upper-class deportment and etiquette that curious people flocked to the theatres to see what high-society manners were like, what styles were worn, and what was being ordered in fashionable French restaurants.

Ironically enough, DeMille is not known so much for his sophisticated films as for his very unsophisticated spectacles. Most DeMille films were lavish and opulent affairs; his *Cleopatra* (1934), and some that were biblical in origin, *The Ten Commandments* (1923 and 1956), *The King of Kings* (1927) and *The Sign of the Cross* (1932), were the most sumptuous of all (Figure 67). One critic suggested that when God sent a hurricane, it was DeMille who had directed its course. He was probably the only director to make an extravaganza out of Calvary, a circus out of Cleopatra's bath, and a bonanza out of the Red Sea crossing. Although there had been many films with historical or biblical settings before DeMille, it was he who really popularized the genre. In adapting both the Bible and recorded history to the screen, DeMille extracted only what could be translated into the most exciting of visual terms and tended to ignore the rest. Patching exciting scenes together with fabricated stories of intrigue and passion, DeMille certainly came up with some audacious and sensuous imagery, but he also reduced his distinguished sources to the rank of dime-store novels. His films could be counted on for a fair share of savagery, violence and seminudity. Since the wicked were invariably punished at the end, guardians of morals did not seem to mind these excesses.

While there may be doubts as to the intelligence of DeMille's more spectacular films, his straightforward adventure films, usually set in the West, are direct and replete with breathtaking action (*The Virginian,* 1914; *The Plainsman,* 1937; *The Buccaneer,* 1938; *Union Pacific,* 1939; *North West Mounted Police,* 1940; *The Greatest Show on Earth,* 1952). These are compelling stories told with verve and vitality; these are films of the sort by which pure and simple entertainment can well be measured.

It was with one of these films that DeMille first established himself. Renting a barn and shooting right in among the animals, DeMille collaborated on *The Squaw Man* in 1913. Not only did this early full-length feature prophesy the coming of longer films and the eventual death of the two- and three-reelers, but its popularity assured DeMille of the freedom to make films as his own producer.

67. *The bath of the empress, from DeMille's* Sign of the Cross, *with Claudette Colbert and Fredric March.* (Courtesy of Universal Pictures)

(Its success also helped establish one of the great studios: Paramount.) DeMille died in 1959, but throughout the length of his career, making seventy-odd pictures, he had remained fairly independent.

It used to be that America was a country of competence. As I write this book in 1971, the phones no longer work properly, the mails take a week to cross the country, letters are lost on the way, and the public transportation systems have become notorious for their delays. While there is very little that can be relied upon, one can depend on the films of John Ford and Howard Hawks. Both men represent a classical American style of doing things. Their films are neat and immediately effective. Although the films do not call attention to technique, they are not as simple as they seem. Their stories and the relationships between the characters are most important. They are unadorned; they are models of restraint. Every cut, every camera angle, and every gesture contribute to the development of the narrative; there are no distractions. Working within the studio, both men mastered their art during apprenticeship days with silent films. Although both excel in the handling of the adventure story, each has made fine films with more somber and sober themes.

Ford, who has directed well over one hundred and twenty-five films, began as a stunt man. It was not until he was about a third of the way into his career that he made *The Iron Horse* (1924) and received critical attention. One of the original locomotives that first crossed the continent was used in this saga of the building of the transcontinental railway (Figure 68). Corruption and an attack by the Cheyenne obstruct the progress of the Iron Horse, but the logic of history wins out in the end — and so does our hero.

Ford's Westerns all have a dimension beyond that of mere surface action. In a way, they are like myths. Like the stories of the ancient Greek and Latin gods, they deal with the human condition. While many more could be listed, *Steamboat 'Round the Bend* (1935), *Stagecoach* (1939), *Young Mr. Lincoln* (1939), *My Darling Clementine* (1946), *She Wore a Yellow Ribbon* (1949) and *Two Rode Together* (1961) are among Ford's more interesting films of pioneer and prairie America.

Two films that were set in the British Isles are major peaks in

135

68. *This is the Iron Horse of John Ford's drama.* (William Fox, © 1924, All Rights Reserved)

Ford's reputation. *The Informer* (1935), a film noted more for its mood and atmosphere than for its story, told of an unfortunate man who informs on a comrade during the Irish rebellion against the British. (Another director, Jules Dassin, used essentially the same story in his *Uptight,* released in 1969, but he transported his characters to an urban black ghetto.) The fortunes of a Welsh mining community and a closely-knit district family are romantically chronicled in *How Green Was My Valley* (1941).

In 1940 Ford directed *The Grapes of Wrath,* a stark, powerful and faithful translation of John Steinbeck's graphic novel of the Depression (Figure 69). Tenant farmers in Oklahoma are forced off their land, which has turned into a dust bowl. Dispossessed, they are lured to California on the promise of work as migrant farmers. They reach California and are cruelly exploited by the landowners on whose fields fruit remains ready to be harvested. The local authorities conspire with the landowners to keep the migrant workers in a state close to slave labor. The family finally comes upon a federally administered camp intended to assist the migrants by providing work to help them keep their dignity. This momentous film records the dispossession, the difficult journey west in which a large family is at the mercy of a ramshackle car, the agonizing experience of the harvest, and the help extended by the government's social involvement. The

136

film astounded audiences all over the world. Did such poverty exist in America? It certainly did. Would Americans treat their fellow men like cattle? They certainly would. *The Grapes of Wrath,* made at the close of the depression decade, is one of the very few Hollywood films that treated a domestic problem in a realistic and uncompromising manner.

During the Second World War, Ford made a number of documentaries for the Armed Services. His last film, *Seven Women,* was completed in 1966. In June 1971 it was announced that a documentary Ford had been working on for the United States Information Agency on American involvement in Vietnam during the past several years would be scrapped.

While the differences between the films of Ford and those of Howard Hawks can be discussed in detail, what they have in common is that they appear so deceptively simple that they hardly appear to have been directed at all. They flow. Hawks' films range the globe from the American West (*Red River,* 1948; *Rio Bravo,* 1959) to Africa (*Hatari!* 1962). His action films are more than just adven-

69. *The Joad family, evicted from its homestead, prepares to head west in search of work. Henry Fonda as Tom, on the tailgate, shakes farewell with John Carradine (Cassy). Jane Darwell (biting her nails) gives a most sympathetic portrayal of Mrs. Joad in Ford's version of John Steinbeck's classic novel,* The Grapes of Wrath. (Twentieth Century-Fox Film Corporation © 1940, All Rights Reserved)

ture stories (Figure 70), each touches upon universal feelings and moral situations. His themes frequently concern friendship, and his leading characters tend to be models for heroic behavior.

There is a telling story that arose with the making of *The Big Sleep* (1946), the popular Raymond Chandler mystery story. A number of people, including novelist William Faulkner, worked on the script. Apparently no one — not the writers, not the stars, not even the director — could make much sense out of a very complicated plot; and though certainly the audience was baffled, too, no one seems to have raised any objections. The story moves without effort, and it is so expertly acted that everyone seems to know what he is doing.

Hawks' comedies are hilarious, if a bit screwball, and they are paced with the speed of an expert gun duel (*20th Century*, 1934; *Bringing up Baby*, 1938; *His Girl Friday*, 1940; *Gentlemen Prefer Blondes*, 1953). The Western *Rio Lobo* (1970) is Hawks' most recent film.

If any director has become a household name, it must be Alfred Hitchcock. He needs no introduction; although he has made other types, films of mystery and intrigue are his special province. Generations of filmmakers have tried to master his technique by imitation, but he cannot be imitated. His concern with detail and eccentricity is extraordinary. By the time Hitchcock arrived in America from Eng-

70.   *The heroic John Wayne and his* Rio Bravo *sidekick, Ricky Nelson, tend to law and order in Hawkes' Western.* (From the motion picture, *Rio Bravo*, copyright © 1959 by Warner Bros. Pictures Inc.)

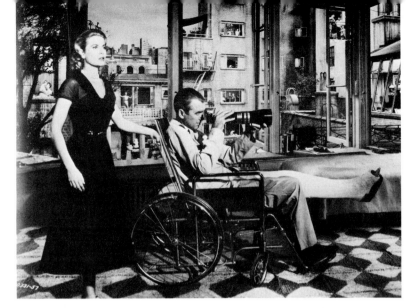

71. *James Stewart sees a bit too much through his telescope in Alfred Hitch-cock's* Rear Window. *Grace Kelly, a popular actress of the fifties (now Princess Grace of Monaco) looks on.* (Museum of Modern Art/Film Stills Archive © Patron Productions 1954)

land, he was already a master director. With such films as *Blackmail* (1929) and *Murder* (1930), he had shown how sound could be used creatively. Had he not made any other films, *The 39 Steps* (1935) and *The Lady Vanishes* (1938) would have established him as a director of consummate talents. But he did make other films, and he continues to do so.

Hitchcock impresses his films with his own hallmarks: the tinge of comedy, the uneasy laugh, the mood of suspense he establishes with a slow or small turn of the camera, or with an actor's minute gesture that smacks of delicious irony, and the establishment of points of interest, objects, visual themes that recur as the film progresses. A cigarette lighter in *Strangers on a Train* (1951), a telescopic lens (Figure 71) in *Rear Window* (1954), the reappearing corpse in *The Trouble with Harry* (1956), and the old, dark house in *Psycho* (1960) seem to have as much character and life as do the actors. Hitchcock lands his protagonists in the queerest and most chilling of situations. The hero of *Rear Window* may be comfortably at home, but when he is pursued by a murderer, he is confined to a wheel-chair. A menacing light aircraft pursues the hero of *North by North-*

west (1959) across an open field. He escapes, only to find himself in a chase across the Presidential faces sculptured into Mount Rushmore. In *Saboteur* (1942), a hot pursuit ends on top of the Statue of Liberty's torch. Earlier in the film the hero and his girl are prisoners at a party. Unaware, the other guests laugh off the suggestion that their magnanimous hostess is a fascist collaborator. Meanwhile, the couple must keep dancing and dancing unless one of the butlers "asks" them into the drawing room and to their deaths. Hitchcock's latest work is *Frenzy* (1972).

The films of Ford, Hawks and Hitchcock all present the same wonderful difficulty. The artistry with which they are made is hard to see. Films, like pieces of clothing, are sewn together. In a well tailored suit the seams are invisible. So it is with these films. The student who is intent on discerning the structure of these films is being seduced continually into their action.

A number of prominent European directors have been attracted to Hollywood, for all sorts of reasons. Men of established reputation were sometimes lured by the promise of unlimited capital. Few realized that a studio contract entailed a loss of some of that creative freedom that they had enjoyed in Europe. But it was not only wealth that attracted these men to America. When the Nazis came to power, many creative talents, in fear for their lives, fled.

On the whole, America has imported more talent than she has sent overseas. However, in 1926 she lost one of her earliest directors of feature films and one of her finest stylists, Maurice Tourneur, because he refused to accept the presence of a supervising producer. Although Tourneur was born in Paris, his first films and his most popular (*The Wishing Ring*, 1914; *Trilby*, 1915; *The Pride of the Clan*, 1917) were made in America. Two European directors of exceptional note, Jean Renoir and Max Ophuls, stopped briefly in Hollywood to direct a number of films before they returned to a continent exhausted by war. *The Southerner*, directed by Renoir in 1945, about an indigent Texas family eking a livelihood from growing cotton, and the romantic *Letter from an Unknown Woman*, directed by Ophuls in 1948, are two distinguished films created by these men during their Hollywood sojourn.

Victor Sjöström (spelled "Seastrom" in this country), arrived in

America when he was only seven months old. His mother died, and his father remarried. Seastrom was sent back to Sweden, where he lived with his aunt. He matured into an accomplished actor, a noted director of both stage plays and some of the first Swedish feature films. Two in particular, *The Outlaw and His Wife* (1917) and *The Phantom Chariot* (1920), have become world classics. When Seastrom returned to America he returned as a celebrity, and completed nine films in Hollywood. Three stand out; one of these is exceptional. *He Who Gets Slapped* (1924) stars the "man of a thousand faces," Lon Chaney. Set in the tinsel of a circus, *He Who Gets Slapped* tells the gloomy story of a scientist whose unique invention is stolen. He becomes a circus clown, and, despite his past hurt, falls in love. *The Scarlet Letter* (1927) is adapted from the once controversial novel by Nathaniel Hawthorne. The story, set in a New England community populated by Puritans, is about sin and punishment. The studio, frightened by the film's theme, and expecting pressure and repression, would not sanction the project until it was approved by the Federal Council of Churches of Christ. Its leading actress, Lillian Gish, had given a brilliant and touching performance in Griffith's *Broken Blossoms*, and was to go on to appear in Seastrom's exceptional Hollywood film, *The Wind* (1928).

The Wind was photographed in the Mojave Desert, where it was so hot that the combustible film needed refrigeration so that it would not explode. A bulky wind machine was constantly used, and so strong was its effect that the operator was required to protect himself from flying debris. When interiors were shot, the "dust" was smoking sulphur blown onto the set. Both the wind machine and the smoking sulphur severely tested the nerves of the actors and the crew.

Taken from a tale in which an unfortunate girl from Virginia is forced to live with her cousins on a lone Texas prairie, the story's original ending was altered by the studio. The girl, forced into a marriage with a coarse man, soon goes insane. The incessant wind, the constant swirls of dust, and her isolation twist both her spirit and mind. In the original, she dies. However, in the film, she grows to love her husband. Given her sensitive nature and his rather barbaric behavior, this seems a bit unnatural; nevertheless, the film still represents a tremendous accomplishment for Seastrom, Gish, and the cameraman, John Arnold, who so expertly caught the never ending onslaught of wind and dust.

It may have been that MGM's publicity department was gearing itself for the promotion of another Swede, the actress Greta Garbo. Or it may have been that in 1928, theatres, some rewiring for sound, were not interested in playing a silent film. Although sound effects were added to the film after it had been completed, *The Wind* was not well publicized, and it was not seen by many people. In Europe, however, it became a critical success and has remained so until the present day, when it is finally getting the attention it deserves in America.

Seastrom directed another two films before he returned to Sweden to become an actor. At the age of seventy he appeared in his last film, titled in English *Wild Strawberries* (1957), an influential work directed by a fellow Swede, Ingmar Bergman.

Ernst Lubitsch had made a series of historical spectacles in Germany and some of them received international acclaim. After the First World War a Lubitsch film was the first German motion picture to appear in American theatres. Then, at the invitation of Mary Pickford, Lubitsch came to Hollywood to direct the star in a historical romance. The film that was made, *Rosita* (1923), certainly was a romance, but it was not historical. Not being what either party wanted, it was disowned by both. Just as Lubitsch's career in the

72. *Greta Garbo as Ninotchka, the Soviet commissar, reminisces with her comrades about those decadent Paris days, in Ernst Lubitsch's comedy.* (© 1939-Metro-Goldwyn-Mayer, Inc.)

73. *Part of the elaborate set F. W. Murnau had constructed for* Sunrise. (Fox Film Corporation © 1927, All Rights Reserved)

States was about to be cut short, he shifted genres and began directing a series of light and sophisticated comedies (*The Marriage Circle*, 1924; *So This Is Paris*, 1926), which were enormously popular. Lubitsch became famous for his "touch." Discretion, tact and taste characterized his films. Like champagne, they were light but with body; like champagne, they were effervescent and refreshing. Although innuendo was a major element in a Lubitsch film, it was unlike the leering suggestiveness found in many films of today.

When pictures began to speak, Lubitsch directed a number of charming musicals: *The Love Parade* (1929), *Monte Carlo* (1930), and *The Smiling Lieutenant* (1931).

Three of his amusing films stand out; they are invariably mentioned in any history of screen comedy. The very elegant *Trouble in Paradise* (1932) tells about a pair of jewel thieves who fall in love. *Ninotchka* (1939) has Garbo playing a purposive lady commissar from Soviet Russia sent to Paris on a special mission (Figure 72). With the irresistible assistance of a dashing American (Melvyn Douglas), she herself falls prey to that city's "decadent" and "materialistic" ways and becomes deliciously corrupt. In *To Be or Not to Be* (1942), Jack Benny plays a Shakespearean actor in Occupied Poland who is forced to use his talents to outwit the Nazis.

If Fritz Lang had not come to America, he would still be remem-

143

74. *George O'Brien is the husband who considers an unholy way out of his marriage in one of the last American silent films,* Sunrise. *This still gives some indication of the film's poetic quality.* (Fox Film Corporation, © 1927, All Rights Reserved)

bered as a director of exotic, dark and moody "nightmare" films. Lang found nightmares enough in America, and the exotic landscapes of his work were the very real cities and towns of the United States. There is a sense of lingering paranoia in the films of Lang; in *Fury* (1936) he presents a memorable picture of a lynch mob, and in *You Only Live Once* (1937) an innocent man is hounded to death as a criminal. *The Big Heat* (1953) pictures corruption in high places.

F. W. Murnau's life was cut short by an automobile accident. Although he worked on four films in the States, it was his first, a parable on love threatened and love triumphant, *Sunrise* (1927), that is most remarkable (Figure 73). Shot as a silent, it was released at a time when sound was making its introduction. A musical score was recorded for the film. The score is fine, but if ever a director's films did not need sound, they were the films of Murnau. (In Germany he had completed *The Last Laugh* [1924], which did not contain a single explanatory title.) For *Sunrise*, this "song of two humans," he constructed a small city, complete with a fairground and a trolley line extending into the country. The camera, handled by Charles Rosher and Karl Struss, moving over great expanses, was used in a manner as graceful as it has ever been. The story becomes a poem,

144

the poem a lyric, and the lyric a memorable experience (see Figure 74).

When sound was introduced, both filmmakers and critics thought it might be no more than a novelty. They said that silent films like *Sunrise* and *Intolerance* were true motion pictures; imagery could never be that fluid again. The first sound-recording apparatus was so primitive that it prohibited camera motion and severely cut the amount of action possible within a frame. Would films regress to the state they were in before Griffith? Would films once more become a static chronicle of staged events? What was the problem with sound?

In the late twenties sound was recorded at first on discs and then photographed directly onto film. To put it crudely, on the set there were two "cameras" working. Both were housed in one box; one photographed the action, the other the sound. The actors spoke into a microphone; the microphone was attached to a sound "camera." Sound waves were translated into electrical impulses of varying strengths. These, in turn, were translated into light waves of varying

75.   *This was a piece of equipment from an arsenal needed to record sound on film. One look at this monster should suggest why it was feared that sound recording would restrict camera motion.* (Museum of Modern Art/ Film Stills Archive)

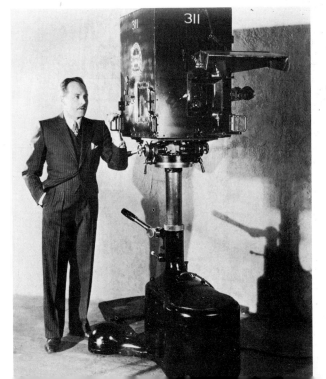

intensities. Unexposed film was exposed to this flickering light and an image was "recorded" on the film. This image was not the same type as the sort recorded by the picture camera, but was instead a continuous band of light that ran down the side of the film. This

76. *The sound track and image "married" on the same ribbon of film. Since it takes longer to project the sound track than the images, the track runs ahead of the image (by twenty-six frames in 16mm) it is to be heard with. This is a strip of 16mm film, and while the track runs along one side, only one edge is sprocketed. In 35mm film, sprockets appear on both edges.*

band is called the sound track. Either the density or the width of the band varies, and it is these fluctuations translated that form the specific words and music finally heard.

The sound camera (see Figure 75) made noise: a huge, heavy box, the blimp, had to be constructed around the machine lest the microphone, sensitive to all sounds, pick up whirrings. Even though the camera might move with the box, it could not move within it. Given the bulk of the blimp, it was not frequently trucked or tracked. So much for camera motion.

The sensitivity of the microphone was another problem. In order to record performers clearly, the mike had to be fairly well on top of them. The microphone, however, would also pick up any other faint noises on the set. Thus the actors had to stay relatively still; everyone else had to remain absolutely motionless. The director could no longer yell his orders, as he had during filming of silent pictures and while a scene was being shot, the crew had to stop work.

When both the picture and the sound track were satisfactory, they were "married" in the laboratory. The laboratory would integrate the two strips of film (one with the band of flickering light running down its side; the other with pictures) into one composite print. In a composite, or married print, the sound track is laid to the side of the images (Figure 76). In this way the sound and the image are in constant synchronization.

When sound technicians came to the studio, the front office told the directors that the latter were to take orders from the new arrivals. If directors had done so, the sound film most certainly would have been a passing fad. The technicians were very conservative in their estimation of the capabilities of their machines. Directors like Victor Fleming, Rouben Mamoulian and King Vidor insisted that they would not be hampered by this equipment. They obliged the technicians to make improvements in the machinery. Directional microphones were developed that recorded only particular sounds in particular places. Mikes were thus given "focus." These directors insisted on mixing various sounds, music, and speech onto one track so that films did more than just speak. Even though the recording equipment was cumbersome (there were no tape recorders) and not portable (trucks were needed), men like Fleming (see still of *The*

Virginian) and Vidor brought the camera out into the field to record natural sounds. Sound was used not only to create mood and atmosphere, but also to create tension between itself and the visual image. The original fears about sound proved wrong. The spoken word was to be recorded not merely as the voice of the actor, music was used for more than just song, and natural sounds were more than mistakes.

Mamoulian was one of the chief innovators in developing sound's creative possibility. Although his techniques were flamboyant, they were well suited to his theatrical subjects. In *Love Me Tonight,* a musical of 1932, there are at least two scenes that illustrate striking use of sound. The first sequence shows the city of Paris awakening. The film opens silently, and within the first few moments the early sounds of morning (hammering, the cries of vendors) begin to be heard. These build up and up as more and more people hurry to work. The noise breaks into a rhythm, a pattern that becomes more and more intense as the number of sounds grow. At its crescendo, the camera cuts to the hero, who breaks into song. A perfect introduction — especially for Maurice Chevalier. Soon afterward, our hero sings another song. A customer in his shop hears the song and carries it out into the street. A cabdriver picks up the song, as does his passenger, who is then seen on board a train riding with a group of soldiers. As the soldiers march along an open field they can be heard marking time to the same song. A passing gypsy, enchanted with the tune, plays the melody on his violin by a campfire. The music is carried over a meadow on the night breeze to a balcony. And who should happen to be on this balcony but — the heroine! She too is enchanted by the song and begins to sing. An orchestra in the background accompanies her. And although the hero and the heroine have no idea of each other's existence, their future relationship is established in the minds of the audience via the music.

Other Mamoulian films which are often cited in film history texts are *Applause* (1929), *City Streets* (1931), and *Dr. Jekyll and Mr. Hyde* (1932). In 1935 Mamoulian was chosen to direct *Becky Sharp,* the first full-length film in a new and rich color process, three-tone Technicolor.

King Vidor was no less an innovator than Mamoulian. *Hallelujah*

(1929) today appears outrageous to those who think its presentation of American blacks was stereotyped. To an extent, it certainly was, but given its time, it is remarkable that Vidor pictured the black community with the concern he did.

A look at another film, one of the most popular musicals of the period, *Whoopee!* (1930), gives a hint at how thorough a consciousness of race prevailed in this country. *Whoopee!* is a light, almost nonsensical entertainment, but its story line, as thin as it is, concerned the love between an American Indian and a rancher's daughter. It was absolutely unthinkable that they should marry, and indeed, in spite of the fact that they want to, they don't even try. Of course when the hero discovers he's not Indian, the film ends happily. What is interesting is that in such a film, the story is not really as important as the musical numbers and the performers. So the story must be a throwaway, an excuse for having other things happen. Well, if the plot was to be a throwaway, the situation had to be so obvious that it went without questioning, and in 1930 miscegenation was never considered within the realm of possibility.

Hallelujah broke new ground for the sound film. It may have been one of the first films to achieve an effective mix of various sound tracks — natural sounds, recorded speech, and music. It was also one of the earliest films to have part of its sound track recorded on location outside the studio.

77. *One of the opening scenes in King Vidor's* The Crowd. *No titles are needed to explain that something dire has happened.* (© 1928-Metro-Goldwyn-Mayer, Inc.)

Vidor's career began long before sound came to film. He started directing one-reel adventure films in 1913, and was soon on his way to making features, of which *The Jackknife Man* (1919) and *The Sky Pilot* (1921) are splendid examples. Considering the genre in which Vidor originally worked, it was remarkable that he should make two such films as *The Big Parade* (1925) and *The Crowd* (1928). Neither had a plot in the traditional studio sense of the word. Both were comprised of a series of dramatic incidents, compelling variations on two important themes (see Figure 77). *The Big Parade* was concerned with the horror and waste of war, while *The Crowd* pictured the anonymity of contemporary urban life.

The theme of *Our Daily Bread* (1934) is notable. As the depression had made city life more and more intolerable, Vidor's film offered a suggestion for a way of life similar to one which has been pursued in recent years by countless young Americans: communal living on the land.

Like Griffith, Preston Sturges had been both an "inventor," playwright, and screenwriter before he was given the opportunity to direct. This was an occasion for which he fought for eight years. Sturges had written the script to one of the most "screwball" of the screwball comedies of the thirties (*Easy Living*, 1937), which although wild was still civilized enough to be an effective comedy of manners. After the success of *The Great McGinty* (1940), a wry look at political machines, which he both scripted and directed, he was given a free hand in adapting his works for the screen. Sturges may have used several star names as leads from film to film, but his secondary players came from his troupe — a group of character actors with whom he continually worked.

In his notable films, Sturges cast a jaded eye on the American success story. Sure, a guy *could* reach the top of the heap — *if* he were a gangster. Bluff, pluck and good fortune had a lot more to do with getting wealthy than hard work did. Sturges' cynicism is evident in *Sullivan's Travels* (1942). Sullivan, a rich and successful Hollywood director, wants to make a film about poverty. Knowing nothing of the subject from direct personal experience, he masquerades as a hobo. Some hobo! Sullivan knows that he has money, that his costume is a put-on, that a warm bath waits for him at home. With

150

studio yes-men trailing him, how can he ever get at the psychological state of mind he wants to understand? He simply cannot. He cannot, that is, until, by a perverse stroke of fate, he goes broke and is rendered a nonentity: penniless, lost, and part of that brigade of restless disenfranchised souls who were "on the road" during the depression.

One look at a film by Josef von Sternberg immediately explains what might otherwise take countless words to define. If nothing else, von Sternberg's films are glorious and opulent exercises in style. Mood and atmosphere dominate, and actors are choreographed like marionettes. Von Sternberg controlled every aspect of his production. He designed sets; he wrote the musical score. There is no mistaking a von Sternberg film. If ever the *auteur* theory makes sense, it makes sense in respect to his films.

At the age of seven von Sternberg emigrated with his family from Vienna to America. He later said that he learned the craft of filmmaking by lighting cigarettes for other directors. He profited from their mistakes.

Von Sternberg worked inside the studio. Only within its stages could every element of the film be put under the director's total influence. He built sets so that the camera could travel across them in a

78.   *Marlene Dietrich as* The Scarlet Empress, *Catherine the Great of Russia, in a palace with atmosphere by Von Sternberg.* (Museum of Modern Art/Film Stills Archive)

certain way. He placed lights so they would cast shadows in specific patterns. Costumes were designed to suit the director's conception of the characters. Everything was executed in the best way to satisfy his carefully made plans. Von Sternberg did not leave anything to chance.

The stories von Sternberg used were romantic. Usually two men fell deeply and passionately in love with the same woman. It was not this familiar, maudlin, and sometimes absurd story that impressed the audience. What was impressive was the way in which it was presented (style). The locales were exotic: Morocco (*Morocco,* 1930), the East (*Shanghai Express,* 1932), Czarist Russia (*The Scarlet Empress,* 1934), Royalist Spain (*The Devil Is a Woman,* 1935). Believing this last-mentioned film to be a portrayal of its military incompetence, the Spanish government was upset. It threatened to ban all of Paramount's films from the country and ordered the studio to burn all prints and the negative of the film. The Spanish government was being unduly sensitive. *The Devil Is a Woman* was no more about Spain (Figure 78) than *Morocco* was about Morocco. The locales were used to evoke a romantic quality; they were fantasy, fairy-tale places where love conquered all.

Even when von Sternberg set his story in America, he chose bizarre, out-of-the-way locations. In his first film, *The Salvation Hunters* (1925), and in *The Docks of New York* (1927), von Sternberg's vision of the city harbor had more to do with fog and mist than with ships and wharves. In 1927 von Sternberg's camera eye turned to new material; his *Underworld* was one of the first gangster films to come out of Hollywood.

Von Sternberg must have known about the telegram Lewis J. Selznick was said to have sent the Czar of Russia. In his *The Last Command* (1928), the protagonist is an exiled Russian nobleman deposed by the Revolution, who finds the only work he can possibly be suited to: as an actor in bit parts in motion pictures, playing out his own story. The studio itself was used by the director as the set for this drama.

Since this book is an *introduction* to the American film, the entire roster of significant directors cannot be covered here. If the reader is especially interested in any director, he can try further investigations of his own. Some other men should be mentioned here, however, if merely in passing. It is not that they are not important, but we need to get on to other aspects of American film history.

May I invite the reader to do more moviegoing, to see more of the work of the following men? Study the folksy, good-natured, quickly paced films of Frank Capra (*American Madness*, 1932; *It Happened One Night*, 1934; *Mr. Deeds Goes to Town*, 1936); the elegant films of George Cukor (*Dinner at Eight*, 1933; *Camille*, 1937), the romantic films of Frank Borzage (*Seventh Heaven*, 1927; *A Man's Castle*, 1933), the adventure films of Allan Dwan (*Robin Hood*, 1922; *The River's Edge*, 1957) and those of Raoul Walsh (*The Thief of Bagdad*, 1924; *What Price Glory*, 1926; *They Died with Their Boots on*, 1941); and the tightly edited and exciting films of William Wellman (*The Public Enemy*, 1931; *The President Vanishes*, 1934). Henry King directed two films of exceptional quality which are repeatedly mentioned in the history books: *Tol'able David* (1921), for its rewarding silent film style, and *The Gunfighter* (1950), as a classic and powerful example of the "adult" Western, in which moral questions are as important as the action. *All Quiet on the Western Front* (1930), an early sound film directed by Lewis Milestone, is one of the most compelling antiwar epics to have been produced in America. All of these men worked within the studio system; the following four are exceptions. Two left the studio and established their own particular brand of moviemaking (and one, another studio); the other two were put out of work.

One of America's most popular stars was not human at all; he was a mouse named Mortimer. Eventually his name was changed to Mickey, and as Mickey Mouse he helped to build an empire for his creator, Walt Disney.

Disney came to film work as a commercial artist. In Kansas City he was the fellow who designed the advertising slides the theatres showed on the screen between reels ("Men, please use your new so-and-so handkerchieves when you sneeze! Thank you!"). With a group of artist friends, Disney produced a series of simple animated films based on fairy tales. The shorts were composed of black-and-white line drawings that moved. With the money these films earned,

79.   *Mickey Mouse in* Steamboat Willie. (© Walt Disney Productions)

Disney moved to Hollywood and found himself a job as an animator with an established company. He worked well and saved hard. He tried to offer his employer suggestions; they were continually ignored. He quit the studio to go into business on his own. Setting up a very small company to produce short animated films, he tried to find distributors who would release his cartoons.

His independent venture floundered at first, but it was buoyed by the coming of sound. Disney was shrewd. He saw that in the early days of sound live actors could not move about the set as freely as they once had; he knew that the sound camera was encased in the blimp. His "actors," on the other hand, could be made to move and speak quite freely — the hand-drawn, animated films were loaded with action and sparkled with sound.

Although he had appeared in two "experiments" earlier, Mickey Mouse made his public appearance as the captain of a scow in *Steamboat Willie* (1928), the "first" sound cartoon (Figure 79). Mickey not only appeared; he had a musical accompaniment. Over th next few years Disney produced several hundred cartoons in which Mickey appeared as an explorer, a musician, a boxer, and in just about every guise imaginable. In Italy he became known as Topolino, and as Miki Kuchi in Japan. At first he was Michael Maus in Germany, but when Hitler came to power he banned the cartoon character as denigrating to national concerns. Disney soon created

154

80. *Note the difference in drawing style between the human figures and those of the dwarfs in this still from* Snow White and the Seven Dwarfs. (© Walt Disney Productions)

popular companions for Mickey. The dog Pluto came into being, and so did Goofy, the whatsit, and the duck, Donald.

Disney also produced many non-Mickey cartoons in a series entitled *Silly Symphonies,* in which there was more experimentation in color, design, and the creative use of sound. Perhaps he was leading up to one of the grandest Disney film of them all, the first full-length animated American film, *Snow White and the Seven Dwarfs* (1937), which took three years to complete. Hundreds of thousands of drawings were executed for this film, the running time of which was less than an hour and a half. Snow White and Prince Charming were drawn in too realistic a manner to be in complete harmony with the fantasy fairy-tale world depicted (Figure 80), but essentially the imagery developed smoothly, with form, design, color, and sound in perfect synchronization. To enhance the fantasy each character was given his own musical theme. The Wicked Stepmother was so horrible and so terrifying that in some countries there was talk of banning the film lest it upset children who were easily frightened.

155

81. *The ballet burlesque to Ponchielli's "Dance of the Hours" in Disney's* Fantasia. (© Walt Disney Productions)

Disney followed the enormously successful *Snow White* with another full-length animated feature, *Pinocchio* (1939). Disney went further into the creative possibilities of the animated film in *Fantasia* (1940). "Fantasia" is a term denoting the free development of a musical theme. In the Disney film of this title musical themes are animated, visual correlatives are designed, and these designs are synchronized with the mood and rhythm of the fine classical pieces. Using his drawn creatures as dancers, Disney and his collaborators choreographed eight selections with imagination and vitality. For a particularly dramatic piece, Stravinsky's "Rite of Spring," a battle of prehistoric behemoths is drawn; for a lighter piece, Ponchielli's "Dance of the Hours," a ballet burlesque is staged in which hippopotami perform in pink tutus (Figure 81). Perhaps the most successful blend of image and sound was the "Sorcerer's Apprentice" sequence, set to the music of Dukas, with an inspired use of Mickey Mouse as the naughty assistant.

Even though one of the world's great conductors, Leopold Stokowski, led the Philadelphia Symphony Orchestra, and even though the film was introduced and "explained" to audiences by Deems Taylor, a popular musicologist, first audiences found the concept too bizarre, and the film did not do well on its initial release nor on its second, under the title *Fantasia Will Amazia*. Re-released in the sixties, *Fantasia* has grown enormously in popularity during the past several years.

Made in 1944 and released in the first month of 1945, Disney's medium-length film *The Three Caballeros* was a pioneering work in which live actors and animated figures appeared in the same frame and interacted with each other. However, this effect was not altogether new, and primitive variations could be found in the films of Méliès, and even in Porter's *Dream of a Rarebit Fiend* (1906).

It would be wrong to imagine that Disney was the first American film cartoonist, or that he himself personally drew the cartoons for which he became famous. He gave ideas *to* his staff, and he took ideas *from* his staff. Indeed, it may have been an early collaborator, Ub Iwerks, who first drew the famous mouse. The actual work of

82.   *Mr. Magoo, designed by John Hubley, was produced by UPA, founded in 1945 by Stephen Bosustow. This character, like Gerald McBoing Boing, was one of the many delightful figures produced by that company.* (Courtesy Columbia Pictures)

drawing, coloring and photographing the images, frame by frame, was done by many, many Disney studio employees.

Like other studio executives, he gave the orders, and he gave direction to every facet of his company's activities. It was he who decided on the tone and the over-all design each film would take. And when a number of talented and independent-minded animators made suggestions that were not heeded, they left the Disney studio to strike out on their own, much as Disney had done when he had been ignored by former employers.

So it was that an independent organization, UPA, was formed in 1945, staffed with a number of former Disney malcontents. The Disney style, they felt, had become too cute, too coy, too sentimental. UPA cartoons (*Gerald McBoing Boing,* 1950, and the *Mr. Magoo* series) attempted to use design and color more freely, and the wit contained a dry and more sophisticated quality as an attempt to introduce a different sort of tension to this not-always-comic art form (Figure 82).

If Disney's cartoons were too sugary to suit some of his staff, then his documentaries engendered dismay for the way animal life was presented. By the fifties Disney had redirected his energies so that his studio was no longer working solely with animated films, the original Disney hallmark. The studio turned to live-action family adventure stores, and sent crews traveling all over the world to shoot some stunning documentary footage on wildlife. While the visual images in most of the documentaries were exciting and informative (*The Living Desert,* 1953; *The Vanishing Prairie,* 1954), the narration was insipid and inappropriate. Animals were not respected for the creatures they were but were portrayed as if they were endowed with human traits: Bobby Beaver is "married" to Bella Beaver and thinks of the swell time he's going to have picnicking in the woods with Baby; water birds coordinate the movement of their wings to the musical sound track; the woods seem to be alive with the movement of miniature people. Enough *was* enough.

Current trends in filmmaking show how inadequate the traditional or classical definition of a documentary film is. This definition suggests that a documentary film is one in which actuality is treated in a creative manner, that reality is somehow molded by the filmmaker.

What do these words really mean? Don't all films treat actuality or reality creatively? Aren't all films based on some experience or other, and isn't all experience real? Moreover, when a film is made aren't real things being photographed — trees, houses, people, families? If all films are concerned with reality, then what makes the documentary film so distinctive? Is it the *way* in which actuality is molded, handled and treated? Perhaps the strongest clues may come from the "children" of Robert J. Flaherty, the father of the documentary film.

Flaherty spent his younger years living off an iron ore mine in Michigan. When the mine failed, he followed his father and prospected for gold. Living like a vagabond, Flaherty developed a thirst for exploration. This drive led him to an area of Hudson's Bay near the Arctic Circle, where he charted an island that now bears his name. He had a constant companion with him — a motion picture camera with which he recorded his adventures. Soon after he returned to America all his footage caught fire and was destroyed completely. Determined to go back to capture scenes of wilderness existence, Flaherty accomplished a most remarkable feat. With no prior professional experience to recommend him, he convinced a fur company to sponsor his trip back to the Arctic. During the expedition he filmed the beautiful and exciting *Nanook of the North* (1922), which

83. *Nanook listens in amazement to a new item from the "civilized" world.* (Museum of Modern Art/Film Stills Archive)

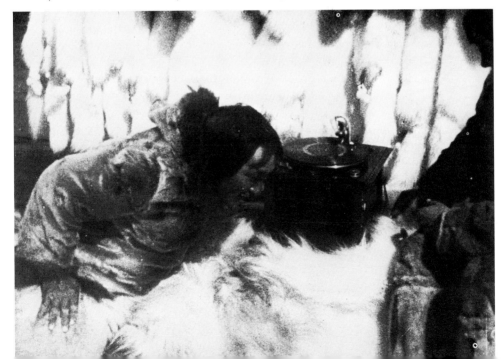

he edited himself, fashioning what must be considered a unique human document.

Flaherty found that distributors were reluctant to release so unusual a film. Some of the first theatres in which it was shown put the film on the lower half of a double bill, but the mysterious location on which the film was shot and the honest quality emanating from the life portrayed soon touched the interest of audiences, and the film created a not inconsiderable sensation.

Nanook of the North is not a travelogue; it is a natural drama, a moving document, a poetic chronicle of one man's heroic struggle against a demented Mother Nature. Nanook, the Eskimo, isn't just one Eskimo, but all Eskimos (Figure 83). Indeed, the theme seems to be broader than the Eskimo's fight for survival. It is a testament to man's ability to adapt to his particular environment.

We may now be getting to the core of the matter. Flaherty's films have a significance beyond what they show. A newsreel (and there have been newsreels for as long as there have been motion pictures) is simply a passive *record* of events, visual note-taking. For example, the President steps out of his plane, the camera makes a record of it, and it doesn't really matter if the cameraman is there or is not, for the actions of the President do not depend on a cameraman at all. The President would emerge from the plane whether or not a cameraman were present.

True, Nanook would hunt and fish and build his igloo even if Flaherty were not there; these are the things the Eskimo must do as part of his survival. But *what* the filmmaker chose to show, and *how* he showed it, made Flaherty a very relevant participant in the action. His perception, his vision, his feelings — they help us to get to the heart of Nanook's life-style.

Flaherty lived with Nanook and his family for a considerable time; he got to know the Eskimo and his ways well. He knew that he could not shoot *every* aspect of Eskimo life. Some things were more important and more dramatic than others. Hunting brought food, and building an igloo provided shelter against the cold. Without these there was no life. Flaherty asked Nanook to do these things, and to do them while he was there. Each man seems to have been keenly aware of the other's role. Flaherty did not just sit back, spy and shoot. He knew he had to participate in the Eskimo's life to grasp its meaning; the *flow* of that life had to be captured photographically. The viewer of the completed film can actually sense that Nanook, too, had a strong grasp of the situation and that he took as serious a view of the work Flaherty was doing as Flaherty had of the Eskimo's efforts. The respect and recognition exchanged by the two men contributes to the profound feeling of verity the film evokes. Flaherty did influence reality, and this is something newsreel cameramen are not in a position to do. The film is a compelling personal document, something constructed by a human being endowed with very strong feelings and with the clarity of purpose as well as the vigor to express his feelings in an artistic fashion.

Although *Nanook of the North* may have been the first American feature film to be conceived without professionals in a locale as foreign as the Arctic, *Grass*, photographed by two adventurers, Merian C. Cooper and Ernest Schoedsack, soon followed in 1925. Impressed with Flaherty's moving record of man's triumphant struggle for survival, Cooper and Schoedsack went to Persia and documented the hazardous trek of the Bakhtiari, a tribe of Mongol descent, who crossed swift-moving rivers and peaks over ten thousand feet high and who faced both perilous blizzards and avalanches in securing grassy lands for their herds. While one man is chosen to represent the tribe in *Nanook*, it is the whole group that emerges as a single determined entity in *Grass*. *Chang*, made by the same team two years later in Siam, has exciting footage of wild animal life that was used repeatedly in studio-shot jungle films several years later. While *Grass* may have been less a constructed film than *Nanook* in that its filmmakers are reputed to have remained more passive, recording original events without asking the participants to simulate them, the filmmakers soon changed their methods, and *Grass* remains an exception in their careers. Their films became narratives, adventure stories with exciting documentary location footage. They became involved in fiction films, and in 1933 produced one of the most memorable adventure stories of all, *King Kong*, in which an ape of gigantic proportions is captured, brought to New York, and after escaping, battles airplanes atop the easily scaled Empire State Building.

Paramount, impressed with the success of *Nanook of the North*, hired Flaherty to go to the South Seas to the unspoiled island of Savaii and to bring back the story of another Nanook. But no counterpart was to be found there. The elements of life in a tropical paradise do not have the same drama as those in a cold white hell. Man's struggle is about something else where Mother Nature is a good provider. Flaherty lived among the natives in Savaii, and he began filming only when he had familiarized himself with their ways. The scenes he photographed were exceptionally beautiful and showed the apparently charmed and idyllic (it wasn't) existence of the islanders. But where there is no tension between man and nature, there is no immediate drama, and drama was what the studio wanted. To pacify the studio, Flaherty arranged to photograph a painful tattooing ritual. The custom had ceased being performed years before, and Flaherty had to pay his "actor" a high price to submit himself to the torment. Despite the inclusion of this ending, the studio was not satisfied and decided ludicrously to promote *Moana of the South Seas* (1926) as a passionate love story. Girls in grass skirts were hired to dance the hula-hula in front of the theatres in which it played.

Shortly after this, another unfortunate experience with a studio followed, and Flaherty left for the British Isles, where he influenced a generation of British filmmakers.

Following his return to America, the Shell Oil Company gave Flaherty a large sum of money to make a film, on which its name would not appear. Naturally, *Louisiana Story* (1948) was meant to have something to do with oil, but only in a subordinate way. The film is about a Louisiana bayou and a Cajun boy who lives by the water and enjoys exploring its winding byways. The story tells of the boy and his pet raccoon coming across what seems to be an invader from another planet. It turns out to be an oil derrick. At first they treat the machine as an intruder, but as they get to know the massive piece of equipment and its operator, they begin to accept and even befriend them as another part of the natural environment. Today the oil derrick might be pictured as a detrimental polluter, but in 1948 it was a symbol of progress as it drew wealth from the untapped resources of the bayou. When the derrick makes its appearance, the boy's relationship to the bayou is altered irreversibly, and the boy must and does live in new ways. *Louisiana Story* tells of more than just a boy and his world. Like *Nanook of the North*, it is a testament to man's ability to adapt to his environment.

Flaherty died in 1951. Even now in the seventies, the remarkable accomplishments of the man continue to stimulate excitement. The catalytic effect of his films is spreading ever wider as young filmmakers focus their attention on the varied ways of life in the nation.

Reality meant one thing to Robert J. Flaherty, and another to Erich von Stroheim. Von Stroheim insisted on accuracy and exquisite detail; the fanatical lengths to which he pressed this insistence lost him job after job and finally expelled him from the studio. There is no question of his genius, but he was extraordinarily eccentric.

Like Josef von Sternberg, he was born in Austria, and had worked himself up within the film industry. He had a small part in *Intolerance,* and later had been one of D. W. Griffith's assistants.

In 1919 von Stroheim had a conversation with the head of Universal Pictures, Carl Laemmle. The conversation must have been impressive, for he somehow sold the executive on the idea that he should direct *Blind Husbands,* a story he had written, and that he would star in it as well. The film was concerned with moral decadence, a theme prevalent throughout von Stroheim's work. It was a cold and cynical piece in which von Stroheim's uncanny eye for detail was continuously at work. The film was so successful that he was assigned to direct a number of subsequent features. These films, however, were not released exactly as von Stroheim had designed them. I have mentioned that the cutting and altering of "finished" films were not unusual in the studio system. What was unusual was what was done to von Stroheim's works.

Whole subplots were excised by the studio to make a film more "commercial." And it was not only the length of von Stroheim's features which exasperated the studio, but the pains (and expense) to which he went to create a feeling or a certain mood. One story about him said that in order that a number of bit players would better *feel* the parts they were playing as royal guardsmen, von Stroheim insisted that a royal crest be woven into their underwear. (The men were never shown out of uniform!) Von Stroheim soon acquired the most damaging sort of reputation a director could have in a Hollywood studio. He was both difficult and expensive. He became known as "von \$troheim," and his last film at Universal was taken from him.

On the basis of past popularity, the newly formed Metro-Goldwyn studio gave von Stroheim almost free rein to do as he wished. What he did was breathtaking, but he was martyred in the process. Von

Stroheim directed one of the most incredible films ever to come out of Hollywood, *Greed* (1924). *Greed* was based on a novel, *McTeague*, written in 1899 by Frank Norris. A simple, affable fellow, McTeague worked in a mining camp. At the suggestion of his mother he starts to practice dentistry. He moves to San Francisco and falls in love with an attractive young patient, whom he marries. In two unrelated incidents she wins a small fortune in a lottery and he loses his job. She becomes possessed by greed. She hides her money, and as she grows more and more miserly, her mind becomes unbalanced. The marriage deteriorates and ends in murder. The novel, an indictment of money's evil power to corrupt human sensitivity, so impressed von Stroheim that he announced that he wanted to film it word for word.

Not only did the director move his entire cast to San Francisco, but he rented a block of houses out of which he tore the walls so that the camera might move freely and with great effectiveness. The climax was shot in Death Valley, where the sun was so strong that many of the cast and crew were made prostrate with the heat. Whether he ever shot the book word for word we may never know.

84.   *Zasu Pitts as the bride in Von Stroheim's* Greed. (© 1924, Metro-Goldwyn-Mayer, Inc.)

We do know that he brought back more than eight hours of finished film. The studio demanded that he cut it, maintaining that even if the showings were split over a period of two days no audience would sit through an eight-hour film. Von Stroheim cut the film by half, refusing to cut another scene at any cost (Figure 84). Irving Thalberg, the young producer who had taken from him the last film he was to make at Universal, was assigned to "rescue" *Greed*. Without von Stroheim's approval Thalberg ordered the film cut in half again. Today the footage that was cut from *Greed* is presumed lost, and as they scout through old vaults, attics, and other tucked-away places, film collectors dream of discovering the missing reels of the epic.

Though the film that was ultimately released appears choppy (logically so, with three quarters missing), it is still a spectacular knockout. The atmosphere is as strong as that in the Flaherty films: details are carefully observed by the camera, characters are drawn with extraordinary shrewdness, and those psychological changes left intact by the cutters are handled sensitively. Each sequence is precisely composed and the camera moves with grace and intelligence. The quality of the photography is beautiful. Both the indoor sequences and the exteriors were directed with the same exacting control.

Although the cost of making *Greed* was substantial, it was not an enormous nor an uncommon sum. Von Stroheim contended that the studio had decided to use the film both as a tax loss and as a lesson to other independent-minded directors. The film was not advertised nor promoted properly, and it was a failure at the box office. Disgusted at the way it was cut and distributed, von Stroheim refused to see the "rescued" version of his film. He tried to disown it, but history turned out to be a better judge of the film's merits than either its public or those who reviewed it. If the critics of 1924 did not see the tremendous quality of the film, future generations have seen it.

The studios seemed to agree that von Stroheim was an original talent, but they also agreed that it was a talent for which they would not pay, and his last two films were again taken from him. After 1932 Erich von Stroheim did not direct again. From that time until his death in 1957 the former director appeared as a capable actor in a number of films that varied from poor to magnificent. In one of the latter category, *Sunset Boulevard* (1950), von Stroheim played an ex-director turned manservant to an aging Hollywood star, played by Gloria Swanson. Ironically, it had been Miss Swanson, the producer and star of the director's next-to-last film, *Queen Kelly* (1928), who had had von Stroheim removed from the production before shooting had been completed.

Although there are certain parallels in the career of von Stroheim and the boy wonder Orson Welles, Welles had the good fortune to be born later, and so he has been able to sit out the demise of the studio system. Just as von Stroheim's reputation peaked on a film closely tied to the American landscape, Welles' did, too.

While in his early twenties, Welles formed The Mercury Players, a theatrical troupe that achieved considerable fame. When he moved his company to radio, the group scared the living daylights out of America one evening by broadcasting a version of H. G. Wells' *War of the Worlds*. The invasion from space was presented as if it were actually happening. Listeners were convinced they were hearing an actual news broadcast. After his experience with the government-sponsored Federal Theatre Project in New York, Welles, at the age of twenty-four (1939), was invited to Hollywood. Two years later he made what was probably the most spectacular debut in the history of motion pictures. The boy wonder of radio became the boy wonder of film. In 1941 *Citizen Kane* appeared, and was to be followed the next year by *The Magnificent Ambersons*.

There was almost as much prepublicity about *Citizen Kane* as there had been about *Gone with the Wind* (1939). Although everyone knew what the latter film was about, and wondered who would be selected to play the leads, no one, apart from the crew, seemed to know just what young Welles was up to. The production was shrouded in secrecy, and only as the production was nearing an end was the story "let out." There was good reason to keep the project in silence; if the studio had known what Welles and his team were plotting, it might very well have withdrawn its support.

The story of *Citizen Kane* is familiar: it is the story of the American Dream gone sour. The way it is told is what makes the film exceptional. Kane, builder of a publishing empire, is dying as the film begins. His last word is "Rosebud." Within minutes a newsreel recapitulates the accomplishments of the financial titan. But what does this word, "Rosebud" mean? A persistent reporter tries to find out, and in doing so pieces together a life of the magnate not covered in the introductory newsreel. What the reporter discovers from interviews with close acquaintances is the story of a principled, ambitious young man who turns into an unprincipled bitter billionaire. The reporter does not discover the precise meaning of "Rosebud"; the audience does.

When the details of the screenplay became public, William Randolph Hearst, the publishing king who made his newspapers sell by sensationalizing the news, took himself to be the model for Kane. (And to a certain extent, he was correct in this assumption, for he was the man who was credited with fanning the journalistic fires that led to the Spanish-American War of 1898.) Needless to say, he and his mammoth organization were not too flattered by Welles' interest. We do not know whether or not they were acting on orders but some of Hearst's newspapers at first refused to carry advertisements for the film, some criticized it for attacking the techniques of American business, and some Hearst-owned concerns went so far as to ask their employees to boycott the film.

It was more its unusual quality than the crusade mounted against it that prevented the film from being an immediate public success. Even though most critics did applaud the work heartily, it was not as popular as had been hoped. Today, however, it is regarded as one of the supreme achievements of the American cinema.

The achievement of *Citizen Kane* is not Welles' alone but that of the tremendously talented group with which he worked: Herman J. Mankiewicz, the co- or sole author of the screenplay (there is a controversy as to how much Welles contributed to the fine script); Gregg Toland, ace cinematographer, who the year before had shot *The Grapes of Wrath* and who, by means of original lighting techniques, executed some stunning deep-focus photography (the shot is in clear, sharp focus all along its depth from foreground to background); Bernard Herrmann, composer and conductor, whose moving score at times provides a subtle counterpoint to the film's images; Robert Wise and Mark Robson, two of the film's editors, who were to become popular directors, Wise with *The Set-up* (1949), and *The Sound of Music* (1965) and Robson with *Champion* (1949) and *Home of the Brave* (1949); and the actors themselves, Joseph Cotten, Everett Sloane, Agnes Moorehead, and Ruth Warrick. In addition to directing, producing, and collaborating on the script, Welles played the part of Kane magnificently, effortlessly aging a good forty years during the course of the film.

Whether or not Mankiewicz wrote the whole forceful script or not, it was Welles who translated an exciting screenplay into the most stunning of film experiences. In doing so, Welles used his training in radio most rewardingly. Indeed, if there is one single aspect of this film that may be unique, it is the way in which the director orchestrated conversation and narration. Conversations trail off and lead to another set in an aural "dissolve." Conversations are half heard, as a few words or sentences are emphasized. The quality of each voice is as integrated into the total "sound" of the film as is the voice's pitch and the rhythms of speech. Of course, it is not only the sound itself that is striking but the several ways in which it is synchronized with the images of the film.

85. *Orson Welles as Citizen Kane at the top of the stairs. The eccentric camera angle shown here is only one of the many to be found in this remarkable film.* (© RKO Radio Pictures)

Apart from this, Welles may not have introduced anything absolutely new to American film technique, but he did use the resources of film so well that many of the film's effects came to be adopted as current and important devices in the unfolding of film narratives. In Welles' hands effects became more than effects; like exclamation points and quotation marks, they functioned as a sort of cinematic punctuation, emphasizing particular aspects of the story. Welles and Toland used wide-angle photography, in which a broader-than-usual range of vision was condensed into a normal frame area. Distortion resulted, and this distortion is used in scenes in which personal relationships deteriorate.

As if the use of this distortion (Figure 85), both visual and aural, were not enough to baffle an unsuspecting audience, the narrative proceeded in jigsaw fashion from present to flashback as the reporter sought the "Rosebud" secret. Moreover, the camera moved, swirled, circled, pirouetted in a ballet of composition.

Technique is not so forthrightly displayed in *The Magnificent Ambersons*. Welles' second film was adapted by himself from a popular novel by Booth Tarkington. Both the novel and Welles' treatment of it dealt with the disintegration of a prosperous and prominent Midwestern family. The decline of the family is contrasted and, of course, affected by the coming of mechanization and industrialization to the town with which it is involved. The automobile is just as strong a dramatic personage in the film as are an unholy mother and a spoiled son.

The film appears to be more conventional than *Kane*, but is indeed as original. Perhaps it is because the film's surface appears less sensational than *Citizen Kane's* that the second film tended to be overlooked by students in favor of the first. There is another reason. Like *Greed, The Magnificent Ambersons* appears choppy. It is. After the shooting was completed, the editing was taken from Welles. Scenes showing the growth of the community and the effect of this change on the nature of the family were eliminated. It was felt that the film was too long. In shortening it, certain clues as to why characters behaved the way they did were excised.

Welles made a number of films in which intrigue figured prominently. While all the films were ultimately changed by other hands,

86. *Orson Welles and Rita Hayworth in* The Lady From Shanghai. (Courtesy Columbia Pictures)

Touch of Evil (1958), in which Welles himself appeared along with Marlene Dietrich and Charlton Heston, is the one film that emerged closest to the form the director himself would have liked. A most bizarre chase sequence climaxes *The Lady from Shanghai* (1948) with a frantic and dazzling pursuit through a hall of distorting mirrors in a deserted amusement park (Figure 86). Welles also directed three controversial and low-budgeted adaptations from Shakespeare: *Macbeth* (1950), *Othello* (1955), and *Falstaff* (1967; also known as *Chimes at Midnight*). The last two films were realized in Europe.

Now that the director has come to be recognized as a prime creative force in the making of films, Welles will probably be able to find the financing to complete another American film. Rumor has it that in the same way that he completed *Citizen Kane* in secrecy, Welles has already finished shooting a film in America which he is presently editing.

If Hollywood represented the only film activity America had, this chapter could end here, but there were others. We have little definite information to go on at present, but motion picture trade papers in the late twenties estimated that, starting about 1915, over thirty small production companies were formed. These companies were special because they were black companies making black films on black capital for black audiences.

In both the South and the North, all of the nation's approximately twelve million blacks were segregated into their own communities. These communities included cinemas. Not surprisingly, these cinemas did fair business by screening films made and distributed by black men such as Noble Johnson, an actor who started the Lincoln Motion Picture Company, one of the earliest production companies.

Most of these films now appear to be lost. So are most records kept on this unique phenomenon. Perhaps, somewhere, copies of the films still exist in a collector's secret atelier. Let us hope so. Here is a subject that needs much investigation.

One of the first black films, *The Birth of a Race* (1919), was made in response to the racism inherent in *The Birth of a Nation*. The film was to have chronicled "the achievements of the colored people." It was conceived in this way in 1916. What emerged three years later was a travesty of the original conception. An advertisement called it "a story of sin." We do not seem to have information on the "company" that produced *The Birth of a Race,* but there is the suggestion that fraud was used to raise capital for the venture.

Information is also lacking on the Ebony Players, who in 1917 (?) made a film, a copy of which now exists in the American Film Institute Collection in the Library of Congress. During the First World War, a spy scare swept America, and citizens were "finding" the Kaiser's agents just about everywhere. *Spyin' the Spy* manages to satirize both this scare and the costumed rites of the Ku Klux Klan.

Oscar Mischeaux was born in South Dakota and gained some fame as an author. Excited by the potential of the new medium to translate his written works into visual images, Mischeaux decided to go into production for himself. Traveling through his home state, Mischeaux sold shares in a film unit. He managed to raise enough capital to launch an organization that lasted twenty-four years and produced about twenty films. *The Homesteader* (1918), was Mischeaux's first film, and like most of his others it was filmed in his Harlem studio.

All of these companies operated under extreme financial hardship. White banks have never been sympathetic to black business, and loans were difficult, if not impossible, to obtain. The studios wanted their films to play in black theatres, and were jealous of any competition. They attempted to put black theatres under contract and to squeeze out rivals. Whereas the Hollywood film had a universal market, the audience for the black film was limited. Films had to be produced cheaply; there was little possibility for high financial return.

With these odds it is a wonder that an industry existed at all. The films made tended to be "quickies": filmed on a very low budget and over a period of no more than two or three days. Each sequence was shot in one, perhaps two, takes. Although the films that have been preserved appear primitive today, they provide an interesting clue as to the conditions under which blacks lived and the way their communities were structured.

The companies were founded on very shaky financial ground, and when the depression sapped the economic resources of the country, most units had to fold. Those that survived could not find the money to convert to sound. If a company did not disband it went into white receivership. While blacks still acted in the films, whites produced, wrote, and sometimes directed them. Themes began to change, and a racist note was felt: the heroes had the lighter skins, the villains the darker. But there appeared to be some interesting black melodramas (*The Scar of Shame*, 1927; *The Black King*, 1932), black mysteries

87.   Bronze Buckaroo, *one of several black Westerns.* (Courtesy Ken Jacobs)

(*Gun Moll*, 1933), black musicals (*Bronze Venus*, with Lena Horne, 1948), black film poems (*Broken Earth* by Clarence Muse), and even black Westerns (*The Bronze Buckaroo*, 1938). Just as there were white stars, so there were stars within the black community. The lead of the last title mentioned above, Herbert Jeffrey, was billed as the "black Roy Rogers" (see Figure 87).

At this moment there are not many other facts about these black films that can be added from present sources. These films must have been seen by a number of people and perhaps those who were alive in the twenties have vivid memories of them betwen 1915 and 1940. But memories only give us hints. They are not the real thing. With each passing year it becomes less and less likely that copies of these films will be saved from advanced deterioration or complete oblivion.

Blacks had little opportunity to make any technical contribution to film. Discrimination effectively kept them out of the studio, and until recently, out of the unions as well.

In 1914 when a black actor and not a white in blackface appeared in a film, *Dark Town Jubilee*, its screening caused a small riot in a

88. *Clarence Muse, the great black actor, in one of his most moving performances,* Hearts in Dixie. (© 1929 Twentieth Century-Fox Film Corporation. All Rights Reserved)

white section of Brooklyn. Although a number of blacks acted in Hollywood, they had no choice of roles. Cast as comic figures, porters, maids, and those outside the law, performers like Louise Beavers, Hattie McDaniel and Butterfly McQueen, all ladies of fine talent, and Paul Robeson and Clarence Muse tried to transcend the sorry limitations imposed on their careers by a racist society. Robeson was probably the most successful (*The Emperor Jones,* directed by Dudley Murphy from the play by Eugene O'Neill, 1933), but eventually he too had to leave America to find roles equal to his talent. Indeed, if the popular series of Roach-produced short comedies, *Our Gang,* is any indication, it would seem that blacks were allowed roles similar to those of whites only as juveniles.

In exceptional films like *Hearts in Dixie* (1929) and *Hallelujah,* when the cast was almost all black, there was more of a dramatic range. *Hearts in Dixie* (directed by Paul Sloane), which predates *Hallelujah* by six months, has only recently been found after resting in a studio vault for close to forty years (Figure 88). Not only is it as accomplished as is *Hallelujah* in its use of sound, but like the other film deals with a rural black community. Clarence Muse is a concerned father worried that, should his young son stay in the South, he will remain uneducated and, like his father before him, no more than a worker in the cotton fields. The father sells what little property he owns in order to pay his son's steamboat passage North, where the boy might go to school, free himself from superstition, and enter society as freely as whites. Looking at the film forty years later one sees what discrimination in the North did to the poor father's vision. Although most of the cast were not professionals, the acting is remarkably smooth and honest.

After the black soldier had distinguished himself in the Second World War, Hollywood's attitude toward the black community slowly began to change. The year 1949–50 saw at least four pioneering dramas dealing with the diseased relationships between the races. In the adaptation of Arthur Laurents' play *Home of the Brave* for the screen, the leading character, who was bullied and threatened by other members of his platoon because he was Jewish, becomes black. *Pinky,* directed by Elia Kazan, although it told of a singularly uncommon case (a mulatto returns to the southern town where she was raised), dealt with the problem in candor. A lynch

89. *Young Sidney Poitier with Richard Widmark, a fine character actor, in a scene from Poitier's first film,* No Way Out, *directed by Joseph Mankiewicz.* (© 1950 Twentieth-Century-Fox Film Corporation. All Rights Reserved)

mob gathers in *Intruder in the Dust. No Way Out,* a prophetic film of 1950, told of the instigation of race riots. It featured Sidney Poitier in his first "starring" role (Figure 89), and in examining the roles given to Poitier from this film and *The Defiant Ones* (1958 — two convicts, one black, one white, are chained together in an escape and so *must* learn to live together) to *The Bedford Incident* (1965), one can see Poitier's graduation from films where his color was the focus of the film's drama to the point where it had little, if anything, to do with the dramatic action.

It was not until the sixties that blacks broke through union discrimination in Hollywood, and Gordon Parks, an expert fashion photographer, was allowed to direct. *The Learning Tree* (1969) was the first major American film to be directed by a black. Based on Parks' own autobiography, the film nostalgically recalled the director's boyhood years forty years ago in rural Kansas. Parks' second film, *Shaft,* about a private detective in Harlem, opened in July of 1971.

The story of Melvin Van Peebles is interesting. Having completed a number of short films, Van Peebles, unable to earn a living in the industry, left for Paris. He learned French and became the author of several books. With his membership in a society for French artists, he was assisted in the making of his first feature-length film, which

175

90.   *Godfrey Cambridge in Melvin Van Peebles'* The Watermelon Man. (Courtesy Columbia Pictures)

gently told of a black G.I.'s affair with a French girl: *The Story of a Three-Day Pass* (1968). The film was exhibited at a number of festivals, and as a French film earned favorable criticism in America. On the basis of its modest success, Van Peebles returned to Hollywood to direct a film with Godfrey Cambridge: *Watermelon Man* (1970). In it Cambridge plays a white bigot who wakes up in the middle of one night to find himself black (Figure 90). The first part of the film is similar to a domestic "situation" comedy. Cambridge tries all sorts of ridiculous potions to return to whiteness, but as soon as Cambridge leaves the safety of his home, and faces the street and town outside, the film assumes a fairly serious and sinister tone. Originally, the film's producers insisted that the film's ending be "happy" and that Cambridge become white. He does not return to his original color, but the film does have a happy ending. Cambridge, at first ashamed and horrified at his skin, not only wears his skin proudly at the film's conclusion, but learns to take offensive action against anyone who troubles him over his color.

Van Peebles' recent film *Sweet Sweetback's Baadasssss Song* was financed by the director, writer, composer and star himself. It is independently produced, and because it is independent, Van Peebles has no one to modify his particular stance. The film is a very inventive but very strong portrayal of persecution: it ends violently with an unmistakable warning of social danger.

176

5 Big Breaks

Appearances are deceiving. At the end of the Second World War, it appeared that the studios of Hollywood had become permanent American institutions. Their contribution to the war effort was colossal. Their films expressed a unity of purpose that buoyed morale both at home and on the front. War bonds were cleverly advertised in short films produced by the studios. Directors were loaned to various war offices to make documentaries that would both inform and propagandize; cameramen became combat photographers; actors were released from contracts so that they could join the armed forces; actresses, comedians, singers and dancers were all organized into troupes that toured battle zones and entertained the fighting men. Studios donated thousands of prints so that projectors could be set up in combat areas and men might relax for a short while away from the horrors of war.

The year 1946 is quoted as being one of the most profitable in the history of American motion pictures. Hollywood films, playing in cinemas all over the world, earned well over two billion dollars in box office receipts.

The Production Code was still very much in force and had lost little of its censorial power. It was primarily concerned with social morality, but in 1947 the threat of political censorship frightened the industry into a desperately self-righteous act. During the war, Russia had been America's uneasy ally; after the Second World War, relations between the two nations grew strained and then froze. The Iron Curtain made a neat, if figurative, division between the West (Capitalism) and the East (Communism), and the Cold War was fought in the diplomatic arena.

177

American politicians, not really understanding the ideological nature of Communism, saw only the ruthless and brutal tactics of the Soviet premier, Joseph Stalin. As Stalin eliminated all his opposition, America fearfully took this barbaric suppression for the essential Communist doctrine.

A number of senators submitted "evidence" to Congress that the most vital aspects of American society were being infiltrated by Stalin's henchmen. It was believed that there were Communists in positions of importance, that these spies had no minds of their own and were acting under instructions from Moscow. Their orders were to subvert national ideals and promote anarchy. Once anarchy reigned, it would be followed by a well organized take-over. Because motion pictures so influenced an audience's image of the world, film was cited as a distributor of Communist propaganda.

The leading senator in this "revelation," Joseph McCarthy, was himself later exposed on television as a fearful, unbalanced individual. However, when his accusations first appeared they were much too dramatic to be ignored. The senator believed that if Communists directed, wrote and acted in films, their political commitments would outweigh their creative talents; the resultant films would be clever vehicles for the "destruction of America." The senator, apparently unaffected by these hidden persuaders, raised a hue and cry that set off witch-hunts by several government agencies across the country, and much attention was focused on the subsequent government investigation.

Inquiries were conducted by the House Committee on Un-American Activities, and an investigating subcommittee of the Senate. Hollywood personnel, including studio executives, were called to testify before these bodies. Although few offending films were actually cited, the examiners asked for the names of alleged Communists. While some witnesses named names, ten "unfriendly" witnesses invoked the Fifth Amendment and would not answer any questions about their own or their acquaintances' political activity. As a result some landed in jail and all were placed on a blacklist.

A group of prominent film executives met in New York, and anxious about federal interference in the making of films, declared that no known or suspected Communist would receive employment at any studio. Even though the Fifth Amendment had been written to protect the individual from self-incrimination, the executives felt that its invocation was incriminating enough. The "unfriendly" witnesses were suspended from work. A blacklist was compiled, and many left-wing sympathizers were unable to find employment. Many retired, some became celebrated directors in Europe, and some, utterly shaken by the investigation, suffered mental collapse.

Unfortunately for Hollywood, some of the most exciting talents were among those proscribed. Not only did the town find itself without its most promising young men but it was also in an ugly temper characterized by fear and betrayal. It has recently been admitted that the studios did not abide as closely by the blacklist as they publicly promised. So long as the "unfriendlies" wrote under pseudonyms, and agreed to keep their identities secret, they were allowed to write certain screenplays. Yet the blacklist, like the code before it, did succeed in its primary purpose. It held back official intervention into the affairs of the industry. The executives remained masters of Hollywood, and the blacklist caused films made morally antiseptic by the code to become politically cautious as well.

During the war tremendous developments had been made in film hardware. America designed battle cameras that had to function well during combat. They were portable, sturdy and dependable and used 16mm film (Figure 91).

91.   *During the Second World War, motion pictures entertained the fighting men in all theatres of combat.* (Museum of Modern Art/Film Stills Archive)

A 16mm frame was about a third the size of the standard 35mm film. Although the 16mm image could contain as much information as 35mm, its image would not be as sharply defined. The new gauge was more easily damaged, but its flexibility and portability made it ideal for active duty. It was cheaper to manufacture, and with certain developments, in time its image quality almost duplicated that of 35mm.

With the popularization of 16mm film, the nature of the film base changed. Originally 35mm film was manufactured on a nitrate base which, if not stored under ideal conditions, decomposed speedily and was extremely combustible. Acetate film was known as safety film, and it was on an acetate base that 16mm film was released. While an acetate or safety film could still burn when exposed to extreme heat, acetate was not nearly as fire-prone nor as explosive as nitrate. Not inclined to decompose under standard conditions, acetate films could be indefinitely stored. In the past, extreme precaution had been needed in the handling of film; now all that was required was common sense. By 1948 Hollywood was moving all its 35mm production onto acetate film. With elaborate safety measures no longer needed, and the transport of film simplified, time and costs were cut.

During the war, the Germans perfected a means of recording sound onto a small ribbon of tape which was magnetized and coated with minute particles of metal. Not only was the sound quality improved, but the means of recording was also made easier than it ever had been. Tape recorders were portable and could be operated easily by one person. No longer were sound trucks, equipped with complicated machinery, required for recording in the field.

There were open-air theatres very early in the history of projected film. Screening films in fields or on rooftops was safer, and certainly more comfortable, than showing them in a sweltering theatre in the heat of summer. In 1914 one exhibitor hired New York's Ebbets Field, usually reserved for baseball, to screen Ince's spectacular hurricane film, *The Wrath of the Gods,* for an audience of twenty-one thousand people. However these screenings were not usual; projecting under open skies had to wait for the drive-in.

The first drive-in movie theatres had opened prior to the war.

They were modest ventures that banked on the American public's mobility for their success. The first builders viewed them as experimental. By 1940 there were not only a hundred drive-ins but plans for hundreds more. The size of the screen had jumped in the late thirties from forty feet wide and thirty high to sixty by fifty; the acreage of the lots more than doubled. Whereas the first theatres might accommodate eighty cars, some could now house eight hundred. There was only one speaker, which had to be heard across the distance of the field. There were no provisions to heat cars during the colder months, so these theatres had to remain inoperative during the winter. With the war there was a hiatus in construction. All building materials were diverted to the struggle overseas, so no new theatres could be erected. However, by the time 1945 drew to a close, old blueprints were dusted off, new lots acquired, and new plans composed. With the recall of gasoline rationing, the boom was on, so much so that in 1950 drive-ins numbered about three thousand.

With all this activity, what could go wrong for Hollywood? Its films were making more money than ever, it had staved off government interference, it had the respect of every American who appreciated its wartime contributions, it had cut down production costs with the introduction of both safety film and tape recording, and it suspected that the newly established drive-ins would attract considerable capital. Surely it would seem that the system was as strong as ever. What could go wrong? Plenty!

Plenty came in the form of strikes, the appearance of television, and a Supreme Court decision.

In 1945 studio employees called a strike to force management into recognizing and bargaining with their various unions. One strike lasted eight months. In 1946 the studios' dissatisfied laboratories decided on another tactic: they would hold release prints in the chemical vats and refuse to develop them until contract demands were met. Employees finally won about a 25 percent wage increase.

The settlement of labor problems did not necessarily damage the strength of the studio. The studios' increased costs could be passed on in the form of raised admission prices to audiences. However, the studios were reluctant to do this, because by the time a calm returned to labor relations, attendance began to drop. This drop was not insignificant, and it was feared that increased admission might aggravate the decline even further.

Although they were reluctant to do so, the studios, by 1948, had to recognize television as a competitor that would soon attract the film-going public in the same way that film had drawn the frequenters from saloons half a century earlier. Prior to the Second World War, only several hundred families had television receivers. During the war, electronic equipment was at a premium, and no sets were manufactured. Soon after the end of the war, stations, organized into networks, offered an incentive to prospective television purchasers. Whereas programs had previously been telecast on a staggered basis of only a few hours every day, the networks formulated a complete day of broadcast. As affluence increased and the price of television hardware decreased, the sale of sets skyrocketed. The national broadcast of the 1948 political conventions provided an important stimulus toward television purchase. One intelligent guess estimated that between the end of the war and 1950, five million sets were sold. This does not mean that five million families stopped going to the movies altogether; they just stopped going religiously every week. Ten years later there were over fifty million television sets, and a fifth of the nation's theatres had shut for lack of business. Many of those that were not closed survived only on candy sales. The theatres' lobbies became marketplaces, and profits were measured in the consumption of chocolate bars and popcorn. One critic was heard to say, "Movies are butter than ever," and attendance continued to drop.

By the time the executives admitted television's threat, it already was a national phenomenon. Rather than think of ways in which the two media might peaceably coexist with each other, the studios reacted sharply. They declared war. Stars were forbidden to appear on television. So television looked elsewhere for its talent. It found it on Broadway, in nightclubs, and ironically, in Hollywood itself, where for every studio contract available there had always been a thousand hopeful actors.

How could the movies recapture their lost patrons? They could not (Figures 92 and 93). Filmgoing had become a habit, a weekly event. That habit was now broken, and in its place, a new habit was cultivated. Evenings were spent in front of the television set. Not only could a home be more comfortable than a theatre, but viewing the set did not require spending extra money on an evening out. During the mid-fifties, television broadcast live dramatic programs that were as sensitive and intelligent as were the films Hollywood was producing. There was no good reason to leave the living room.

Hollywood did not seem to understand this. The studios could have left the casual, easy, and often simpleminded entertainment to television. They might have questioned the restricting code, and begun to have tackled more mature themes. But like film's first executive, Edison, and the trust members who followed, the studio executives saw only their immediate business interest imperiled, and failed to keep pace with the taste of the American public.

Instead of changing the quality of film subjects, they changed the shape of the screen. The film image became streamlined, longer and wider. The American audience was never as stupid as the executives seemed to assume. Of course it resisted the temptation of the wide screen. After all, if shape and size were all that films had to offer over television, then they offered very little.

The wide screen was not a new idea. Not only were there "talkies" at the World's Fair held in Paris in 1900, but also there was a process called Cinéorama. Each of ten projectors cast part of one continuous hand-colored image that swept 360° around a room. The film surrounded the spectator in a complete circle. Since the range of human vision is at best about 160°, the 360° effect was not appreciated and remained a novelty. We have already seen how Griffith simulated a wide-screen effect in *Intolerance* (1915) merely by masking the regular frame. He did not really change film's width nor did he resort to special projection devices. When during their premiere exhibitions certain epic sequences in *The Iron Horse* (1924), *The Big Parade* (1925), and *Chang* (1927) were presented in panoramic wide screen, the image was actually made larger and wider through an ingenious projection procedure called Magnascope.

There was, besides, a compelling argument for changing the shape of the screen. The standard screen did not make use of peripheral vision, the ability to see those objects at the edges of our sight. Whatever is on the peripheries of our vision may hardly be noticed,

92–93. *The power of television. Once an ornate theatre . . . and now . . .*
(Museum of Modern Art/Film Stills Archive)

yet these scarcely glimpsed objects act as orientation points in providing depth to our vision.

It was Edison who, in the designing of his films for Kinetoscope use, determined the shape of the film frame as oblong. Screens, which needed to correspond in shape, were a third longer than they were high. They made no use of peripheral vision, and so the illusion of depth had yet to be introduced as a popular feature into the commercial American cinema.

This illusion is what Hollywood thought might be the trump card against television. Two depth processes were introduced in 1952. Neither of them came from a major studio. Each was an independent production. However, their success prompted the studios to adopt other more feasible processes that would better present an illusion of depth.

This Is Cinerama came to Broadway in 1952. Cinerama was projected on a screen that was almost three times as long as it was high; the screen was deeply curved in toward the center so that its sides were closer to the audience than its recessed middle. Using three projectors, which presented three adjoining segments of one continuous image, Cinerama's picture filled the immense screen. The shape and size of the screen imitated the latitude of man's vision, and if members of the audience were fortunate enough to sit toward the center of the auditorium, they experienced the sensation of depth. This illusion, in turn, reinforced the idea of "being there" wherever the Cinerama travelogue took its audience.

While the feeling of depth may have made films more "real," Cinerama proved self-defeating. Whatever may have been gained by the illusion of depth was lost by a constant reminder that this experience was a film experience and not a real one. The image on the screen was being cast by three different projectors. The seams between the adjoining images, two very straight and narrow lines, showed. Even though there was an elaborate method of synchronization between the working projectors, it was not uncommon for the image cast by one to be brighter or darker than the other two.

Equipping a theatre for Cinerama screenings was a notoriously expensive affair. Not only would the front rows of seats have to be removed from the auditorium so that the huge screen might be accommodated, but also the booth from which the film was projected had to be altered. Now there were three booths of two projectors each. (Any booth from which 35mm is projected should come equipped with a set of two projectors. Thirty-five-millimeter film is usually wound onto a core holding one thousand feet — eleven minutes' worth — of film, or it is wound onto a reel holding twice this amount, and 35mm projectors are so constructed that they may not be loaded with more than a double reel of film at any one time. At a standard number of frames before the end of a reel a white dot, printed on the film, flashes on the upper right of the screen. This is a signal to the projectionist to "change over" or switch to the adjacent projector, on which the next load is ready. The projectors are so synchronized that the audience is unaware of a smooth transition. A theatre equipped to show Cinerama was therefore outfitted with three sets of two projectors each.)

Cinerama became an attraction in only the largest of cities, and even in these, only one theatre to house the process tended to be built per community. And it must be added that the subjects of Cinerama were not the most vital. Most of the films presented in the process were travelogues that made use of the illusion of reality.

The new 3-D, viewed privately the year before, made its public appearance in 1953 with a jungle adventure, *Bwana Devil* (Arch Oboler). Using a principle known as early as 1600, *Bwana Devil* presented its audience with lions that leaped from the screen, and African feather headdresses that brushed against its noses. Men gasped, women screamed, and children giggled. The 3-D experience became a fad, and typical of most fads it was considered such box-office poison two years later that the first fine films to be photographed in 3-D were released in the usual flat process.

Relying on stereoscopic vision, 3-D's illusion of depth was much more sensational than that of Cinerama. Stereoscopic vision springs from the physiological fact that each of our eyes sees a little differently from the other. When the information from both eyes is correlated in the brain, the perception of depth results. In shooting a stereoscopic film, two cameras, each as far apart from the other as is one eye from the other, photograph the same scene. When the scenes are projected, they do not appear side by side, but rather one scene is projected "on top" of the other. The result is not an immediate illusion of depth but a jumble. If an audience wears special spectacles equipped with a particular polarizing filter, the spectacles unscramble the network of lines and translate the experience into one image that has the illusion of depth. What helped to destroy the popularity of the device was that it was originally used for a series of films noted for their cheap thrills (pies in the face, arrows in the back). Had it remained popular, something interesting might have developed. Hitchcock was shooting the rather tranquil murder story *Dial M for Murder* (1954) in the process when 3-D failed. Even though the spectacles were inexpensive, an audience resented buying or renting them. They were nuisances and particularly difficult to adjust if one already wore glasses.

It was not Cinerama nor 3-D that made a lasting impression on the screen. It was CinemaScope. CinemaScope had been developed earlier by a good quarter century by Professor Henri Chrétien before Twentieth Century-Fox released *The Robe* (1953), the first full-length American film photographed in this process. CinemaScope used the same camera as regular film did; the difference was in the lens. Remember that Orson Welles, for one, in the making of *Citizen Kane* and other films, used a lens with wider vision than lenses usually encompassed. Because more visual information had to be squeezed into an area designed for less, distortion resulted. When that distorted image was projected on a screen, the figures appeared uncommonly thin and all bunched up. Indeed, if you look at a frame from a CinemaScope film, the characters appear this way. An "anamorphic" lens with a wide range of vision squeezes much information into a small area. When the film is projected, another anamorphic lens, attached to the projector, straightens out the image and spreads it over a large area that imitates the scope of the original lens. At first the CinemaScope screen was almost three times as wide as it was tall, but now the wide screen's contrast in proportions is hardly that dramatic. The new rectangular screen brought peripheral vision into use. Although its depth illusion was not as stunning as Cinerama's and could not compare with 3-D's, it was an improvement over that of the standard oblong shape.

In the new processes, speakers strategically placed around the auditorium transmitted high-fidelity stereophonic sound to enhance the feeling of depth. For a few months toward the end of 1959, two processes with the self-explaining names of AromaRama and Smell-O-Vision attempted to bring a very real dimension to the illusion of reality. Pleasing manufactured whiffs were synchronized with the images of *Behind the Great Wall* and *Scent of Mystery* so that they would be released throughout the auditorium in concert with certain images.

Each company sought its own wide-screen process and although the anamorphic lens was not always used, and the shape of the frame itself may have altered, it seemed that the rectangular screen was to stay.

The switch from the nearly square to the wide rectangular frame perplexed producers and exhibitors. The question of standardization arose, and the industry wondered what process would win out. Confusion was increased when Cinerama kept its name but changed its process. Still maintaining a screen of panoramic proportion, it dropped two of its three cameras and, using 70mm film width (the largest used commercially), chose to shoot with an anamorphic lens that gathered almost as much information as three standard lenses.

If this transition confused the industry, it delighted filmmakers. Now there seemed to be a choice of frame. While intimate dramas could be more forcibly presented on the standard screen, Westerns, shot on vast expenses of territory, could be better accommodated on the epic wide area.

Actually this choice did not last for long. When the screen changed shape, it did so for good. Theatres made their screens wider so that they could present the new wide films. As screens were made wider, they were also made thinner. Tops and bottoms were shorn. If a film that was made before the introduction of the wide screen was to be shown on this new screen, its top and/or bottom would also be cropped. While the cut is small, it does interfere with films whose images have been carefully composed. When *Gone with the Wind,* originally shot at 1.33:1, was recently rereleased, every single one of its three hundred thousand or so frames had to be rephotographed within new broader borders.

The shape of the screen changed in such a way that television sets of the fifties could not mimic. So the shape changed. So what? Audience levels continued to fall.

The film industry, finally seeing the futility of battle with television, wisely decided to sue for peace. It began to advertise its films on television, and encouraged its stars to enhance their popularity through selected television appearances.

In one sense television is a medium for broadcast. Television itself does not preserve its programs. Television is certain signals transmitted over wires. Television programs have only a present tense; they exist only while they are being transmitted and received. When broadcasting was live, the programs had no life beyond the television set. In order to remain permanent, the broadcast had to be recorded on some substance which would preserve the information.

As broadcasting became a daily affair, and as that daily affair spread from the early evening into night, into the afternoon, and the hours of daylight, television needed to consume more and more material. Some of this material would have to be programs already broadcast. But television could not rebroadcast a program unless it was preserved. Film preserved broadcasts, and although it is not the only means of recording and preserving broadcasts, it was, until the advent of videotape, the important one.

As broadcasting increased, television studios became overworked, and other facilities were required. The motion picture studios, in need of income, were only too happy to make their superbly equipped sound stages available. In 1951 Columbia Pictures' subsidiary, Screen Gems, entered the field of producing filmed series (a season's worth of programs) for television. The studios that did not rent space to television producers entered production themselves. By 1957, Film City was well on its way to becoming Television City.

Unfortunately, the economics of television broadcasting operated in the same fashion as the motion picture industry. The respect for the dollar overpowered the concern for quality, and soon, with the great number of television films produced, an assembly-line system developed. Even audience response was planned: laughter, recorded at another time and in another place ("canned" laughter), was added to comic programs as a signal to home viewers that certain incidents were supposed to be funny.

Television's appetite was fantastic. It could consume vast amounts of material. What the film industry lost in paid admissions it almost made up in sales of older films and rental of shooting facilities to television. In the middle fifties the broadcast rights to nine thousand theatrical films made before 1948 were sold or leased to television. Each was a ready-made program with a built-in appeal; yet they were quickly used up by the new media.

After 1960 the industry began to sell its post-1948 productions, and with each succeeding year the time gap between the year of production and the date of broadcast becomes narrower and narrower. Some films made today never see the inside of an American theatre. Low-budgeted films made abroad, horror films and Westerns, may appear only on late, late, late television shows, and new American films that are made for television here may find their way to foreign theatres.

The studios, once so fearful and anxious about the appearance of television, turned their competitor into an uneasy ally, and reaped a bonanza. The ally, realizing the tremendous market for film material, has now taken the offensive and become intimately involved in the production of theatrical films.

Watching a film on television may introduce you to the work of an interesting director or give you the opportunity of seeing an important work that you no longer would be able to find in a theatre. It can also be an unsatisfactory experience. Commercial interruptions are annoying, but, depending on the film, they can be tolerated; wholesale reediting of the film cannot be. Sometimes whole plots are removed and beginnings and endings of sequences are lopped off so that the running time of the film may fit into a prescribed time slot. Occasionally, the fellow who cuts up a film to insert commercial breaks puts the pieces back together in a bizarre order. A recent film I saw on television had a gangster shot dead in one scene and in the next had the same man taking his girl out to a movie.

The proportions of most television screens are those of the old oblong screen; it is very difficult to accommodate a wide-screen film for television broadcast. Part of the image is usually missing. On the whole it is best to stay away from films on television if you tend to think of film as primarily aesthetic experience. If you are most interested in the narrative and social aspects of film, then watching it on television is better than not seeing it at all.

Television must be thanked for preserving some of the heritage of American filmmaking. Most of the studios, acting as if the film industry were nothing more than a business, were not inclined to keep old copies of films lying around for sentimental reasons. When the vaults became crowded or material began to decompose, the studios methodically cleaned out the storage areas by destroying old, unused copies of film. Even original negatives were not always saved from the garbage bin. Luckily, institutions like the Museum of Modern Art in New York, George Eastman House in Rochester, and the Motion Picture Division of the Library of Congress in Washington tried to restore and preserve a limited number of classic American films from disappearing. Recently the American Film Institute Collection in Washington joined these ranks. Although these institutions were successful, their small budgets prohibited ambitious efforts. What finally saved many films (a good number seem to be lost forever) was the prospect that they would make more money. Copies in 16mm could be circulated for television broadcast.

It was not television that ultimately changed the nature of the industry. It was no less a force than the United States Department of Justice. The government maintained that the film industry had created a monopoly, and that its practices restricted trade and made a mockery of free enterprise. Most theatres, if they were not owned by the studio, were at least controlled by them through a series of contractual agreements. Through these theatre chains, studios practiced "block booking" and "blind selling." A theatre, wanting to exhibit a particular film, would be obliged to play a number of others as well (block booking). Sometimes the theatre was obliged to exhibit a film it had not yet seen (blind selling). The studio, not the theatre, fixed the price of admission and determined the length of the film's run.

The government, as early as the late thirties, had been scrutinizing the economic practices of the studios. By 1940 the courts had asked the studios to stop their purchase of theatres. The studios complied, and the most flagrant incidents of block booking and blind selling were stopped, but although a stranglehold can be loosened, a grip may still be tight. The studios loosened their hold somewhat, but their grip on the industry was still suffocating.

In 1945, in the United States District Court of New York, the studios went on trial. It took four years before a verdict was reached; it was several years later before the court orders were translated into standard practice. The verdict, issued in a number of decrees, cut to the bone. Five companies — Metro-Goldwyn-Mayer (MGM), Paramount, Radio-Keith-Orpheum (RKO), 20th Century–Fox, and Warner Brothers — were told to divest themselves of their theatres. Three others that did not own theatres — Columbia, Universal–International and United Artists — were ordered to desist from negotiating prohibitive contracts with theatres. (Two other minor studios, Republic and Monogram, were not engaged in these practices and were left alone.) In short, production was divorced from exhibition.

What did this immediately mean for the studios? It meant that the films they produced were no longer guaranteed a theatre for their exhibition. Of course, a big studio film would always find a theatre in which to play; but the studio now would have to negotiate with the exhibitor. The studio could not automatically assume that its film would play in this or that theatre. The studio, having built a self-perpetuating system in which box-office receipts were cycled back into future production, had to stop counting on this continual flow. Box offices no longer belonged to them.

What did this immediately mean for the exhibitor? He was now free to choose what films played in his theatre. He could open his doors to films made in other nations as well as to the independent American filmmaker. The exhibitor now was not obliged to change his film weekly or whenever the studio ordered him to do so; a film could be engaged for as long as an audience attended.

What did this mean to the independent filmmaker? He still faced considerable financial odds in the making of films, but he no longer had to align himself with a studio in order to find a theatre. Now the independent film could compete on an open market with studio-made films. However, the studios continued to have considerably more bargaining power than the independent filmmaker, and the "divorce" decree did not at first mean all that much to the independent.

What did the court's ruling mean to the audience? Theatres had the whole world of cinema from which to choose. When theatres began to exhibit foreign-produced films, audiences could broaden not only their appreciation of film but also their understanding of other cultures.

Usually, going to the movies had been similar to spending an evening at a fancy restaurant in which the customer is served several dishes before the main course. The main attraction at the theatre was preceded by a digest of the news, a cartoon, a short film on sport or travel or a one- or two-reel comedy, and trailers of coming attractions. Sometimes there was an intermission before the feature, and every so often after the final screening the national anthem would be played. When television began to broadcast the news as it was being made, the industry saw no need to duplicate this information: it turned the newsreel into a film compiled of interesting sport, fashion, society and travel events. Meanwhile, to cut down on their theatrical output, the studios dropped the making of short films. After theatres were freed from studio control, the studios no longer felt the need of supplying the exhibitor with a "complete dinner." From now on, the main course, the featured attraction, would have to suffice.

The studios had been geared to maximum production. Every film made by the studio had been guaranteed a theatre in which it could begin to earn back its production cost. No more. Audiences had diminished, and the box office had been wrested from the immediate control of the studios. The studios could not afford to keep up demanding schedules; production was severely cut back. Low-budgeted programmers, or "B" films, which often accompanied an expensive production in second runs, followed the short films in being cut from production.

Sound stages remained idle. Technicians went without work. Even though studios cut their staffs by a quarter or more in the fifties, they still had tremendous overhead. The sound stages, although empty, had to be maintained for the times when they would be used. Costumes still had to be stored and catalogued, sets warehoused until they could be incorporated into future films. While their activity slowed down, studios still had the expense of total upkeep. When the studios geared for television production, the renting of facilities helped pay for some of this overhead. Yet so draining was this cost, that they began to divest themselves of their various properties.

When the first studios were constructed they were built in huge empty fields and occupied hundreds of acres. Los Angeles was then a nothing town, and Hollywood a suburb of nowhere. But in forty years, Los Angeles became a sprawling, bustling metropolis which grew up around many studio lots. As studio acreage was falling into disuse, real estate values were climbing steeply. At handsome profits, studios rid themselves of unneeded land. Not only were apartments and factories constructed on the land on which vampires and Texas sheriffs once roamed, but oil speculators installed drilling machinery as well.

Property that was not sold was used for the shooting of television serials. The sound stages became home to more and more television serials and fewer and fewer films destined for theatres. Indeed, the Ponderosa may once have been Dracula's Transylvania.

The most dramatic divestiture of property was highly advertised when in 1970 MGM auctioned off its warehouses of costumes, sets and properties. The dresses worn in *Gone with the Wind* were sold, along with mock Sherman tanks, saloon bars, fake airplanes, and a real steamboat. Twentieth Century–Fox conducted a similar auction. Columbia, in June 1971, went one step further. It announced that it was selling all its real estate, and moving into the Warner Brothers lot, where it would lease space from its Burbank competitor to shoot films!

Studios eased out of the production of theatrical films, but this does not mean that they ceased to be interested in film. They shifted attention to the distribution of motion pictures that were independently produced. In 1938, American studios produced over four hundred films; in 1962 the studios produced only twenty-five. Independent producers, however, made about one hundred and fifty, many of these abroad, and the majority of these films were distributed by the studios.

The studios no longer held directors, actors and writers to long contracts. With the stopping of the *continual* flow of money coming back to the studio from the theatre, the studio could no longer afford to keep its artists on a regular weekly salary. For the most part these

194

artists were freed to negotiate for employment on a free-lance basis. When contracts are written now, they tend to be written for the making of one particular film. The long-term contract has all but disappeared. Artists are in better control of careers than they have ever been. If they do not find suitable work after scouting around, then, like Frank Sinatra and Jerry Lewis, they have the option of becoming producers themselves and doing their own thing in films of their own making.

Studios now welcome the independent producers. As a rule it is the independent producer who takes part of the financial risk. It is he who originates an idea to shoot this or that property. It is he who assembles "a package" with which he tries to raise money. A package is assembled from commitments by certain performers and a director who agree to work on a project devised by or for a producer. With these promises the producer usually approaches a studio with the hope that the studio will be interested.

If the studio does not produce films, why should the producer be concerned about the studio? The studios, although they do not own theatres, maintain an extensive distribution system in which films may be released. The studios still have contacts with major networks of theatres. If a studio is interested in a film, it may guarantee to distribute the film once the work is completed. Distributing a film involves investing money. (Some films cost more to advertise than to make.) Promotion campaigns must be designed; hundreds of release prints must be struck in the laboratory.

If a studio thinks that a film has a potential to return a profit, then a bank, impressed by the studio's agreement to distribute the film, may interpret this guarantee as a favorable credential, and loan the producer perhaps up to 50 percent of the film's budgeted costs.

At times a studio might think so favorably of a certain idea that not only will it loan the producer the use of its technical facilities, but also it may advance him almost the complete cost of the production. Advancing this money does not mean that the studio is producing the film, but the studio does expect to make some money releasing it and the money advanced is part of what the studio expects to make.

Although studios may offer their facilities to the producers with whom they work, many producers prefer to shoot out of Hollywood on actual locations. More than half the films photographed for American producers today are shot away from Hollywood sound stages. A healthy portion of feature filmmaking has returned to the city which incubated the industry, New York. Until recently, foreign nations like Spain, Italy and England induced American crews to shoot abroad. Not only was labor inexpensive but in many cases there was no need to build sets. Real temples, mosques and jungles were at hand. Some countries even invested in American productions so that their own economy might be stimulated. In India, for instance, the rupees paid at the box office cannot be translated into American dollars. The money must stay in India; it cannot leave the country. The only way an American producer may see his profit is by making a film in India.

When equipment became portable and shooting apparatus flexible, there was no need to remain inside the confines of a Hollywood sound stage. Audiences also became suspicious of productions that had a studio-manufactured appearance, with sets that looked like those that could be seen on any television situation comedy or action program.

New alliances between the artists and producer began to grow. At times, when actors, directors or cameramen believe very much in a film on which they have been invited to work, they participate in financing the film by deferring their salaries. Waiting until the film is completed and released, they share the profits, if any, with the producer. Such a film *might* (there is no one tried and true formula) pay for itself in the following way.

When a film is exhibited, the exhibitor makes up his expenses by taking his cost from what is paid by the box-office receipts. What is left of this gross is called the net. This is sent to the distributor, who, after making up his cost and his advance, forwards a major percentage of his net to the producer. The producer pays back those who invested in his film. If he has taken a bank loan, it must be returned at an interest. Only then is there a profit, and it is this profit which must be divided up among those who worked and collaborated on a deferred-payment scheme. (This is an ideal situation; the actual payment is usually more complicated.)

196

The studios have become distributors, and irony of ironies, these old monopolies have slowly been absorbed into new conglomerates. Paramount Pictures is no longer an autonomous organization. It is now a subsidiary of Gulf & Western Corporation, which owns many smaller companies to which it may dictate policy and business procedure. Although Paramount operates with a degree of independence, its role in the corporate structure is like a child to his parent — the parent in this case could put this child up for adoption at any time. Universal Pictures and its lot, Universal City, a tourist attraction, are almost completely devoted to the making of television films, and this studio, the first of the majors, is an arm of the Music Corporation of America — perhaps the old studio heads, now mostly retired or dead, had a charisma that kept their organizations together and independent.

With the decline of the studios came the decline of the code. The studios had enforced the code. If a film did not have code approval, it would not play in a studio-owned theatre. Since the studios controlled most of the theatres, a code seal had to be obtained. After the "divorce" decree, the theatres were freed from studio scrutiny, and could book films as they saw fit. Theatres were free to exhibit films whether or not they carried a code seal.

Otto Preminger was an independent producer/director who did submit his films for code approval. Twice this approval was turned down. The reason for refusing approval to *The Moon Is Blue* (1953) was adultery, which is not committed in the film but is treated with some jest; the film also made mention of that unutterable word "virgin." The golden arm in *The Man with the Golden Arm* (1955) belonged to a junkie (Figure 94). Addiction to drugs was not considered a fit subject to be exploited in the popular media. In both cases a fine of twenty-five thousand dollars was levied on Preminger for releasing nonapproved films. It was never collected. Preminger not only found theatres to exhibit his films, but each attracted a large audience. Their popularity warned the code administration to ease its stultifying standards. The code took the hint and continued to modify its standards until those that were left were truly valueless. (However, we really should not mourn the code. It seems simply to have moved on to television.)

94. *Frank Sinatra is the Man With The Golden Arm in Otto Preminger's film.* (Museum of Modern Art/Film Stills Archive; Courtesy Otto Preminger Productions)

Theatres, freed from maintaining ties with the studios, nevertheless remained with Hollywood. Stars of the fifties such as Marilyn Monroe (*Bus Stop,* 1956; Figure 95), Elizabeth Taylor (*A Place in the Sun,* 1951), James Dean (*Rebel without a Cause,* 1955; Figure 96), and Marlon Brando (*On the Waterfront,* 1954) could still attract millions (Figure 95). Theatre owners realized that American films had a luster, a type of professional gloss that European films lacked.

At first, only a handful of small cinemas in the largest of cities played foreign films. Those films that were imported into the States were usually more intelligent and sensitively made than the colorful American films of the period. They were also made inexpensively — frequently in black-and-white. American films had graduated to full Technicolor, wide screen and stereophonic sound, and the European ones still lacked these techniques. To the untrained eye, these films appeared "primitive." On the whole, though, those foreign films that were imported into America were imported with good reason. They tended to be realistic, honest and stimulating. They also demanded more concentration and understanding than their American counterparts.

198

Still fearing disguised Communist propaganda, the average American audience tended to look on imports with suspicion. Failing to understand the economic situation in which many of these films were made, many viewers thought them unprofessional. The way in which the language in these films was translated into English caused problems. Some people complained that English subtitles printed at

95. *A gifted comedienne, a most attractive star, Marilyn Monroe in a touching performance as a reluctant passenger at a* Bus Stop. (Twentieth-Century-Fox Film Corporation © 1956, All Rights Reserved)

96. *James Dean in* Rebel Without a Cause. *The film was one of the first from Hollywood to recognize that not all youthful rebellion was synonymous with delinquency. Dean, who starred in two other films,* East of Eden *(1955) and* Giant *(1956), was the symbol for a restless and inarticulate generation. He was well on his way to becoming the most idolized actor in decades when he was killed in a car crash.* (From the motion picture *Rebel Without a Cause,* copyright © 1955 by Warner Bros. Pictures, Inc.)

the bottom of the screen during scenes of conversation distracted from the action; others complained that foreign films dubbed into English made the actors sound hollow and untrue and that the new voices were not synchronized with the original actors' lip movements.

Despite the language problem, European films slowly became popular. They often dealt with social problems unsentimentally and were not hampered by a code of "morals" that forbade realistic portrayals of life problems. They had a frankness American films of the fifties tended to lack. For this reason European films appeared candid to unsophisticated audiences, and the term "candid" soon became interchangeable with "notorious." It was more the notoriety of

the films than their quality that brought audiences into newly established art houses, and it was their notoriety that caused cries of censorship to be raised once more. Many foreign films screened in this country did not bother with the code. Their distributors knew that the code insisted on a dream world; they also knew that they could find theatres that would show the films without code certification. And so they did.

The Legion of Decency still reviewed films for classification, and handed down more "condemned" ratings than it had before. State censor boards, knowing that the code was not examining foreign films, became very active in reviewing these films before they were licensed for public exhibition.

As we have seen, censorship of films was a long-standing practice and in fact had been sanctioned by the Supreme Court. In 1915 the Supreme Court termed film no more than a "spectacle" and equated its exhibition with circuses. Motion pictures were judged "not an organ of public opinion," and so lacked the protection of those constitutional amendments that guaranteed freedom of speech. Since 1915, however, the art of the motion picture had matured considerably. As the century reached its halfway mark, film's social value was beginning to be recognized. After all, had not film made an invaluable contribution to the war?

An Italian film, *The Miracle* (1948), directed by a great filmmaker, Robert Rossellini, opened in New York in December of 1950. The film shown was actually part of a larger production, but it was as *The Miracle* that this film accomplished a small miracle of its own. The film tells of a simpleminded peasant girl who thinks that she is pregnant with God's child (Figure 97). The townspeople mock her and finally drive her from the community. Even though the Vatican had honored the filmmaker for his works, the Archdiocese of New York took strong exception to the film. It found *The Miracle* offensive and sacrilegious. The film was condemned by the Legion of Decency, but after it was reviewed, New York state's licensing agency passed it without cuts for public exhibition. The film found an exhibitor, but was promptly boycotted by Catholics, who threw a picket line around the theatre. The boycott was self-defeating; it drew publicity to the film, and lines of interested people began to

97. *Anna Magnani in* The Miracle. (Museum of Modern Art/Film Stills Archive)

form. In exasperation, the archdiocese pressured the state's agency of review to take another look at the film. It did, and the film was again declared sacrilegious and banned from further exposure.

The film's distributor, Joseph Burstyn, argued that this ban was unconstitutional and sued the state. In a decision that has become historic for film, the Supreme Court, in 1952, reversed its 1915 "spectacle" decree. The Court ruled that film indeed was part of the press and its exercise of free speech could not be abridged by Congress (First Amendment, 1791) nor by a state (Fourteenth Amendment, 1868). Indeed, to censor a film on the charge of sacrilege would be to open almost any film to censorship. After all, there are, the Supreme Court argued, thousands of religions, sects and cults in the United States, and some film is bound to offend someone somewhere. Sacrilege was thrown out as a ground for censorship as being too vague.

In 1954 the Supreme Court threw out another ground for censorship — the advocacy of ideas that are not approved by the commu-

202

nity. What meaning did freedom of the press have if the press could not print ideas that were unpopular? With the exception of obscenity all grounds for censorship were gradually eliminated by the courts. Even obscenity was defined in the broadest terms possible. Currently a work is deemed to be obscene only if it is found to have no redeeming social value; the burden of proof is on the censor. If a filmmaker argues a censor's decision and brings the censor to court, then the censor must show that the work has *no* social interest whatsoever, and this should be an extraordinarily difficult thing to do.

In the case of a Swedish sex education film which customs had refused entry to this country on the grounds of obscenity, the Second Circuit Court of Appeals recently ruled in favor of the importer. The court stated that *Language of Love* was not obscene because it neither insulted nor debased sex. Perhaps this criterion may provide a start toward a needed feasible definition of obscenity. But if subjectivity is taken into account, it may not.

Why do any censorship boards exist at all? If a film is deemed to be part of the press, its freedoms are protected from abridgement by the Constitution. Then, aren't the review boards altogether unconstitutional? As of this writing, the Supreme Court has not ruled on the constitutionality of the various boards. All the Court has done is to say certain film boards were behaving unconstitutionally when they banned a film for a particular reason.

If no organization examines newspapers before they appear on the stands or in the doorways of your home, and if no organization licenses books to appear in stores, should there be any government agency that examines films prior to public screening? Should every film not have the same opportunity as every book and newspaper?

In discussing offensive films, another question arises. A film may have "no redeeming social merit," and its audience may know this. Knowing this, customers may still want to pay their admission price; they consent, agree to see the film. Since adults consent, and since the judgment to see the film is their own, then does anyone or any group have the right to prohibit the film from being screened? If we think a man is unwisely spending his money to see films of questionable value, we may think him a fool. We can speak to him and try to argue with him, but if he is to stop, the decision must be his, not ours. *It will be his decision not to see a film that will effect the removal of that film.* After all, no film will play to an empty auditorium.

It is one thing for adults to be able to choose what they see; it is quite another for children. Theatres exhibiting controversial films began to refuse admission to children and teenagers. Although there was some question as to the legality of this move, there have been no definitive court cases arising from the action. Communities in which there was no prior reviewing agency welcomed this control. Parents wanted to be informed as to the suitability of certain films, and theatres that prohibited young people from entering obviously gave parents the information they required. This form of control did not jeopardize an adult's free choice but did provide the needed clues for parental guidance. Classification has become the accepted manner of control in the States. Instead of having films banned, admission is restricted to adults.

Classification of films is a concern of the industry. When films are rated, they are not rated by an official government bureau but by an organization created by producers, exhibitors represented by the National Association of Theatre Owners (NATO), and various distribution agencies.

The ratings, which went into effect in 1968, embrace four categories. Although there is no law requiring that films be rated, most theatres in America will refuse to exhibit a film without posting a rating. A film that does not carry a rating is assumed not to be suitable for children; admission to the theatre will be restricted to adults. A rating of "G" (for "general") signals that the film in question is suitable for all ages. Originally the "GP" rating ("general but with parental guidance") was an "M" ("mature"). Each of these ratings indicates that the film is recommended for general viewing only with reservations. Parents or guardians of young people might find the film potentially disturbing. A film rated "R" ("restricted") will admit a young person only when accompanied by a parent or guardian. Age limits vary from community to community, and anyone under the age limit will be prohibited from viewing a film rated "X." Even though there have been problems about which films deserve which ratings, and although there have been some difficulties

204

in enforcing the ratings, this system seems to be the most responsible method of indicating suitability: that is, this is the best method short of censorship, which is no method at all. Freedom of choice is maintained, yet there is some control imposed.

Although during the fifties bastions of film censorship began to crumble, the screen changed shape, and the use of color became more frequent, it was not a decade of great originality in the production of American films. It was, however, the decade in which science fiction came of age.

There had been science fiction films before *Destination: Moon* (Irving Pichel, 1950), but these films were not representative of a continuing trend. They were usually adapted from famous sources such as Jules Verne or H. G. Wells, and most came from Europe. With *Destination:Moon,* science fiction became a standard but not exclusive American genre, and the genre has been growing and expanding continually ever since (Figure 98). Produced by George

98.   *American astronauts land on the moon in the prophetic* Destination: Moon. (Museum of Modern Art/Film Stills Archive)

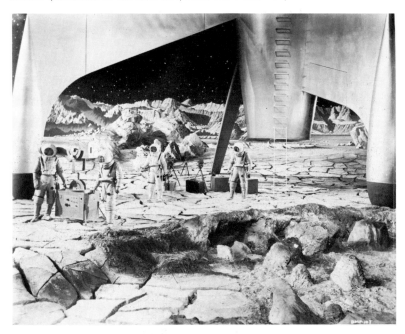

Pal, a one-time puppeteer, whose films have become celebrated for their imaginative use of ingenious special effects, *Destination: Moon,* almost a documentary of the future, pictured man's first moon landing nineteen years before the actual event.

The American public was not only fascinated with the remote possibility of space travel, but it also had strong anxieties about the future of atomic energy. It was worried that world leaders could not cope with the tremendous power unleashed by the atom. This fear manifested itself in a number of films. *Five* (Arch Oboler, 1951) was not only one of the first American films about the lives of the last survivors of a technological holocaust; it was also an early film to touch directly on the race question in the States: the fact that one of the survivors is black seems to affect some of the group more forcefully than the realization that they may be the only human beings left alive on earth.

In the same year as *Five,* anxiety about the bomb gave rise to a paranoia that was triggered when people all over the nation sighted unidentified flying objects (flying saucers?). In *The Day the Earth Stood Still,* directed by Robert Wise, a flying saucer lands on a lawn near the White House, and Klaatu, a messenger from space, arrives with a warning. He also arrives with a most formidable robot, Gort (Figure 99). If Klaatu is hurt, and if the message goes unheeded,

99.   *Gort, the robot, stands guard on his master's flying saucer in* The Day the Earth Stood Still. (© 1951 Twentieth Century-Fox Film Corporation. All Rights Reserved)

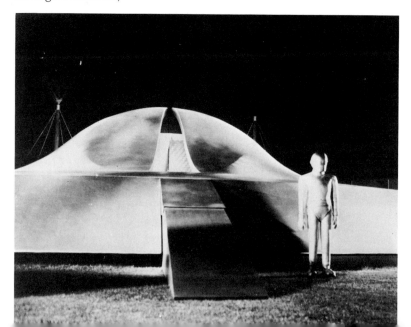

Gort is programmed to destroy the planet. What is this important message? Advanced powers in space realize the grave potential of nuclear weapons. Not wanting chaos in the galaxy, they have issued an ultimatum to our planet's leaders. Statesmen must cease the military deployment of nuclear weapons.

Several of the science fiction films of the decade showed that some advanced powers came with a "friendly warning," but there was a host of films in which the visitors from space did not behave so altruistically. Some visitors were invaders, cruel and intelligent; they were intent on colonizing the planet. The most frightening and probably the most chilling of these appeared in *Invasion of the Body Snatchers* (Don Siegel, 1956). These colonizers from the beyond were absolutely insidious; they came in peapods, each the size of a coffin, in which lay an identical "twin" to someone on earth whose mind the invader would soon inhabit.

Atomic fallout was also credited with a multitude of mutations. One of the most dramatic was *The Incredible Shrinking Man* (Jack Arnold, 1957). A man on vacation is surrounded by a field of radioactive dust. It has the unsettling effect of shrinking him. He continually diminishes in size. Having outshrunk the dollhouse in which he has lived for a brief while, the hero shrinks right out of sight and into the microscopic world of infinitely small particles. As he enters the world of atoms and their nuclei the film ends.

Some science fiction films were really little more than adventure stories in bizarre new settings. In *This Island Earth* (Joseph Newman, 1955), elaborate sets and dramatic views of future architecture were the main points of visual interest and were more startling than the plot. Another film with intriguing design and an intriguing story was *Forbidden Planet* (Fred Wilcox, 1956), which was adapted from Shakespeare's *Tempest*.

While science fiction films helped create a new genre, the fifties were also known for the production of a few other fine genre films. Stanley Donen and Vincente Minnelli directed a number of striking musicals (respectively, *Singin' in the Rain,* 1952; *An American in Paris,* 1951), Samuel Fuller and Robert Aldrich did several intriguing and moody gangster films (respectively, *Pickup on South Street,* 1953; *Kiss Me, Deadly,* 1955), and Anthony Mann and Budd

Boetticher staged a group of hard-hitting Westerns (respectively, *The Naked Spur*, 1953; *Seven Men from Now*, 1956).

A limited number of films like *High Noon* (Fred Zinnemann, 1952), which tautly told of one particular gun "duel," have become classics. The mysterious hero of *Shane*, played by Alan Ladd (George Stevens, 1953), is now a Western legend. Stevens also directed *A Place in the Sun* (1951), a sentimental version of Theodore Dreiser's famous novel that cast a jaundiced eye at the American Dream, *The American Tragedy*. If self-honesty and humanity were not the virtues of the antihero of *A Place in the Sun*, they certainly were of the protagonist in *On the Waterfront* (Elia Kazan, 1954). Almost single-handedly the hero of the film attempts to stop gangsters and hoodlums from infiltrating the labor unions of dock workers (Figure 100). This stark, uncompromising and often brutal film, actually shot on the Brooklyn docks, is regarded as one of the high points of the decade.

Two directors, Stanley Kubrick and Arthur Penn, who were to make three of the most absorbing and telling films of the sixties (*Dr. Strangelove*, 1964; *2001: A Space Odyssey*, 1968 [both Kubrick];

100.   *Marlon Brando, one of America's most exciting actors, and Eva Marie Saint in* On The Waterfront. (Courtesy Columbia Pictures)

101. *To emphasize their subordinate position at their courts-martial, Stanley Kubrick photographs the soldiers from under the table in his film* Paths of Glory. (Museum of Modern Art/Film Stills Archive. Courtesy Stanley Kubrick Productions)

Bonnie and Clyde, 1967 [Penn]) made auspicious debuts as film directors in the fifties. Kubrick made three low-budget exciting crime films before he attracted international attention with *Paths of Glory* (1957). This film, originally banned in France, is considered by some to be a most cogent antiwar statement (Figure 101). It is rather a frightening exposure of military thinking. An officer of the French Army during the First World War orders his men into a suicidal and worthless offensive. The men balk. As a punishment, selected platoon members are sent to the firing squad. So many of the preparations for the execution are carried on with pomp, ceremony and coldblooded calculation that what the military had hoped would be "an example" turns into nothing less than sanctioned murder.

In *The Left Handed Gun,* Arthur Penn's first feature film (1958), Billy the Kid is illuminated with psychologically revealing light. His notoriety is reassessed, and indeed, he emerges more of a kid than the black villain history has pictured.

Two of Billy Wilder's films bracket the decade. *Some Like It Hot* (1959), an exceptionally funny period comedy with Marilyn Monroe, Jack Lemmon, and Tony Curtis, anticipates much of the confusion, the reversal of sex roles, and the anarchy of the sixties.

Sunset Boulevard (Billy Wilder, 1950), which began the decade, may be one of the most interesting films made about Hollywood morality and mortality. In it, Gloria Swanson, an actual star of the twenties, plays Norma Desmond, a star of the twenties living in the late nineteen-forties. Other members of the cast are reminiscent of the twenties. Her faithful manservant is acted by Erich von Stroheim, the man from whom Swanson actually took a film in mid-production. Buster Keaton appears briefly as a once-popular actor, and even Cecil B. DeMille plays Cecil B. DeMille.

Forgotten both by the public and by the studio she claims to have saved from debt, Norma, a recluse in her palatial home, imagines herself to be both young and still the object of popular affection. Time has stopped for her. When the studio finally does call her, it is not to use her talent but to use her car, which by now has become an antique. Her vision of reality and fiction has become so distorted that when she commits murder, and the press, flash cameras in hand, rush to the scene of the drama, she believes the time for her "comeback" has arrived. She fixes her hair and chooses her costume with care. As

102.   *Gloria Swanson as Norma Desmond descends the stairs for her comeback, in* Sunset Boulevard. (© Paramount Pictures Corporation)

she descends her staircase waiting for the world's applause, she is seen as a noble if tragic figure (Figure 102), duped by the morbid values of the industry in which she still believes.

Sunset Boulevard, a bitter and brilliant film, was about an aging has-been; it was also a requiem to the old Hollywood. The system that produced such women as Norma Desmond had by mid-century changed radically. It was these changes that have concerned us in this chapter.

But all this has to do with commercial filmmaking in America. Meanwhile, underground in basements and overground in artists' lofts, a new network of independent film poets was growing. When this network emerged it upset just about everybody's notions about what films were and what they could be.

6 Another Cinema

On a pilgrimage from Canada to New York in the early sixties, I spied a soiled leaflet. It was posted on one of the few trees left in Greenwich Village. The leaflet announced a special "private" screening of "underground" films. The presentation was to be held Sunday afternoon in the attic of an art gallery.

That particular August was the hottest and most humid month in several years; the attic must have been the stuffiest room in town. A battered and cranky 8mm projector was set up; the screen was a patched sheet. Sweat soaked through shirts and blouses; the small audience was exhausted by the weather. But the group was both interested and dedicated. It had to be. Not only was it willing to endure the temperature; it was willing, I thought, to endure the films.

I was flabbergasted at what I saw. My orientation to film was thrown out of kilter. I had learned how to appreciate "story" films; I did not know how to react to such eccentric and outrageous works as these. My first impulse was to dismiss them. However, the audience seemed able to "understand" the films; it knew what to expect of the films and what not to expect. It applauded, laughed and groaned at times when I could see no reason why it should. The audience obviously was reacting on a different wavelength from any I could comprehend. Rather than think that both the films and the audience were crazy, I assumed it was I who lacked something. It was at that point that I realized that films, like paintings and poems, can be subject to many different styles and forms of expression.

When all the films were screened, the wiry man operating the old equipment passed a paper cup around the audience and asked for a small donation to cover the cost of maintaining the machinery. Intrigued by the situation, I asked the fellow why the exhibition was conducted in such an out-of-the-way place and under such trying circumstances. He replied that it had to be. The screening was illegal. New York State still required that films be submitted to a board of review before they could be screened publicly.

I replied that the censor would not have found anything objectionable in what was shown; indeed, I doubt whether the gentleman would have had the patience to sit through them. One film was for the most part unrelieved black. Occasionally the darkness was interrupted by stabbing flashes of pure white. While a Beatles album played on the tape recorder, the imagery of the second film was contained in a single shot of an open fire hydrant whose spray was aimed directly at the camera. There was no soundtrack on the third film. A young man dressed as a witch wandered and wandered and wandered through rows and rows of tenements. Old ladies stared; young children threw garbage. The camera used for the film was hand-held; it shook; it jerked; it let its principal walk out of focus. At one point it even fell to the ground. The man-witch walked back to where it had been dropped, picked it up, and kept shooting himself in super close-up. None of the films had either credits or titles.

The fellow answered me by saying it was not that the censor would find the films objectionable. It was that he would never be given a chance to judge them. "We refuse to cooperate with him." Why?

The filmmakers represented in the program that day considered themselves, no matter what anyone else thought, to be artists. Art, they insisted, could not be licensed. No one can pass an official public judgment pertaining to the world of private experience. Film artists do not think of the exhibition hall where films will be screened as a theatre so much as a gallery where their films will be "hung." This reasoning provided the clue to my future appreciation of the films of the American avant-garde.

In any discussion of this type of American filmmaking the following terms keep popping up: "avant-garde," "independent," "personal," "experimental," "abstract," and "underground." I shall try to define them before going further.

Avant-garde is a French term that comes from military language.

Members of the "avant-garde" were those soldiers in the advance guard. They paved the way, cleared the brush so that others might follow. In Paris, a group of painters, poets, and later, at the end of the First World War, filmmakers rebelled against "bourgeois" (middle-class) standards. Their works ridiculed conventional deportment and signaled a new direction in the arts. These strange new forms confused most critics because the works could not be measured by those standards critics thought self-evident. The new creations were iconoclastic, refreshing, and somewhat revolutionary. The press may have been facetious when it called the films of this phenomenon "avant-garde"; it may not have believed that others would follow the path cleared by these works. But in both Europe and America, others did. "Avant-garde" is now applied to forms of creative expression that are believed to establish precedents.

In our discussion about Hollywood, we became acquainted with the word "independent." Certain directors and producers worked independently of the studios and yet remained within the framework of commercial filmmaking. In this chapter, the word is applied in a different way. An independent filmmaker is one who works independently of regular commercial channels. An independent producer is not an independent filmmaker. The producer is an organizer, a hustler. The independent filmmaker chooses to be an artist.

A personal film is one that represents the feelings or ideas of its maker. Many people participate intimately in the making of a commercial film, and most of the time too many of these "cooks" tend to spoil the "broth" of a singular feeling. By definition the films on which only one person, the filmmaker, works are more personal than others.

"Experimental" and "avant-garde" are two words that are usually used synonymously. Experiment implies that there is doubt as to the result of performing certain actions. When an experiment is performed, the performer literally does not know what he is doing. He may know that he is adding this to that, but he does not know what the outcome will be. If he knows what will happen, he is not experimenting. If he knows the outcome there is no need to experiment. This suggests that the experimental filmmaker is not certain of what will happen when he shoots something in a certain way, or adds sound to an image in another way. But in a sense all filmmaking is experimental. No camera shoots precisely what the eye sees. Different eyes see differently. No tape recorder picks up exactly what the ear hears. The quality of projection varies from auditorium to auditorium. Even prints of the same film from the same laboratory are hardly ever identical; colors, for example, may be shaded differently. There is a surprise factor to all of filmmaking.

As if these aspects were not enough to make filmmaking experimental, consider that a film's effect may be impossible to predict. Its reception depends not only on all the contingencies just described but on the personality of its audience as well. "Experiment" really is a misleading term. In an important way the "avant-garde" filmmaker does know what he is doing; he realizes that he is trying novel techniques and proceeding in an original way.

An "abstract" film may be avant-garde; today, few are. That ground has already been broken. Abstract films are interested in pure shapes, colors, designs, patterns, rhythms and sounds. They are also known as "absolute" and "concrete" films. They eschew plot and characters. Movement and form are the foci of these films. The image of swirling waters, deep colors, the outlines of New York skyscrapers, the scratches on a used print and even the "grains" that ultimately constitute a film image are some of the concerns of the abstract filmmaker. Abstract films are now sometimes programmed on computers.

Amateur films are those made by nonprofessionals. Who is a professional? The answer varies. To someone working within the industry, a professional is someone whose films make money. To an artist, money is not the criterion. Dedication and sincerity are. Both groups tend to use "amateur" in a derogatory manner. Now that home movies have added another horizon to motion pictures, some critics have begun to regard home movies as a type of folk art. Seen in this light, the idea of the amateur takes on a richer significance than it had before.

We have already discussed "underground." When the filmmakers took their stand against censorship, they had to go underground to exhibit their films. They initiated a series of "guerrilla" like screenings in various theatres at midnight, in art galleries on Sundays, in friends' lofts and even on the sides of tall buildings. As these presentations attracted more and more incipient filmmakers, public interest grew. With the public came the press. The press, always eager to promote new social phenomena, found an attractive name for these screenings. They dubbed the films "underground." "Underground," with its sound of mystery and intrigue, raised public curiosity.

"Underground" really says nothing of the films themselves. It refers only to the manner in which they were screened. Indeed, some "underground" films were very conventional. What made the films underground was the filmmaker's conviction that the censor had no right to interfere with the presentation of alleged works of art. In the past few years the word has taken a nasty turn and is used to denote films that some critics believe celebrate sexual amorality.

Actually, "underground" had been applied to certain low-budget action films a little earlier in American film history. Since it is now an almost meaningless term, let's drop it from further use in this chapter.

If we discuss films of the American avant-garde, we discuss films that have set precedents which may or may not have been followed. And we talk about films made by "artists" who, for the most part, work independently of commercial considerations.

Until the sixties, if motion pictures had been anything in America they had been an industry. They were produced to be sold; they were made to make money; they were merchandise to be marketed at a profit. This is not to say they were bad; it is to say that first and foremost they were a product. To be successful products they had to be popular, and to be popular they had to delight, amuse, entertain or intrigue their audience. However, those films I saw that hot afternoon seemed to spring from another motivation.

They revealed that there were films made that were so personal that they required another standard by which to judge them and a different mode of appraisal by which to "understand" them.

To say that the films I saw that afternoon were poor because the camera work was jerky would be like saying that a car is poorly manufactured because, unlike a boat, it cannot stay afloat. Cars and boats are both vehicles, both methods of transport, and yet each is as different from the other as the two functions are. A car is not designed to ride across water; an independently made film is not necessarily designed to amuse. Something cannot be faulted if it does not live up to a standard for which it was not designed. If a commercial film does not entertain or amuse it is a failure. If an independent film does not, it's often quite another matter.

Just as a painter can use his genius to paint for himself or for money, so may a filmmaker. A painter may create a beautiful canvas which he might not otherwise produce had he not needed money for sustenance. Again, this is not to say the work is any the less valuable; it simply draws a distinction between two of the most important motives (perhaps the only two) that compel an artist to work: the need to express oneself and the need to earn a living. The two motives should be treated differently. The artist who works for material gain considers his audience foremost. The artist who works to express his own feelings and notions does not necessarily consider any audience outside himself. He is his own critic. The distinction is not always this neat.

The traditional vocabulary of filmmaking originated from the commercial filmmaking experience. Some of this language makes no sense when applied to the artists' cinema. I described the film about an open fire hydrant. What sense is made in speaking about directing and editing it? In the film that is all dark, where are the actors? Indeed, what could be meant by the credit "Written by"? In both cases the films were not so much written or directed as simply made.

Of course, personal filmmakers perform certain functions necessary to the completion of their works. At times they do what the editors, cameramen, scriptwriters, actors and directors of commercial films do. But in each instance they also do more than this; they *make* the film. They do not regard themselves as directors or writers; they see themselves as complete filmmakers. Directing and writing and acting all may be parts of filmmaking, and the filmmaker may solicit and accept assistance, but like America's first film artist, D. W. Griffith, the creator, and not the public and not the producer, is the final arbiter of what the film is. A painter signs his canvas with his signature, a poet ends his lyric with his initial, and the filmmaker is credited with the title, "A Film by So-and-So."

This credit is simple enough, but until the sixties few American

217

artists, critics and members of the motion picture audience considered film to be a true medium for personal expression. Many thought that both the complexity of making films and the cost involved prohibited individual expression. The attitude toward film that was most difficult to change was the one that insisted film *should* be nothing more than a vehicle for commerce, that each film must be designed for public consumption. In 1952 the Supreme Court realized that film was no longer merely a "spectacle"; it took most people another fifteen years to change their orientation.

D. W. Griffith is regarded as America's first film artist, but it is difficult to divorce him from the industry of making films. Although *The Birth of a Nation* and *Intolerance* sprang more from Griffith's mind than from economic formulas, they were made as commercial films. The brief sketches that follow are of the work of those filmmakers who, whether by choice or circumstance, remained outside the field of commercial filmmaking.

Manhatta (1921) has been cited as one of the earliest of avant-garde American films. Made by a painter, Charles Sheeler, and a photographer, Paul Strand, this short film alternated rather static views of New York City with excerpts taken from a poem, "Mannahatta," by Walt Whitman. These titles reinforced the tone of the shots which emphasized the energy of the metropolis.

The shapes and the activity of New York always have attracted sensitive eyes, and New York City is the subject of many semiabstract films. *N.Y., N.Y.* (Francis Thompson, 1957) is one of the most successful of these (Figure 103). (Two urban environments in

103.   *Lenses fuse automobiles in Francis Thompson's* N.Y., N.Y. (Museum of Modern Art/Film Stills Archive)

California have also been the subject of interesting treatment: Richmond [*Castro Street,* by Bruce Baillie, 1966] and Sausalito [*Sausalito,* by Frank Stauffacher, 1948]. Although Tom Palazzolo of Chicago is celebrated for his telling perception of parades in that city [*America's in Real Trouble,* and *Your Astronaut,* 1970]; for his vision of the circus [*O,* 1967] and for his warm portraits of sad and lonely individuals [*Pigeon Lady,* 1968] ultimately underneath every image in his colorful films is felt the forceful presence of the great Windy City.) Flaherty's visual tribute to Manhattan, *Twenty-four-Dollar Island* (1925) suffered a most ignoble fate. Even though the film was shown in the grand Roxy, it was not screened as a film. It was cut and used as a background (back-projection) to a stage show sequence in which chorus girls kicked and danced to a song extolling the personality of the city. A full print of *Twenty-four-Dollar Island* was recently located, of all places, in the mammoth film archive in Moscow. It is a sad testament to our past concern for American film heritage that our lost works keep being found with Russian and Yugoslav titles.

What is probably the first full-length avant-garde American film, *The Last Moment* (1927), is now lost. Made outside the studios by a Hungarian émigré, Paul Fejos, it described the last moment of a suicide before drowning (Figure 104). Its theme is that of the dying

104. *Sometimes when the negative and prints of a film are lost, a still is all that remains of a motion picture. This is one of several stills from Paul Fejos'* The Last Moment. (Museum of Modern Art/ Film Stills Archive)

man who sees his whole life flash by in his mind's eye a split second before he passes away. As *The Last Moment* opens, a hand is seen emerging from the water and grasping at air. A jumble of images is said to flash by in double and triple exposure. The images proceed at a chaotic pace, but soon the pattern of the man's unfortunate life emerges. The imagery is distorted by his own psyche, and time sequences do not appear in chronological order. The audience must participate in putting together the jigsaw of the man's life. As *The Last Moment* ends, the hand retreats under the water and a few weak bubbles rise to the surface. This film, called a landmark by critics, was followed by Fejos's studio-produced semitalkie *Lonesome* (1928), a more conventional romance, but still in its silent sequences a strikingly original film. Fejos, who worked very closely with his cameraman, Hal Mohr, made two more films in the United States before he returned to Europe (*Broadway*, 1929, and a bit of *King of Jazz*, 1930).

In 1928 an independent film produced in a garage accomplished the remarkable when, like *The Last Moment*, it created so much interest that it was exhibited in theatres across the country. *The Life and Death of 9413 — A Hollywood Extra* (also known as *The Life and Death of a Hollywood Extra*) was conceived by three men who were later to become well-known filmmakers working within the Hollywood system: Robert Florey, Slavko Vorkapich and cinematographer Gregg Toland. The film, constructed among the utensils of the kitchen, made ingenious use of household hardware as set constructions. Shot mostly in miniature and magnified, the film was a satire on Hollywood values. A fellow, recommendation in hand, comes to the office of a casting director. The director stamps a number on the hopeful's forehead; at that point the young man becomes an automaton. He is pressed into a system. While our friend, #9413, searches for work, another actor, attractive #15, finds a film in which to appear and becomes popular. His number is removed and a star is placed on his forehead. Stardom does not bring him riches so much as an ill change in temper. Meanwhile, #9413 can no longer dream of earning great sums of money; he cannot even afford the cheapest meal. He starves. Only in heaven is his number removed. If he can no longer be a man, at least he can be a self-respecting angel.

Many critics think that when a filmmaker adapts a book or short story for the screen, he is primarily obliged to retell the original story. Why should a filmmaker be tied to such a restrictive policy? It may not have been the story that originally attracted the filmmaker; it may have been the mood of the piece or one of the characters or the manner in which the narrative was developed. For example, *The Fall of the House of Usher* (1928), made in Rochester by James S. Watson and Melville Webber, was based on a short story by Edgar Allan Poe. From the tale of a doomed environment the filmmakers extracted the feeling of impending disaster (Figure 105). Settings were distorted in a sinister way; smoke and fog contributed mystery. Rather than dwelling on the original story, the film emphasized its mood. An intriguing musical score was later added to the film after the team had completed what is regarded as the first American avant-garde sound film, the atmospheric *Lot in Sodom* (1934).

105.   *Mood and atmosphere predominate in Watson and Webber's* The Fall of the House of Usher. (Museum of Modern Art/Film Stills Archive)

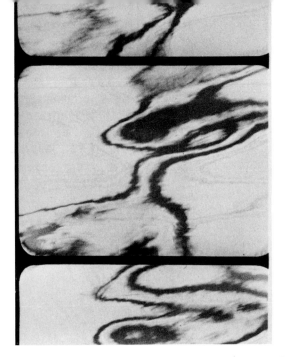

106. *Ralph Steiner took the ever-changing patterns of water as the subject of his abstract (or absolute, or concrete) film,* H_2O. (Museum of Modern Art/Film Stills Archive)

Ralph Steiner's films tended to be purely formal. While the images of *Manhatta* are of buildings and people, those of H_2O (1929), and *Surf and Seaweed* (1931) are lines, dots, curves and moving swirls. These were patterns that Steiner, a photographer, saw in nature (water and plant life) and abstracted with his camera (Figure 106).

Primarily concerned with visuals, the early film artists at first avoided sound. Sound was expensive and its technique was for use outside the studio. However, in 1932 MGM invited a celebrated German animator, Oskar Fischinger, to continue his film abstractions in America. Fischinger's shapes moved in concert with a musical track and colors that changed hue and tone. His *Optical Poem* (1938), set to the music of Liszt, won an Academy Award, but the work he did subsequently for Disney on *Fantasia* was eliminated for being too abstract. Shortly after this experience, Fischinger turned to painting and, with the exception of the memorable *Motion Painting No. 1* (1949), produced few films (Figures 107, 108).

Not only did the depression wipe out black production companies but it eliminated many independent filmmakers as well. Mary Ellen Bute made a number of attractive animated films, abstract "color symphonies," through the middle thirties and into the forties, but on the whole very few avant-garde films were produced between the early thirties and the war years. Some of these garnered a little attention, but none were really influential.

107–108.   *Since it is absurd for one still to suggest the motion of an abstract film, perhaps these two from Oskar Fischinger's* Motion Painting No. 1 *might do better. Although we can't see the motion in these stills, we can note the shapes and forms that the lines and shadings take during the course of the film.* (Museum of Modern Art/Film Stills Archive)

Until the Second World War, the inspiration to use film as an artist's medium came from Europe. Most "artistic" American films were patterned after French and German models. Adolf Hitler's rise divested Europe of her creative talents. Men who insisted on keeping their minds their own emigrated. Those who remained stopped work or perished. After the war it was America's turn to embrace the avant-garde.

The voracious appetite of the war placed a premium on all motion picture equipment and mechanical devices. The superb technical advances that were made during the war already have been described. Filmmaking became a simpler procedure, and as it was made less complex it could become more personal. When the war ended, cameras and recorders became surplus material. They were put up for public sale at inexpensive prices.

The remarkable Maya Deren did not wait out the war's end to start filmmaking. She made her stunning debut with *Meshes of the Afternoon* (1943), a film that determined the course that many young filmmakers would take. *Meshes* is a nightmare which suggests a psychological disorder in the dreamer. A woman, played by the filmmaker, seems to be upset by a number of seemingly insignificant and unrelated incidents. A figure turns a corner; a knife is seen fleetingly. The girl discovers a room, and feeling herself trapped inside, begins to suffocate as the room sweeps her from one wall to another. Deren's next film, *At Land* (1944), has the filmmaker once more wandering through "life." She comes upon a sumptuous banquet being conducted by a seaside, and crawls along the banquet table, upsetting the dishes and glasses.

Deren's later films *A Study in Choreography for Camera* (1945), *Ritual in Transfigured Time* (1946), and *Meditation on Violence* (1948) were more interested in the rhythm of dance than with symbolism (Figure 109). Film could accommodate the dancer in ways the stage could not. For example, Talley Beatty, the dancer in *A Study in Choreography for Camera,* makes a leap. The movement appears as one grand, graceful gesture, but it starts in one room and ends in the Egyptian Hall of New York's Metropolitan Museum of Art. Both aspects of Deren's filmmaking suggested new possibilities to young American filmmakers. While one group attempted to express emotions or neurosis in terms of striking and elaborate visual

109.   *Dance is the major element in* A Study for Choreography for the Camera, *by Maya Deren.* (Museum of Modern Art/Film Stills Archive)

symbols, another involved itself with presenting the dance on film, or better yet, with choreographing the entire film image itself.

Perhaps Deren's most important example to young filmmakers was her life-style. She lived by her films, and in so doing became one of the earliest avant-garde artists to eke a sustenance from her works. She rented her films, and, for a fee, lectured on campuses and at film societies across the country. Filmmaking was not a sometime occupation for this woman. Deren showed the possibility of an independent filmmaker living by his work. Her behavior encouraged other artists to take to film, and other filmmakers to hope that one day their art would be sufficient to earn a livelihood.

225

Like Maya Deren, Shirley Clarke came to film through her experience in dance. Although Clarke began photographing choreographed action (*Dance in the Sun,* 1953; *Bullfight,* 1955), she soon shifted to a dance film, where the image itself was choreographed either in the camera or, after shooting, in the editing. In *Bridges-Go-Round* (1959), the bridges themselves seem to execute a most appealing turn.

Ed Emshwiller illustrated science fiction magazines before he turned to dance film. His first, *Dance Chromatic* (1959), involved two very different sorts of images which are seen as one. A dancer performs, and over her image Emshwiller painted abstractions on the film frame. Emshwiller eventually moved from the patterns of human dancers to the rhythms of the universe. *Relativity* (1966), one of Emshwiller's major works, seems metaphysical in its concern with galactic movement. It is fascinating to note how interests in film, dance and science fiction can fuse so successfully into one work.

There have been two main centers of independent filmmaking activity in America: San Francisco and New York. Although it is misleading to generalize, it can be suggested that the San Francisco filmmakers were more immediately concerned with spiritual and mystical matters, while the New Yorkers tended to concern themselves with the pressing problems of a chaotic urban environment. The number of independent filmmakers in both cities grew prodigiously between Deren's 1943 appearance and the sixties; and, as their ranks grew, the network of communication between them became smoother. Since the late thirties, the Film Library (now the Department of Film) of the Museum of Modern Art had been distributing European and American avant-garde works to film study groups across the country. In New York, Amos Vogel's Cinema 16 Film Society, and in San Francisco, Frank Stauffacher's Art in Film Series introduced audiences to the works of contemporary independent filmmakers. *Film Culture,* "America's Independent Motion Picture Magazine," founded in 1955, did much to promote the new cinema. It was distributed nationally, and its pages recorded descriptions and critiques of the independent and avant-garde cinema.

A number of independent filmmakers found it difficult to secure exhibitions for their feature-length films. In response to their problems, *Film Culture* assisted by issuing the call to form an organization of independent filmmakers. The call was heard, and on September 28, 1960, a new chapter was begun in the history of the film artist in America. The New American Cinema Group was formed.

In *Film Culture* the group issued both a call for a new generation of filmmakers, and a manifesto articulating the spirit that would motivate filmmakers to join this free and open organization. There were no rules, no regulations, no membership records. All that was (and still is) required is the conviction that film may be something other than a product, a commodity, merely a commercial entity. To the filmmakers of the New American Cinema Group, human sensibility and not the desire for capital gain is the major factor in the making of film. The group, citing the assembly-line procedure in commercial filmmaking, decried the product film as "unreal" and lacking in any real moral or spiritual values. The group understood that commercial films mimic or imitate the social standards of their times, and so while they may make good study for the sociologist and historian, they do not picture anything not already reflected in the nation's popular press. As far as life-styles are concerned, the commercial cinema does not present its audience with suggestions that have not already confronted it in newspapers, on television, over radio.

The group insisted that "rough, unfinished" films which dealt directly with problems were morally and aesthetically preferable to "slick, polished, rosy films which reflected only the cheapest of dreams." The group promised to make films "the color of blood."

The group took its hardest stand against censorship. They considered censorship not so much wrong as a senseless waste of energy. It was irrelevant. How can one censor the human spirit? You can try to mold it, educate it, but you cannot censor it. What is felt by an artist is authentic, and that feeling is what the filmmakers of the group attempted to convey.

While the group did not succeed in its immediate aim of finding exhibitions for its feature-length films, it did succeed in establishing the groundwork for an organization which would cater to the needs of the independent film artist. One of the major achievements of the group was the founding in 1962 of the Film-Makers' Cooperative. The cooperative functions as a distribution agency from which nontheatrical exhibitors (film societies, schools) can book independent films. The cooperative began with a catalogue issued on mimeographed paper. About twenty-five filmmakers and fewer than a hundred films were listed. Only nine years later, the fifth edition of the catalogue, which was distributed early in 1971, had over four hundred and fifty filmmakers listing sixteen hundred and fifty films on three hundred and fifty pages.

What are the principles of the cooperative, and how does it function as a service to filmmakers? Anyone who has made any film may deposit a print of his work at the cooperative. When the filmmaker brings a film to the cooperative he also is requested to bring a description of the film that will be printed in the cooperative's catalogue. The filmmaker himself names the rental fee he wants to receive for a single screening of his film. In calculating this sum, the filmmaker must realize that the cooperative will retain 25 percent to help defray its operating cost.

The cooperative pools the work of the American avant-garde, and seven thousand film societies interested in this aspect of cinema can use its catalogue to find such films. Since the cooperative is a true cooperative, it does not promote one film at the expense of any other. Therefore the filmmaker is encouraged to look for other distributors who may be in a position to advertise his films. The cooperative issues no information other than the catalogue. Since the catalogue descriptions are written by the filmmakers, some are notoriously obscure. What can be learned about a film simply described as "A Celebration"? Well, at least you have a clue to the tone of the film.

The success of the cooperative has provided a model for many others both across the country and abroad. On the West Coast, Canyon Cinema probably has the most extensive listing of independently made films.

The main problem with the early independent films lay in the area of exhibition. If films were not seen, they could not be reviewed or discussed. After the New York state licensing agency passed out of existence, guerrilla screenings turned into a "floating" cinema, which moved from auditorium to auditorium. Filmmakers brought new films to constantly changing locales to be screened and seen. Reviews of these films might appear in *Film Culture* or in the weekly Greenwich Village newspaper *The Village Voice*. Once the floating theatre, the Film-Makers' Cinematheque, won a grant to build its own permanent home, the house was closed down by civic authorities. It apparently violated New York City's zoning and fire safety regulations. The Museum of Modern Art, the Jewish Museum, the Whitney Museum of American Art, the Milennium Film Workshop, a private organization called Film Forum, and several churches have since contributed their auditoriums for the screening of new avant-garde films in New York. In December, 1970, the Anthology Film Archives opened its specially designed "Invisible Cinema," in which all the "essential classics" of film would be screened once every six weeks. A good number of these films turned out to belong to the American avant-garde.

One figure stands out in all this organizational and creative activity, the Lithuanian émigré, Jonas Mekas. Mekas, who as a young man collaborated in publishing an underground newspaper during the Nazi occupation of his native land, was one of his country's leading poets. For five years after the war, he and his brother were displaced persons in search of a country to which to emigrate. Three days after they arrived in America, Jonas Mekas acquired an army-surplus camera and began to record in diary fashion the sights about him.

Having completed a number of personal films, Mekas helped found *Film Culture*. The magazine first attacked the existing American "avant-garde." Mekas wrote that these films were little more than a "superexcess" of unintelligible details. Soon he realized that the crudeness of the films was due not so much to a lack of a discipline as to an urgency and passion felt by the filmmakers. Mekas the poet began to sympathize with the avant-garde. *Film Culture* quickly turned into the champion of the independent and avant-garde.

Mekas continued to edit *Film Culture*, but he also continued to make films. As Mekas continued to make films, he became more and more interested in establishing distribution outlets for the works of the avant-garde. It was partially his idea to call the independent filmmakers into an affiliation. The New American Cinema Group's Film-Makers' Cooperative, mentioned earlier, was born out of discussions in which Mekas played an integral part. Mekas has always sat on the Cooperative's board of directors. He promoted the idea of the Film-Makers' Cinematheque, and often, when help was scarce, he would be found projecting films himself for audiences that varied in size from moderate to only Mekas and the filmmaker.

After seeing a film, Mekas published "reviews" in the *Village Voice*, and acquainted hundreds of interested readers with the new films he had screened earlier in the week.

The Brig, made in one evening in 1964, is Mekas' most widely seen work (Figure 110). The film is a recording of an unusual performance by the Living Theatre. The play was a harrowing chronicle of "life" in a bestial Marine stockade. One humiliation after another was visited on the prisoners. In the original performance the audience sat separated from the action by a wire fence which was placed where the curtain ordinarily would have been. Mekas' camera went behind the cage and captured the clawing claustrophobia of confinement. Filmed stage productions usually lose dramatic punch, but *The Brig* is a powerful experience.

Mekas collaborated on several other films. *Hallelujah the Hills* (1963) has been called "the most liberated" film in cinema. It may

110.   *Jonas Mekas shooting* The Brig. (Courtesy Jonas Mekas)

not be, but it is close. Made by Jonas' brother Adolfas Mekas, *Hallelujah the Hills* is a confirmation of life, a celebration of nature, and an explosion of wild and wacky goings-on. All that can be said of the plot is that two young men woo the same girl. The girl is played by two actresses. Each suitor sees the object of his affection in his own way. Girls grow on trees; men run naked through the snow; an ape appears — and yet in the zany context of the film all these incidents seem to make perfect nonsensical sense (Figure 111). Dominating the film is a feeling of affection for the Vermont countryside. Many American films take their landscapes for granted; some, mostly Westerns, make dramatic use of their terrain. *Hallelujah the Hills'* landscape becomes a comic spirit, living, breathing, and dropping all sorts of strange and wonderful things into the laps of its inhabitants.

Jonas Mekas has been working recently on releasing his film diaries, *Walden.* In 1969 he screened the first volume of this work, *Diaries, Notes & Sketches, 1965–69.* This volume runs about three hours, and its mood changes with the events recorded. Each image is glimpsed for a fraction of a second; it takes a trained eye to absorb the wealth of detail.

111. *A still showing the antic quality of* Hallelujah the Hills. (Museum of Modern Art/Film Stills Archive)

Although not all "diary" films proceed in the same frantic manner, there is a great interest among independent filmmakers in recording casual experiences of sight. The "diary" film is a popular form of expression; often the filmmaker wants to share his experience first-hand with his audience. Sometimes the filmmaker records what he sees (filtered of course by the camera's "eye"); at other times he takes what is experienced and molds it into a poem or statement of sorts.

Quixote, made by Bruce Baillie in 1964–65, welds both these elements of the "diary" film. A record of a trip across the United States (and in this way it very well may have inspired the phenomenally successful *Easy Rider,* 1969; Dennis Hopper), it is a lyric about the feelings and sensibilities encountered on the journey, and a comment upon certain attitudes of the American people and government. It is a complex work, and at times, three images within the same frame are working in three different ways.

What kinds of films are represented in the independent, avant-garde movement? All kinds. Made by all ages of filmmakers. It is misleading to categorize these films. It is unfair to the filmmakers who work with a spirit of individuality to lump their works together with other filmmakers' on the basis of strong but superficial resemblances. The only real way to acquaint yourself with the scope of American avant-garde is to see its films, but I will try to describe some of them.

Robert Breer's lines flow and continually and unexpectedly materialize momentarily into pleasant shapes and figures: *A Man and His Dog Out for Air, Jamestown Baloos* (both 1957). In his later films Breer still uses his endearing shapes, but they have taken a new dimension as their rhythms are associated with colors (*66,* 1966; *69,* 1969; *70,* 1970). Stan Vanderbeek and Larry Jordan have both made collage films using magazine picture cutouts of faces, hands, cars, cows, city blocks, crystal balls and the kitchen sink. The films' figures move in ingenious and surrealistic ways. A face merges into someone's bottom; out of a general's mouth a rocket appears. Vanderbeek's films (*Science Friction,* 1959; *Breathdeath,* 1964) tend to be satirical; Jordan's (*Duo Concertantes,* 1964; *Our Lady of the Spheres,* 1968) "probe" the supernatural and the occult. Vanderbeek has now been working for a while on an extensive series of film "poems" animated by computer (*Computer Art* #1, 1966). While the pioneering computer films of John Whitney, Sr., who began making abstract films in the early forties, are composed of exquisite patterns (*Permutations*, 1969), those of Vanderbeek emphasize words programmed into the machines and emerging crocheted into the screen.

The films of Jordan Belson appear as "mathematically precise" as Whitney's, but Jordan Belson does not work with a computer. His method is secret. Belson, a student of Asiatic cultures, is extraordinarily exacting with his work, and has destroyed completed films with which he has not been totally satisfied. His films are exciting to view, and the patterns, movements and rhythms he composes are most compelling. Of those films which now survive, *Re-Entry* (1964) and *Samadhi* (1967) are two of Belson's more celebrated self-called "recognitions."

Stan Vanderbeek and Larry Jordan made collage films from paper, cardboard and other two-dimensional cutouts, but Bruce Conner has used motion picture footage extrapolated from other sources. *A Movie* (1958) bears some similarity to a symphony. A symphony may play with several independent musical themes, bringing them closer together until they integrate with each other in the final movement. This is what Conner, the visual composer, does with a number of recurring images in *A Movie. Report* (1965), of which there seem to be no fewer than eight different versions — all by Conner — uses the footage of the assassination of John F. Kennedy and other contemporary events to articulate the reaction of the filmmaker to the tragedy.

Some avant-garde filmmakers carry abstraction to radical and extreme limits. These artists attempt to isolate the basic or essential elements of film and motion pictures. (Remember, the first chapter discussed the differences between motion pictures and films.) Paul Sharits' *Ray Gun Virus* (1966) is little more than a succession of rich hues; there is rhythm to the sequence of deep colors presented. In *History* (1970), Ernie Gehr "studies" the most intimate constituent of film itself, the "grains" whose shading ultimately determines just what the photographic image will be.

Michael Snow, a sculptor and musician, took two fairly static environments, an artist's loft and a schoolroom, and made two remarkable films, *Wavelength* (1967) and ⟵⟶ (1969). In a series of staccato shots the lens of *Wavelength*'s camera "zooms" from a full image of a huge loft right into a photograph of an ocean wave, hanging on a far wall. The movement of the camera, for half the length of ⟵⟶ , is just that. The back and forth motion begins slowly in a classroom and gradually speeds up until all detail is lost. The classroom has not changed but the audience's image of it has. It is no longer concrete; all details merge into one undefined whole.

A loop is a length of film the last frame of which is attached to the first. In other words, it has no beginning nor end. When placed in a projector, the same image or shot or scene keeps repeating and repeating. Since a special setup is needed for the projection of loops, filmmakers imitate the action of a loop by printing one scene several times and splicing these copies together. George Landow induces an unsettling effect with loops in films like *Bardo Follies* (1967), in which a worn looped image begins to burn and dissolve, *Film That Rises to the Surface of Clarified Butter* (1968), and *Institutional Quality* (1969). In his *Film in Which There Appear Edge Lettering, Sprocket Holes, Dirt Particles, Etc.,* (1966), the title effectively describes precisely what appears. Everything is extracted in this film, and what is left is the basic film material on which the photographic image is printed. You can't abstract much more.

The photographic image itself is studied in Ken Jacobs' knockout film *Tom, Tom the Piper's Son* (1969). Jacobs takes the moving image and treats it like a piece of sculpture to both photograph and examine. In 1905 the Biograph studio produced a short one-reel film, *Tom, Tom the Piper's Son.* Sixty-five years later, Jacobs projects this film onto a screen, and photographs the projected image. At first he records the whole film directly as it is projected; he then moves his camera up close to the screen, behind the screen, at a distance from the screen. The figures become indefinable shapes, the shapes, dots (grains), and the grains, fluid spaces. The film image is revealed at its most basic.

Will Hindle subordinates technical advances to an extraordinary discipline in creating the most eloquent and haunting of moods. Al-

234

though not a word is spoken in *Billabong* (1968), and although the audience is not aware of why the young men are gathered in a barracks-like cabin, a melancholic atmosphere of anxiety mixed with sadness is deeply felt. The stagnant pool of water that is a billabong reflects, one feels, the immediate future of this unlucky group. In *Watersmith* (1969), Hindle builds the most beguiling and attractive of patterns around the shapes of Olympic swimmers and the forms they create in the water.

The films of Gregory Markopoulos reveal more information in one complex frame than it would take many filmmakers whole works to explain. Images are superimposed in such a fashion that relationships are made clear. A visit to an apartment (*Ming Green,* 1966) becomes a visit to its tenant's mind.

Zorn's Lemma (1970), by Hollis Frampton, is an "exact" film. It is a riddle, a game played with letters of the alphabet, with words photographed on signs and buildings, and with recurring images that come to stand for the letters (Figure 112). Frampton, who has lovingly made a film portrait of a lemon, *Lemon* (1969), and of carrots and peas, *Carrots and Peas* (1969), has designed a unique film puzzle with *Zorn's Lemma.* Frampton says the film derives its name from the story of a philosopher (probably Zeno,) in ancient Greece who specialized in formulating dilemmas. A paraphrase of one of Zeno's dilemmas: Say you want to walk from A to B. Before you get to B you have to cross the halfway point, and before you get to that halfway point you have to cross the halfway point of the halfway point, and so on and on and on and on — infinitely. How do you get anywhere? You do. But how? The tone of *Zorn's Lemma* is very much in the spirit of the question.

The moods and tones of Scott Bartlett's films *Off/On* (1967) and *Moon 69* (1969) derive from the fluent use of various types of complex mechanical equipment such as television monitors, oscilloscopes and videotape units. Much as a concert musician masters the piano, Bartlett plays with the same grace on his image-producing apparatus and precisely "edits" these images in a most exquisite manner.

James Broughton is a pioneer of the new American cinema, and from his dark humored but funny *Mother's Day* (1948) and *Looney Tom, The Happy Lover* (1951) to his spiritual and romantic

112. *Fox stands for F or F stands for Fox, in Hollis Frampton's puzzle film* Zorn's Lemma. (Courtesy Hollis Frampton)

Nuptiae (1969), his films bracket the avant-garde film movement in America.

Kenneth Anger's two most celebrated films, *Fireworks* (1947) and *Scorpio Rising* (1963), are considered "X" viewing. Anger was seventeen when he made his second film, the notorious and harrowing homosexual dream fantasy, *Fireworks*. Legend has it that it was filmed one weekend when his mother was away from home. The avant-garde knows no age limits. *Scorpio Rising* was noted for the ingenious use made of popular songs that comprised the sound track. Like most of Anger's films, *Scorpio Rising* has to do with ritual; in this instance it is the motorcyclist's ritual with costume, chrome and death. Although Anger himself has published his obituary as a filmmaker, he has since completed a short film in London (with a musical track by Mick Jagger), *Invocation of My Demon Brother* (1969), and he is presently working on a feature film tentatively titled *Lucifer Rising*, which is being shot both in England and Egypt.

Stanton Kaye's autobiographical films, *Georg* (1964) and *Brandy*

236

in the Wilderness (1969), made under severe economic circumstances, display remarkable ingenuity of film form.

Then, there is Stan Brakhage. He is America's most prolific independent filmmaker, and certainly one of its most influential. In tracing his career, the growth of an artist can be detailed. His films are poems and they sing of the beauty of the world. Brakhage reacts to Nature and her blessings as a child full of wonder: the child's reactions are pure, in a sense, untainted with inhibiting learned social responses. Much of Brakhage's work is characterized by this wonder and amazement; many of his films are "songs," visions as if glimpsed through "primitive," "young" eyes. This film poet is attempting (with some success) no less a task than to preserve all intuitive universal human experience in film, crystallized on both 8 and 16mm.

The films of the avant-garde are usually not meant for theatres. They are intended for private viewing, and for repeated experience. Poems are read and reread; paintings are reexamined every time someone walks into a room. Brakhage and most independent filmmakers believe that their works should be treated in the same way.

In reading a poem, the reader is alone with the work, and reacts to it intimately. In a theatre, a spectator is continually aware of fellow audience members, and this affects his reaction to the film. Most commercial films, particularly comedies and thrillers, depend for their effect on the reaction of many people laughing or screaming; this is not the case with many of the filmmakers of the avant-garde. A whole different viewing experience is demanded. Perhaps Brakhage and the avant-garde will realize their dreams within the next few years when the possibility of "publishing" films in cassettes or cartridges becomes a reality. At the moment, Brakhage has completed well over thirty "songs," six hours of separate 8mm films.

The desire to make personal films may stem from many sources: a need to express certain psychological disturbances in a symbolic way (*At Land; Fireworks*); or a desire to probe the aesthetic and technical limits of film (*Bardo Follies,* $\longleftrightarrow$). Some filmmakers, motivated by a social interest, wanted to break through the gloss imposed by studio-manufactured sets. They wanted to photograph the real streets and dwellings of the nation. Taking advantage of portable equipment, a number of filmmakers set out to shoot

America, not as she was seen through the rose-colored perspective of Hollywood, but as she "really" was.

Up until recently, the ghettos where blacks lived were as foreign as Ceylon to most white Americans. But the ghettos have never been thousands of miles away. They were downtown, uptown and all around. The ghettos suggested another theme: poverty. It was not that the filmmakers wanted to emphasize the shabby side of American life; it was that they felt someone had to draw attention to forgotten but real aspects of the national perspective.

In 1948 there appeared one of the earliest 16mm features. Made in New York by a team under the supervision of Sidney Meyers, *The Quiet One*, a sad and moving work, told of an emotionally disturbed black adolescent and the treatment accorded him (Figure 113). Its technique was fresh and intimate, and its views of Harlem frightening and startling to an audience ignorant of black life.

Four years later, part of the team that worked on *The Quiet One* — the photographer Helen Levitt, James Agee, one of America's leading writers on film, and Janice Loeb — released the short film *In the Street* (Figure 114). There was no narration because *In the*

113.   *A scene from* The Quiet One. (Museum of Modern Art/Film Stills Archive)

114.　　*A portrait from* In the Street. (Museum of Modern Art/Film Stills Archive)

Street did not tell a story. It was a portrait, a compassionate, candid view of a poor New York neighborhood on East 105th Street. There is no polemic, and the work is populated with some of the most expressive faces and tender moments in all of film.

Lionel Rogosin, Richard Bagley and Carl Lerner's film *On the Bowery* (1956) was an authentic look at a once-proud street. Now a sad and dreary thoroughfare, the Bowery is littered with the bodies of alcoholics so desperate they attempt to distill liquor from shoe polish. *On the Bowery* is not just a casual documentary about a jaded section of New York. It attempts to understand the plight of wasted figures; it is a humane view of purgatory. Instead of condemning what it sees but does not comprehend, *On the Bowery* engages in interviews with residents of the street, who speak for themselves about their grotesque situation.

Made in 1960 as a television production and not an independent film, *Primary* represented a turning point for the American documentary film. It was also a major influence on many personal documentaries that soon followed; indeed, most of its collaborators became celebrated independent filmmakers working within the *cinéma vérité* school of filmmaking. (*Cinéma vérité* is a French term that comes from the Russian expression *kino pravda,* meaning "film truth.")

Flaherty, we have seen, influenced, affected the material he photographed. He was as much of an active participant as an observer. *Cinéma vérité* filmmakers at first took great care *not* to disturb the order that they were interested in filming. Originally, they tried to be passive. They followed their subject and shot and shot and shot. The hope was that the subject, once used to the presence of recording equipment, would begin once more to react naturally to situations, and become somewhat oblivious to the filmmakers. For this hope ever to become a realization, the filmmakers had to work with few pieces of portable, unobtrusive and reliable equipment. The filmmakers who worked on *Primary,* including Richard Leacock, Don Pennebaker and Al Maysles, refined existing equipment so that they could keep themselves mobile and close to their subjects, yet have the apparatus compact enough not to disturb their subjects. Their modifications of equipment and technique were adopted by other documentary filmmakers.

This type of filmmaking involves the shooting of miles of footage, and the final film is theoretically molded on the editing table. Many filmmakers have admitted that they did not know the shape their film would take when they began recording the activities of certain subjects. Each began with the hope that something dramatic, unexpected or unusual would happen to cause much random material to jell. For example, a Hell's Angel murdered an audience member at a Rolling Stones concert in California; this sad event subsequently formed the climax of a film documenting the rock group's American tour (*Gimme Shelter* [1970], Al and David Maysles). Fortunately, *Primary* was filmed before many people worried about political assassinations.

Primary was paced with the breakneck speed of a frantic political campaign itself. The primary contest was between two national Senate figures, John F. Kennedy and Hubert Humphrey. Each tried to win the State of Wisconsin's Democratic Presidential nomination. The participants were keen and open and, under intense pressure, both displayed an ease and a naturalness not usually found among politicians. A rich portrait of both candidates emerged, and so did an exciting, invaluable document of national politics.

The development of apparatus that simplified shooting affected the making not only of documentary films but also of fictional films that used actual locations. Shirley Clarke's *The Cool World* (1964) has documentary aspects, and although the narrative was adapted from a novel, it could have been the story of any number of young people growing up in Harlem. In it a young gang leader moves past the violence which has been his daily bread into a more frightening alienation. The ghetto is not just a canvas against which the young man's drama is played; it is a character that shapes the young man's activities (Figure 115). Clarke made an extensive use of the voice-over. Duke, the young leader, "thinks" his mind aloud as he crosses his home turf. The images of the street give meaning to the boy's thoughts, and again, in this context create a rich dramatic dimension. Offscreen conversations also provide efficient and explanatory bridges between scenes. Clarke's use of the voice-over and the hand-held camera, although expert, upset many critics used to more con-

115. *At home in Harlem, Hampton Clanton, as Duke Curtis, leader of the Royal Pythons, explains strategy to his gang in Shirley Clarke's semidocumentary,* The Cool World. (Museum of Modern Art/Film Stills Archive)

ventional methods. Little did these writers realize how classic these techniques would become within the next two years.

The portable camera soon became a political tool. Young filmmakers began to chronicle the plight of America's dispossessed. The recorded speech of the poor and the discriminated against became as eloquent as any fiery pen. In *Troublemakers* (1966), Robert Machover and Norman Fruchter visited a Newark community-action project in which students attempted to organize ghetto residents into a power bloc. One of the issues involved a stoplight that residents wanted installed at a dangerous intersection. The bureaucratic resistance encountered was monumental, and although the film began as a teaching aid for community organizers it ended as a dramatic record of one community's frustration and anger.

Many politically minded filmmakers, mostly students, were not content merely to record certain social actions. They sought involvement in changing the course of American society. To this end a loose network of radical Left filmmakers declared that they would film those events not broadcast over television nor reported in the press, and would interpret others according to their own dogma. So, the Newsreel, a viable amalgam of cooperating filmmakers, is now established. The participants in the Newsreel project tend to sympathize with activists on the nation's campuses, and Newsreel films have best detailed the turmoil that has so beset these seats of learning. No salaries are given; the work is done out of a deep sense of social obligation. Services are donated. Decisions are made by a committee on which all filmmakers are supposed to sit.

Wreck of the New York Subways (1970) provides a good example of Newsreel technique. An indictment of the recent big fare hike for New York public transportation, the short film uses polemic, interviews with troubled New Yorkers, and shots of enterprising riders trying to avoid the thirty-cent charge.

Frederick Wiseman, a lawyer turned producer (*The Cool World*), then filmmaker, focuses on specific institutions. In films like *Titicut Follies* (1967), where the operations of a Massachusetts house of detention for the criminally insane are coldly and dispassionately examined, the camera and tape recorder seem to have access into every

242

corridor. After exploring the functioning of such an exceptional institution, Wiseman turned to more familiar sources in *High School* (1968) and *Hospital* (1970). While it is in the general interest to see how public organizations operate, there are questions. Does the high school Wiseman "dissects" represent other high schools? Does the high school in one locality operate on different principles from a high school in another? The question does not invite easy answers, because just when one decides that there are differences, one must contemplate how large these may be and to what extent a particular institution reflects its immediate environment. It is not difficult to understand why Wiseman's films invite controversy.

Another film about high schools that raises questions is about high school activists: *Ira, You'll Get into Trouble* (1969), made by Stephen Sbarge. Sbarge became acquainted and friendly with a group of students who wanted to keep the schools open during the teachers' strike which crippled learning in New York City during September of 1968. Never condescending to his subject, Sbarge lets the students behave naturally and so records the formation of a political awareness in young people.

Although some filmmakers would like to retain the illusion of passivity, it is not true that all documentary *cinéma vérité* filmmakers now remain passive. Some provoke and encourage responses from their subjects. The filmmakers from New York University who shot and compiled *Street Scenes* (1970) verbally baited many onlookers attending the Wall Street demonstration for peace. (This was the demonstration that won national news coverage when it was disrupted by construction workers.) The onlookers, perplexed by the events, were asked leading questions; annoyed, some reacted in anger, some in confusion. This verbal confrontation often ended in a dramatic outburst which may or may not have been significant. Thus the interviewers activated many of the scenes photographed.

Just as it has become wrong to suggest that the *cinéma vérité* filmmaker never effects, never brings about the action he photographs, it is equally wrong to suggest that he never photographs "acted" scenes. The filmmaker can place certain actors in a situation and then photograph them in a *vérité* manner, as if he were photograph-

243

ing a documentary film. The camera becomes the eyes of a spectator following subjects, probing the scene, resting for a moment on this or that item, and changing focus as the situation alters.

One of the first filmmakers to bring this "true" informal style to the making of a story film was the actor John Cassavetes. Out of his experience as an instructor of acting technique, Cassavetes mounted an unusual project with a 16mm camera, flexible sound equipment and a group of students. *Shadows,* which took three years to realize (1958–1960), was a closely knit series of improvisations in which the actors, most of whom were appearing in front of the camera for the first time, were given detailed situations and told within these limits to improvise the scene themselves (Figure 116). Cassavetes, of course, had discussed the characters they were to play and each actor discussed his feelings about the character with the others so they could perform as a harmonious ensemble. The film detailed the rather unfortunate lives of a number of young adult New Yorkers.

116. *A pensive pose from* Shadows. (Museum of Modern Art/Film Stills Archive)

(It was one of the first films to discuss interracial love relationships.) To this impromptu manner of acting Cassavetes brought the *vérité* camera. The improvisations carried a certain unrehearsed realistic weight, and the feeling of authenticity was reinforced by the "documentary" camera. What was shot was determined by what was improvised; and in this way the appearance of the film had a most vital, direct feel. Cassavetes' *Faces* (1968), *Husbands* (1970), and *Minnie and Moskowitz* (1971) have the same aura.

When Andy Warhol began to turn from the designing of advertisements (he had been a successful commercial artist) to the making of films, his first works were documentaries in the purest sense of the word. So pure were they that many people considered them to be abstract. They chronicled such everyday activities as eating (*Eat,* 1963), sleeping for six hours (*Sleep,* 1963), kissing (*Kiss,* 1963), and getting a haircut (*Haircut,* 1965). The camera remained static, and although there was some movement, it was slight and remained within a seldom changing frame. This was not caprice; like some other independent filmmakers, Warhol felt that we probably take these frequently performed activities for granted, and that, in fact, we never really "see" them. Indeed Warhol may believe eating and sleeping to be as dramatically intriguing as dancing or fighting. Seen in this concentrated way, mundane activities do take on somewhat more of an exciting glow. (Actually one of Warhol's more noted films, *Empire,* which runs eight hours and is an outside view of the upper floors of the Empire State Building, is not quite in the above category.)

Warhol soon turned to filming eccentric personalities, like those of junkies and transvestites, who spoke to the camera or were put into semiscripted and improvised situations (*The Chelsea Girls,* 1966; *Lonesome Cowboys,* 1969). Because the characters were regarded as sordid and sensational, Warhol's films attracted the curious, and he was one of the few independent filmmakers whose works enjoyed commercial success. Warhol does not moralize, and frequently his films are both sad and funny. His studio is called a factory, and out of it he also produces the semihilarious, semitragic films of a colleague, Paul Morrissey (*Flesh,* 1968; *Trash,* 1970).

Not all independent documentaries are "casual," intimate or in the tradition of *cinéma vérité*. Emile de Antonio, one of the original members of the New American Cinema Group, made a number of socially oriented films which were compiled from many sources. The footage of his successful *Point of Order* (1963) came from 1954 kinescope recordings which detailed Senator Joseph McCarthy's disintegration in the face of televised Army investigations. *In the Year of the Pig* (1969) is not only an excellent construction of footage that was, for the most part, shot from other projects, but it is also the most intelligent film to have been made on our tragic involvement in Vietnam (Figure 117). *Millhouse; A White Comedy* (1971) traces Richard Nixon's career to Presidency.

It is quite unfortunate that today elaborate film techniques have become an obsession with many Hollywood directors. It is in speaking of these techniques — frequent zooms cutting quickly and abruptly to one image before another has totally been absorbed, eccentric camera angles — that we come to the major stylistic influence on the commercial film: not the avant-garde film but the commercials on television. Technically, commercials are wonderful achievements. Their lengths tend to be no longer than those first films produced for the Edison Kinetoscope. Yet they utilize every conceivable cinematic resource (image, sound, the relationship of image to sound), and they do it with great finesse. There is a message to be conveyed, and it must be conveyed both dramatically and forcefully in a very short time. Characters must be established in a fraction of a second, moods have to be effected at a moment's notice. Simplicity must be the key. Commercials tend to be models of lucidity and forcefulness. Interestingly enough, while a dazzling vocabulary of film techniques has been perfected by the makers of commercials in order to accomplish something (capture the viewer's attention and sell the merchandise), these techniques tend to be used merely for thir own sake in many Hollywood films.

Personal filmmaking and Hollywood cinema represent two deep facets of the American personality — the desire to do your own thing in your own way, and the drive to accumulate material wealth. The personal cinema, whether it deals with problems of the individual or with social issues, did *not* spring from an anti-Hollywood reaction. It grew from the very urgent need to have an American art reflect cer-

117. *A young soldier reveals his sentiments in Emile de Antonio's compilation film,* In the Year of the Pig. (Contemporary Films/McGraw Hill)

tain issues realistically and without compromise. It was never a "destructive" type of filmmaking, and for the most part did not preach the downfall of the established commercial order. Rather, it used all its energy to suggest another way of looking at things.

247

7 Future Promise

Where are we now? Just about everywhere. Hollywood makes films; independent artists make films; radical political groups make films; television makes films; admen make films to interrupt television films; film students make films; other students make films; actors make films; kindergarten pupils make films; tourists make films; theatre owners make films; computers make films; and my Uncle Louie makes films.

Films are made in 8mm, Super 8mm, 16mm, 35mm, 65mm, and 70mm. In the making of home movies, 8mm and Super 8mm are used. Although most independent film artists prefer to work in 16mm, a number have taken to the cheaper method of Super 8. Sixteen-millimeter prints of films are circulated to schools, universities, and film societies, and may be used for television broadcast. Although a process called Super 16mm, which is reputed to be more economical to use than 35mm and to give almost as defined an image, has been developed in the States and perfected in Scandinavia, it is not yet readily available. Theatres use 35mm films for standard presentations. For the first runs of special, spectacular attractions (*Fiddler on the Roof*, 1971), 65mm and 70mm are usually reserved.

Theatres show films; television broadcasts films; schools and universities examine film; film societies study film; political groups persuade with film; films function as backdrops to plays, ballets, operas and rock concerts; industry uses film as a means for teaching certain skills; museums exhibit films as a contemporary art form; and my Uncle Louie projects film to the entire family. Like another medium of communication, the telephone, film is everywhere.

Future Promise

Theories abound that state that future learning techniques will use motion pictures solely. This vision seems to be a bit too narrow. Philosophy and theoretical writing of any sort cannot be easily visualized. The purely abstract film can be developed only so far, and film by its very nature can deal only with material phenomena (trees, books, men, drawings, magazine cutouts, even the printed word). We can write about various concepts such as goodness or truth, but we cannot "film" them except by choosing specific manifestations. Writing can deal with ideas and abstractions, but film must always stay with concrete examples.

The novel is not as popular as ever, and filmed stories are becoming more widely sought than printed narratives. But for film to be widely used on a personal basis, methods of film distribution must change, and a film itself will have to become as portable as a paperback book. The hardware necessary for viewing must also become more accessible.

Major electronic companies already have completed the final stages of experimentation, and are preparing to market apparatus that makes the viewing of personally selected motion pictures as available as the television set now in your living room. Imagine an attachment similar to a tape deck that can be fitted to a television set. When a cassette is dropped into this attachment's slot and the set is turned on, what would appear on the screen would not be a television program but a motion picture of your choosing. Your television would become less like a radio, over which you have little program control, and more like your record player, on which you yourself determine which records will be played. Today, in cartridge or cassette you may buy an aural recording which may be played on a tape deck; tomorrow, these compact packages will store both black-and-white and color motion pictures to be played on your television receiver.

When this happens — and during the next decade it certainly will — motion pictures will be published like books; and like phonograph records, they will be distributed in large numbers to thousands of retail sources. You will be able to purchase or loan a complete library of motion picture classics from Griffith's *The Birth of a Nation* to Arthur Penn's "new" Western (Figure 118), the picaresque *Little Big Man* (1970). Like a book you can pick up and read

118. *Dustin Hoffman wards off an attacker in* Little Big Man. (*Little Big Man* starring Dustin Hoffman, directed by Arthur Penn, is a Cinema Center Films presentation)

at leisure, or a record you can play whenever you feel in the mood, there will be a motion picture that you can see on your "television set."

This is not to predict that broadcasting will cease altogether. Some channels will still broadcast old movies, new situation comedies and adventure series; and of course, there will always be the news. Since only television covers events as they are happening and instantaneously transmits them into millions of homes, the reporting of news will become the major function of television broadcasting. Some radio stations are now devoted entirely to news broadcast; it is quite likely that many television channels will restrict their programming in the same fashion.

But in the future there will always be a free channel on which the television owner can choose to play his own motion picture. This motion picture may come from his cassette library, or, with the promise of coaxial cable television, he may be able to dial into a

250

central library and choose his program. In the library concept the viewer would not own a copy of the motion picture, but at the turn of a dial, and for a slight charge, he would always have a motion picture available to him.

The visual and aural information that constitute a motion picture will probably be stored on a variety of materials. Film is only one. Feature-length motion pictures already are stored in cartridges of 8mm film, and less lengthy films have been transferred successfully to EVR. EVR, developed by Dr. Peter Goldmark of CBS, stands for Electronic Video Recording. It is made up of a special ribbon of film, which contains two columns of images printed in frames side by side. Outside the images, on each side, run strips of magnetic tape that hold the sound tracks for these images. EVR film can be played only on an EVR recorder, which can be outfitted to a standard television set.

At the present, there do not seem to be any plans to market an EVR "camera" so that home recordings can be made for playback. But videotape certainly offers this possibility. Films can be and are transferred to videotape cartridges. Already, almost all television broadcasts, including prime-time network films, are presented on tape. Videotape, like regular magnetic tape, is a plain strip of material. Unlike film, on which images are printed in small but discernible frames, videotape must be played, and only then is the image presented. Although this is considered a drawback, there is a tremendous advantage to videotape. It does not need to be processed or developed; like sound recording tape, whatever is recorded is *immediately* recorded (Figure 119). Once an image is taped, it can be played back at once. If it is satisfactory, it may stay recorded on the tape. If it does not prove satisfactory, it can be erased at once and another image can be recorded.

As if tape does not complicate the picture enough, a "tremendous technological breakthrough" was recently unveiled at a European trade fair. Motion pictures were revealed to have been stored on a wafer not unlike a phonograph record; and not unlike a phonograph record, this motion picture wafer was played on a turntable. Instead of being tuned into a sound amplifier, the wafer player was tuned into a television receiver, and reportedly revolving at a frantic speed

119.   *EVR film and player. The film is divided into two parallel channels, each with its own magnetic sound track. The player is compact, portable and easy to operate.* (Courtesy CBS)

CHANNEL B   CHANNEL A

AUDIO TRACK B

AUDIO TRACK A

CHANNEL B
25 Minutes
Maximum Program
Running Time

CHANNEL A
25 Minutes
Maximum Program
Running Time

8.75mm

of 1500 rpm, the wafer supplied the images on the television screen.

Whether motion pictures are ultimately stored, published and distributed in cassettes or on cartridges or wafers, and whether they appear on 8mm, EVR, videotape or any other material, one thing is certain. The quality of the reception will have to improve. Given modern technology, there is no reason why this improvement should not take place. Television receivers may become more sensitive to color and shading, and as motion pictures become a part of our daily experience, screens probably will be built into new homes.

And theatres? What will become of theatres? Spectacular films will still be produced. There will be no home immense enough to accommodate a gigantic wide screen. But that is not the only reason for the survival of theatres. I imagine that if films are published like cassettes, many will first be exhibited as films in cinemas. Here they will be reviewed and brought to public attention. It is in theatres that they will attract interest. On the basis of popularity in theatres, motion picture publishers will be able to judge how many cassettes of a given film will be made. If this is the case, then there may be a need for theatres only in large cities that act as communication centers.

Is this the fate of theatres? I do not know. There does seem to be some sort of social communion, a value, of people meeting, congregating, and acting, reacting as an audience, that would be missing in the privacy of one's home. Does this matter? Maybe.

And filmmakers? Well, they probably will become motion picture makers, and with the future holding so much technical promise, the possibilities for the manufacture and distribution of vital and creative works multiply. As possibilities multiply, predictions become less valid. The future may be good; it certainly is open. Let's leave it at that.

A Highly Selective Bibliography

(For the reader interested in continuing general reading on the American film.)

Behind the Screen: The History and Techniques of the Motion Picture by the late critic Kenneth Macgowan, is a general, accurate and enthusiastic introduction to film, not necessarily American film. As the title suggests, the easily readable text is not confined to the history of film, but touches upon some of the more important aspects of the industry, sociology and technology of film. The book was published in 1965 by Delacorte Press of New York, and a paperback edition (Delta series) appeared in 1967.

One of the first histories of the American film was written by a journalist, Terry Ramsaye, and was endorsed by Thomas Edison: *A Million and One Nights: A History of the Motion Picture through 1925.* Although it is riddled with exaggerations (such as the role Ramsaye has Edison play in the "discovery" of the motion picture), is anecdotal in nature and not researched in any scholarly fashion, it manages very well to capture the spirit of the early years, and reads much like an adventure yarn. Originally published in two volumes by Simon and Schuster (1926, New York), the paperback edition, also published by Simon and Schuster, appeared in 1964 as one giant book.

For a firsthand account of that time Griffith spent in developing the art of film at Biograph, consult the memoirs of Linda Arvidson (at one time Mrs. D. W. Griffith), about those years prior to *The Birth of a Nation: When The Movies Were Young.* Although it is atrociously written, it is interesting in that it not only betrays the

254

deep-seated prejudices of the period and so helps make clear the social circumstances in which Griffith worked, but also is about the only readily available authentic description of the way in which the primitive studios operated. The book was published in 1925 by E. P. Dutton and Company (New York); the paperback edition was published in 1969 by Dover Publications (New York). It differs from the original in that it has a new introduction, an index and a number of additional stills.

Griffith is so important to the history of film that another text, now a classic monograph, should be mentioned: *D. W. Griffith, American Film Master*. This slim hardbound volume, originally published by the Museum of Modern Art (New York) in 1940 on the occasion of the first Griffith retrospective, was written by Iris Barry, who arranged the tribute. The volume includes Miss Barry's essay, an interview with Griffith's cameraman, Billy Bitzer, a descriptive list of Griffith's films chronologically arranged, and many telling stills.

Film Notes, edited by Eileen Bowser, published by the Museum of Modern Art (New York) in 1969, is really a paperback compilation of program notes to selected American fiction films (1894–1950) in the archives of the Museum. The various authors have taken pains to place each film, including several not mentioned in this book, in a historical context and have supplied relevant biographical data about each director. This text should prove valuable to anyone about to see the programs suggested in the section following.

In 1939, Lewis Jacobs, a filmmaker and critic, wrote a "critical history" of the American film. *The Rise of the American Film* discusses the subject as both an art and an industry; the emphasis is critical and social. It was originally published by Harcourt, Brace and Company (New York). The recent paperback edition (1968), put out by Teachers College Press (Columbia University), has appended to it a valuable essay, also by Jacobs, "Experimental Cinema in America, 1921–1947."

Charles Higham and Joel Greenberg, in *Hollywood in the Forties,* divide their subject according to genre (for example, films of fantasy and horror, war propaganda, "women's" pictures), and discuss the films within these groupings. Part of the *International Film Guide Series,* the book was published in paperback in 1970 by Paperback Library.

Just before the studio system began to dissolve, a noted anthropologist, Dr. Hortense Powdermaker, studied the Hollywood colony much as she would have an isolated foreign tribe. Scrupulously applying sociological methods to her research on the studio system, she compared the system with the mores and laws that hold "uncivilized" societies together in a way that is revealing, rewarding and frightening. *Hollywood: The Dream Factory* was published by Little, Brown and Co. (Boston) in 1950. The paperback edition, published by Grosset and Dunlap/The Universal Library, appeared in 1961.

Lillian Ross tackled the same subject as Dr. Powdermaker, but took it in a different direction. Her book *Picture,* which reads like a novel, is a chronicle of the making of the film of Stephen Crane's classic book *The Red Badge of Courage.* Miss Ross befriended the writer-director of the film, John Huston, and was intimately involved in almost all aspects of the ambitious production. The book was published in 1952 by Rinehart; the paperback edition was published in 1969 by Avon Books.

Sheldon Renan's *An Introduction To The American Underground Film,* although embracing the unfortunate word "underground" in its title, is precisely what it claims to be. It gives a short history of the independent and avant-garde film movement in this country, defines terms, discusses key figures in the movement, suggests future directions, and lists a good many of the avant-garde works, along with their running times and sources. Since the book was published in 1967, it does not include the most recent titles. The book is available in paperback and was published by E. P. Dutton and Co. (New York).

Although it is more of a useful reference text than a history, Andrew Sarris' *The American Cinema: Directors and Directions 1929–1968* is a necessary catalogue for anyone wanting an immediate orientation to American directors. This encyclopedia lists all the major directors and almost all the interesting ones. Each listed director's concerns and style are neatly précised in a few concise paragraphs. Not only does a filmography (not always accurate) follow each director's name, but to the whole text is appended a year-by-year (1915 to 1967) chronology, in which the more interesting films of each year are listed according to director. In addition, Michael Schwartz and

James R. Prickett have compiled an index of many more titles than appear in the body of the text. For each title the name of the director and the year of production is given. The book was published in paperback by E. P. Dutton and Co. (New York), in 1968.

If your interest in film extends only as far as your television set and you would like some guidance to the films that are broadcast, let me recommend one light reference book: *TV Movies*, edited by Leonard Maltin. Consisting of 8,000 listings and much information about each title, the book was published in paperback in 1969 by the New American Library (New York), in a Signet edition.

Finally, a note about a book that has not yet appeared. I recently had the pleasure of reading passages from Miles Kreuger's manuscript "The American Musical Film," which when published promises to be a definitive work on this very American subject. Indeed, there will be much new information on a topic that needed more thorough research: how sound came to film. I recommend this chapter in particular. This book will be published by E. P. Dutton sometime in 1972.

One Reel a Week is a book of personal reminiscences. Fred J. Balshofer, one of the industry's first executives, and Arthur C. Miller, a respected cinematographer who not only worked with Porter, Mamoulian and Ford (*How Green Was My Valley*) but with many other directors as well, remember the Edison-versus-everybody days, the birth of the industry, the journey west, Keystone's founding, and the Patents Company on the warpath. Compiled with the assistance of Bebe Bergsten, this hardcover book was published in 1967 by the University of California Press, Berkeley and Los Angeles.

One Hundred Programs Illustrating the Growth and Scope of the American Film

The following list of films, their running times, and the distributors from whom 16mm prints may currently be rented is not meant to be definitive. It is merely a suggestion that should guide the new viewer around (and not too deeply inside) the perimeters of American film expression.

Personal prejudice and informed opinion have had as much hand in the selection as have more objective considerations such as the reader's probable age, the availability of titles, and whether the films have been discussed in the text. Some of the programs listed are compilations of films or film packages and may run longer than the average viewer would find reasonable. I have tried to shorten many of the longer programs but have decided, for fear of omitting an interesting and illustrative film, to err on the side of length.

One note about the silent film programs: although some modern projectors are equipped to show silent films at one slow speed of 18 or 20 frames per second, there was no standardization of speed at the time when many of the films were made. The speed at which the films were photographed (that is, the number of frames shot per second) varied with the speed at which the cameraman cranked his machine. Projectors were outfitted with a device that permitted the film to run through at variable speeds. The operator could adjust his projector to provide the smoothest image. By 1924 most American films were made to be projected at about 24 frames per second, and 24 frames was the speed adopted with the introduction of sound on film. Some silent films should be run at this speed, some a little slower, and some as slowly as 18 frames per second. I have marked with a # those silent films which should run at a speed slower than that of sound films, and have listed the *approximate* running times of the film projected both "silently" and at sound speed. The reader must realize that if a silent film designated with a # is projected at sound speed, a jerkiness of image will result that was not part of the original presentation.

With the exception of certain independent and avant-garde films which often had difficulty in finding a theatre in which to open and to be reviewed, most feature films are dated from their New York openings. Titles may be available from sources other than those listed.

A Chronological Listing of the One Hundred Suggested Programs

(The numbers in parentheses refer to the programs, discussed more fully in the next section.)

1879 History of Animation (39)
1894 Pre-Griffith Films (1)
1908 Griffith at Biograph (2)
1911 Mack Sennett Comedies (3)
1913 Early Western Heroes(4)
1915 *The Birth of a Nation* (5); Early Chaplin Comedies (6)
1916 *Civilization* (7); *Intolerance* (8); *The Mystery of the Leaping Fish* (9A)
1917 *Wild and Woolly* (9B)
1919 *Broken Blossoms* (10); *Male and Female* (11)
1920 *High and Dizzy* (12A); *One Week* (25A)
1921 Early Avant-Garde (70); *The Playhouse* (18A); *Tol'able David* (13)
1922 *Nanook of the North* (14)
1923 *The Covered Wagon* (15)
1924 *The Iron Horse* (16); *Greed* (17); *Sherlock Jr.* (18B); *The Thief of Bagdad* (19)
1925 *The Big Parade* (20); *The Gold Rush* (21)
1926 *Hands Up!* (12B); *So This Is Paris* (22); *The Strong Man* (23)
1927 The Coming of Sound (24A); *The General* (25B); *The Jazz Singer* (26); *Seventh Heaven* (27); *Sunrise* (28); *Underworld* (29A)
1928 *The Crowd* (30); *The Last Command* (31); *The Wind* (32); Laurel and Hardy Comedies (37); *St. Louis Blues* (24B)

260

A Chronological Listing

1929 Musicals of the Thirties (43)

1930 *All Quiet on the Western Front* (33); *Morocco* (34)

1931 *The Public Enemy* (29B)

1932 *Love Me Tonight* (35); *The Sign of the Cross* (36)

1933 *Duck Soup* (38)

1934 *Our Daily Bread* (40); *It Happened One Night* (41)

1935 *A Night at the Opera* (42)

1936 *Mr. Deeds Goes to Town* (44); *Modern Times* (45); *The Plow That Broke the Plains* (46A)

1937 *Camille* (47); *Easy Living* (48); *Snow White and the Seven Dwarfs* (49); *You Only Live Once* (50)

1938 *Bringing Up Baby* (51)

1939 *The City* (46B); *Ninotchka* (52)

1940 *The Grapes of Wrath* (53); *North West Mounted Police* (54)

1941 *Citizen Kane* (55)

1942 *The Magnificent Ambersons* (56); *Now, Voyager* (57); *Saboteur* (58); *Sullivan's Travels* (59)

1943 *Prelude to War* (60)

1945 Avant-Garde Program 2 (83); *The Southerner* (61)

1946 *My Darling Clementine* (62)

1947 Avant-Garde Program 3 (91)

1948 *Louisiana Story* (63); *The Quiet One* (64); *Red River* (65)

1950 Animation Program 2 (90); *Destination Moon* (66); *The Gunfighter* (67); *Sunset Boulevard* (68)

1951 *The Day the Earth Stood Still* (69)

1952 *In the Street* (71A); *High Noon* (72); *Singin' in the Rain* (73)

1953 *Pickup on South Street* (74)

1954 *On the Waterfront* (75); *Rear Window* (76)

1956 *Invasion of the Body Snatchers* (77); *On the Bowery* (71B)

1957 *The Incredible Shrinking Man* (78); *Paths of Glory* (79)

1958 Avant-Garde Program 4 (93); *The Left Handed Gun* (80)

1959 *North by Northwest* (81); *Rio Bravo* (82)

1960 *Primary* (84A); *Shadows* (85)

1961 *The Hustler* (86)

1963 *Hallelujah the Hills* (87)

1964 *The Cool World* (88); *Dr. Strangelove, or How I Learned to Stop Worrying and Love the Bomb* (89)

1966 *Troublemakers* (84B)
1968 *2001: A Space Odyssey* (92)
1969 *Easy Rider* (94); *In the Year of the Pig* (95); *Ira, You'll Get Into Trouble* (96A); *Tom, Tom the Piper's Son* (97)
1970 *Little Big Man* (98); *Watermelon Man* (99); *Wreck of the New York Subways* (96B); *Zorn's Lemma* (100)

and the films you yourself make and those made by your family and friends.

The Programs

1. PRE-GRIFFITH FILMS

Perhaps the best way to begin is with a program devoted to much of the material covered in the first chapter of this book. *The Origins of the Motion Picture* (1955), by Martin Quigley, Jr., visualizes the apparatus that preceded the appearance of our modern cameras and projectors. (20 min.: MT)

MT has also compiled two packages that should be included in this program. The first, entitled "Films of the 1890's," consists of twelve works designed for the peep shows so popular in the decade preceding the Nickelodeons (#18/11 min.). "The Films of Edwin S. Porter" includes those films Porter made for Edison, *The Life of an American Fireman, Uncle Tom's Cabin, The Great Train Robbery, The Dream of a Rarebit Fiend* and *Rescued from an Eagle's Nest* (#55/37 min.). All the Porter films except the last are available also from FG, and other Porter films such as *The Kleptomaniac* and *The Cure* are available in a package from PY.

2. GRIFFITH AT BIOGRAPH

A compilation of five films made by the great director for the American Biograph and Mutoscope Company. Included in this selection are *The Lonely Villa, The Lonedale Operator,* and the socially aware *A Corner in Wheat* (1909). Lillian Gish appears in *The Musketeers of Pig Alley* (1912), and Mary Pickford is the lead in *The New York Hat.* Although these films are short, both provide fairly naturalistic portraits of an urban slum (*Musketeers*) and a rural community (*Hat*) in America near the beginning of the century. From AB and PY a program consisting of *His Trust* and *His Trust Fulfilled* (both 1911) can be rented. Even though the films were made separately from each other, the latter is a sequel to the former, and the two may be enjoyed as one film. In the same pack-

263

age, AB distributes one of Griffith's first two-reelers, *Enoch Arden* (#62/44 min.). PY distributes this title separately. Griffith's first film, *The Adventures of Dollie,* and *Pippa Passes* and *The New York Hat,* each about #11/8 min., are available for separate rental from FG.

3. MACK SENNETT COMEDIES

A compilation of six zany and perfectly timed slapstick comedies: *Comrades* (1911), *Mabel's Dramatic Career* (1913), *The Surf Girl* (1916), *His Bread and Butter* (1916), *The Clever Dummy* (1917), *Astray from Steerage* (1920) (#110/73 min.). *Teddy at the Throttle* (1917), in which Gloria Swanson appears and which satirizes the conventions of the melodramatic stage presentations of the day, may also be rented from MT (#24/16 min.).

4. EARLY WESTERN HEROES

(Broncho Billy, Tom Mix, William S. Hart). Two of Broncho Billy's Westerns have been put together by MT: *Broncho Billy's Capture* (1913) and *Shootin' Mad* (1918) (#48/32 min.). William S. Hart's *The Taking of Luke McVane* (1915), also known as *The Fugitive,* may be rented from the same source (#30/20 min.). FM distributes what many historians regard as Hart's finest film, *Hell's Hinges* (1916; #65/50 min.). MT has the Tom Mix film *Sky High* (1922, #72/48 min.), which was written and directed by Lynn Reynolds. FG also distributes the films of Broncho Billy, William S. Hart and Tom Mix. Of special interest is FG's package of four early (1913–1916) films of Tom Mix (#90/75 min.).

5. *The Birth of a Nation* (#195/130 min.: MT)

6. EARLY CHAPLIN COMEDIES

Chaplin's second film and the first in his celebrated costume, is Keystone's *Kid Auto Races at Venice* (1914, #6/4 min.: G). After leaving Keystone, Chaplin made fourteen films for a company called Essanay (1915). Among the more celebrated films Chaplin completed here are *The Tramp* and *The Bank.* Both films are available from AB and MT, and each runs about twenty minutes at silent speed. Having quit Essanay, Chaplin moved to Mutual, where many critics believe he made his most successful short films: *Easy Street, The Cure* and *The Immigrant* (1917). AB, FG and G list them in their catalogues (about twenty minutes each), and if any of the above are unavailable, one Chaplin is almost as good as the next.

7. *Civilization* (#101/68 min.: MT)

8. *Intolerance* (#191/127 min.: AB or MT)

9. TWO EARLY DOUGLAS FAIRBANKS FILMS

Both may be rented together from MT. *The Mystery of the Leaping Fish* (1916) and *Wild and Woolly* (1917) are directed by John Emerson (#80/68 min.).

10. *Broken Blossoms* (#95/68 min.: AB or MT)

11. *Male and Female* (#120/97 min.: MT)

12. TWO CELEBRATED COMEDIES

Each title may be rented separately from MT. (12A) *High and Dizzy*, directed by Hal Roach, with Harold Lloyd (#32/21 min.). (12B) *Hands Up!* directed by Clarence Badger, with Raymond Griffith (70 min.).

13. *Tol'able David* (#110/85 min.: MT or FG)

14. *Nanook of the North* (#70/55 min.: CT, MT or PY)

15. *The Covered Wagon* (#100/71 min.: AB or MT)

16. *The Iron Horse* (#111 min.: FI or MT)

17. *Greed* (#114 min.: FI)

18. TWO FILMS OF BUSTER KEATON

The Playhouse (#11/8 min.: AB); *Sherlock Jr.* (55 min.: AB).

19. *The Thief of Bagdad* (135 min.: AB or MT)

20. *The Big Parade* (130 min.: FI)

21. *The Gold Rush* (81 min.: AB, CF, CT, FI, FG or JA)

22. *So This Is Paris* (64 min.: CT)

23. *The Strong Man* (78 min.: AB)

24. THE COMING OF SOUND

MT compilation includes excerpts from two early films using sound: *The Jazz Singer,* directed by Alan Crosland, and the first "all-talking" picture, *Lights of New York* (1928), directed by Bryan Foy. The sound for both these films was recorded onto discs, separate but synchronized with the film (the Vitaphone process). The following short films also appear in this program: [George Bernard] *Shaw Talks for Movietone News* (1927), *Steamboat Willie* (1928), and the monologue of humorist Robert Benchley, *The Sex Life of the Polyp* (1928).

By the time this text appears, AB may have a sound program in which will be included pioneering work by Dr. Lee de Forest, who helped perfect the Phonofilm (later incorporated into the Movietone) sound-on-film process.

St. Louis Blues (17 min.: MA) In 1928 an independent production company, Sack Amusements, produced an intriguing sound and musical film with the legendary singer, Bessie Smith. *St. Louis Blues,* directed by Dudley Murphy, may be a pioneer sound film, but made by a white organization with an all-black cast, it unfortunately reproduces racial stereotypes of the period.

25. TWO MORE FILMS BY AND WITH BUSTER KEATON

One Week (#11/8 min.: AB); *The General* (82 min.: AB or FM).

26. *The Jazz Singer* (89 min.: AB, CT or UA)

27. *Seventh Heaven* (125 min.: MT)

28. *Sunrise* (95 min.: FI or MT)

29. *Underworld* (80 min.: MT); *The Public Enemy* (74 min.: UA)

Although there are great stylistic differences between these two titles and each film is recommended viewing in itself, it may be rewarding to compare films the protagonists of both of which are outside the law. "Bull" Weed (George Bancroft in *Underworld*) exists in a fictionalized world of heavy atmosphere, but four years later Tom (James Cagney as the "public enemy") is very much a part of the social landscape.

30. *The Crowd* (90 min.: FI)

31. *The Last Command* (119 min.: MT)

32. *The Wind* (78 min.: FI)

33. *All Quiet on the Western Front* (103 min.: U16)

34. *Morocco* (92 min.: U16)

35. *Love Me Tonight* (96 min.: U16)

36. *The Sign of the Cross*

For its 1944 release, a prologue was added to the film in which the war in Europe was thematically tied to the body of the film. U16 distributes the film as it was originally released in 1932 at 124 minutes. Some of the scenes are fairly savage, and so the film is not recommended for very young audiences.

37. LAUREL AND HARDY

Two of the most successful silent films made by the comic team of Stan Laurel and Oliver Hardy may be rented together in one 42-minute program from MT: *Two Tars* (1928) and *Big Business* (1929). Both are produced by Hal Roach. The former is directed by James Parrott and the latter, J. Wesley Horne. These two films may be rented separately from AB or G, as may be the hilarious

Double Whoopee (1929), directed by Lewis Foster (19 min.). *Brats* (1930), in which the duo play tykes, may be borrowed from AB (20 min.), while their sound film *The Music Box* (1932), an Academy Award winner, is available from G and AB (27 min.). Both films are directed by James Parrott.

38. *Duck Soup* (70 min.: U16)

39. HISTORY OF ANIMATION

Although this program is not restricted to the American film, this compilation does illustrate the development of the moving cartoon. The earliest American animated film which appears in this program is Winsor ("Little Nemo") McCay's *Gertie the Dinosaur* (1909). Gertie was made to move only after McCay spent months completing thousands of similar simple line drawings (see Figure 120).

120.   Gertie the Dinosaur. (Museum of Modern Art/Film Stills Archive)

Actually, Gertie was half a vaudeville act (of which her animator was the other), in which McCay would approach a screen and invite the bashful dinosaur to appear. Emile Cohl (*The Pumpkin Race*) seemed to influence a number of American newspaper cartoonists to take to film. (A Cohl film is included in this program.) *Mutt and Jeff* (1918) and Pat Sullivan's *Felix the Cat* (1924) appear in the compilation. Three Disney films round out the American segment of the program. An "advertising" film, *Newman's Laugh-o-Gram* (1920), made in Kansas City by Disney, is included, as are two Mickey Mouse cartoons, *Steamboat Willie* (discussed in the text) and *Mad Dog* (1932). Compare the Mouse figure in *Steamboat Willie* to the one that appears four years later in *Mad Dog* (60 min.: MT).

40. *Our Daily Bread* (71 min.: JA)

41. *It Happened One Night* (105 min.: CQ)

42. *A Night at the Opera* (93 min.: FI)

43. MUSICALS OF THE THIRTIES

Song and dance arrived with sound. During the thirties a number of musical films were distinguished by elaborate "routines" in which one singer would happen upon a chorus which, in turn, would grow into a whole troupe of dancers executing the most complex and beguiling of formations. Busby Berkeley, dance director, used mirrors and dazzling camera techniques (prisms, odd angles) in choreographing these attractive human mosaics. This program includes some of the more exciting musical moments in the following films: *Rio Rita* (1929; S. Sylvan Simon), *42nd Street* (1933; Lloyd Bacon), *Gold Diggers of 1933* (Mervyn LeRoy), *Gold Diggers of 1935* (Busby Berkeley), *Flying Down to Rio* (1933; Thornton Freeland), *Music in the Air* (1934; Joe May), and *In Caliente* (1935; Lloyd Bacon). The directors listed did not necessarily work on the musical sequences of their films. Appearing in this compilation are such stars as Fred Astaire, Ginger Rogers, Gloria Swanson, Ruby Keeler and Dick Powell. (78 min.: MT)

44. *Mr. Deeds Goes to Town* (118 min.: AB)

Deeds, a folk hero if ever cinema has given us one, a man who puts character before wealth, can be found in even "purer" form in Capra's earlier film *American Madness* (1932). Paced like lightning and taking place almost entirely in a bank, this 70-minute film, coming in the middle of the depression, affirms faith in both the people and banks. Unfortunately, at the time of writing, this second title was not in 16mm distribution.

45. *Modern Times*

At the moment, I know of no 16mm source for this film. However, the Chaplin estate does see that the film is periodically reissued, and at these times it is distributed to theatres across the country. There has been some talk of a distributor buying the 16mm rights to this film, and it very well may be available after this book's publication.

46. TWO SOCIAL DOCUMENTARIES OF THE THIRTIES

The Plow That Broke the Plains was commissioned by the Roosevelt administration (United States Resettlement Administration) as a film "history" of the Great Plains. Written and directed by Pare Lorentz, the film became something more than history. *The Plow That Broke the Plains* is a moving and poetic chronicle of the settlement and farming of this area, its time of fertility, and the disastrous effects of poor ecological practices and drought. It was one of the earliest American documents dealing with questions of national social importance, and its grace and rhythm affected many other committed filmmakers who followed. In 1939 Ralph Steiner and Willard Van Dyke made *The City*, in cooperation with the American Institute of Planners, which financed the production. *The City*, made for exposition at the New York World's Fair, is not only remarkable for the humane approach it takes to a situation that was fast becoming inhuman — city life — but also for its brilliant photography, use of sound, and cutting and for its clarity. It shrewdly anticipates the problems facing so many urban centers today. Both films are available separately from MT or PY. *The Plow That Broke the Plains* is 21 minutes and *The City*, 55 minutes.

47. *Camille* (110 min.: FI)

48. *Easy Living* (88 min.: U16)

49. *Snow White and the Seven Dwarfs*

Like *Modern Times, Snow White and the Seven Dwarfs* is not available in 16mm. It is periodically reissued nationally, and may be seen across the nation at any one of these times. (80 min.)

50. *You Only Live Once* (79 min.: CT or UA)

51. *Bringing Up Baby* (102 min.: FI)

52. *Ninotchka* (110 min.: FI)

53. *The Grapes of Wrath* (127 min.: FI)

54. *North West Mounted Police* (126 min.: U16)

55. *Citizen Kane* (119 min.: AB, FI or JA)

56. *The Magnificent Ambersons* (88 min.: FI or JA)

57. *Now, Voyager*

Made in 1942, this "woman's film" remains a classic tearjerker. It's a Cinderella story played so expertly by Bette Davis and directed so smoothly by Irving Rapper that the romance moves the most hardened of viewers (117 min.: UA).

58. *Saboteur* (108 min.: U16)

59. *Sullivan's Travels* (90 min.: U16)

60. *Prelude to War*

This film was the first in a series of seven films entitled "Why We Fight." The series was produced for the War Department by Frank Capra. As a major, Capra, along with other Hollywood directors, was asked to complete a number of propaganda films explaining to American servicemen the nature of America's commitment to war. (Many films were commissioned by the United States government during the war. Germany and Britain also used film in an extremely capable way in their propagandizing efforts.) The "Why We Fight" series should be singled out in any discussion of the teaching film and ways in which film may be used to convey what might otherwise be visually uninteresting "statistical" information. *Prelude to War* describes in no uncertain terms "the rise of fascism, nazism and Japanese imperialism from 1931 to 1938." Audiences today might find the film a bit hysterical, but it must be remembered that it was produced under the exceptional circumstance of war. This film runs 53 minutes. If it is unavailable, *Divide and Conquer* (1943: 58 min.) or *The Battle of Russia* (1944: 80 min.) should prove as interesting. (MT or PY)

61. *The Southerner* (92 min.: This film is currently out of 16mm distribution.)

62. *My Darling Clementine* (100 min.: FI or MT)

63. *Louisiana Story* (77 min.: CT or PY)

64. *The Quiet One* (67 min.: CT)

65. *Red River* (113 min.: UA)

66. *Destination Moon* (91 min.: IV)

67. *The Gunfighter* (88 min.: FI or MT)

68. *Sunset Boulevard* (110 min.: FI)

69. *The Day the Earth Stood Still* (92 min.: FI)

70. AVANT-GARDE PROGRAM NUMBER 1 (EARLY FILMS)

Manhatta (1921, 9 min.: MT), *The Fall of the House of Usher* (1928, 12 min.: MT), *The Life and Death of a Hollywood Extra* (1928, 14 min.: AB, G or MT), *Meshes of the Afternoon* (1943, 18

272

min.: G), *Loony Tom — The Happy Lover* (1951, 10 min.: AB, CC, CF, G or MT), and for older, mature audiences, *Fireworks* (1947, 15 min.: CF or FM).

71. Two "Street" Documentaries of the Fifties

In the Street (16 min.: MT); *On the Bowery* (60 min.: CT)

72. *High Noon* (85 min.: CT)

73. *Singin' in the Rain* (103 min.: FI)

74. *Pickup on South Street* (82 min.: FI)

With the exception of the brilliant *Underworld* and *The Public Enemy*, this film is the only one in the listing that represents the traditional American genre of the hardboiled, seamy, quickly paced and tightly edited gangster film. While many others (*The Maltese Falcon*, 1941; *The Naked City*, 1948; *The Lineup*, 1958; and recently, *The French Connection*, 1971) are fashioned as carefully and hold as great an interest, *Pickup on South Street* has an amazing photographic quality. Its action is violent and frequently chilling. For this reason the film is not recommended for very young audiences.

75. *On the Waterfront* (108 min.: AB, CQ or CT)

76. *Rear Window*

There is no 16mm listing for *Rear Window*. Like the other films for which there is no listing, it is issued (infrequently) to theatres and has recently been broadcast for the first time over network television. (112 min.)

77. *Invasion of the Body Snatchers* (80 min.: HW or IV)

78. *The Incredible Shrinking Man* (94 min.: U16)

79. *Paths of Glory* (87 min.: UA)

80. *The Left Handed Gun* (102 min.: AB or WB)

81. *North by Northwest* (136 min.: FI)

82. *Rio Bravo* (141 min.: WB)

83. Avant-Garde Program Number 2 (Rhythms of Dancers, Land-scapes and Cameras)

A Study in Choreography for Camera (1945, 4 min.: G), *Sausalito* (1948, 10 min.: FE or MT), *Dance in the Sun* (1953, 7 min.: FM), *N.Y. N.Y.* (1957, 15 min.: MT or PY), *Bridges-Go-Round* (1958, 4 min.: FM), *Dance Chromatic* (1959, 7 min.: G or FM), *America's in Real Trouble* (1967, 15 min.: FM). I saw Ernie Gehr's *Serene Velocity* (1970, 25 min. at silent speed: FM) after this listing had been compiled, and finding it one of the more exciting films viewed in a six-month period, felt that it should be included as a part of this catalogue. Although not a person appears in the film and the camera remains firmly fixed on its stationary tripod, intriguing and absorbing rhythms are established as, staccato fashion, the camera zooms up and down the corridor, causing a strange, compelling effect.

84. Two *Cinéma-Vérité* Films of the Sixties

Primary (54 min.: TL); *Troublemakers* (54 min.: G or FM)

85. *Shadows* (81 min.: AB)

86. *The Hustler* (135 min.: FI)

Directed by Robert Rossen, this parable about ambition is set, for the most part, within the confines of pool halls, yet the wide Cinemascope frame is used with remarkable effect. Three of the more exciting screen performances of the sixties, by Paul Newman, George C. Scott and Jackie Gleason, appear in the film (Figure 121).

87. *Hallelujah the Hills* (82 min.: FM)

88. *The Cool World* (105 min.: ZP)

89. *Dr. Strangelove, or How I Learned to Stop Worrying and Love the Bomb* (93 min.: CQ)

121. *Jackie Gleason, pool champ extraordinaire, meets an ambitious challenger, Paul Newman, in* The Hustler. (© 1961 Rossen Enterprises, Inc., and Twentieth Century-Fox Film Corporation. All Rights Reserved)

90. ANIMATION PROGRAM NUMBER 2

Although *Ragtime Bear* was the first Magoo cartoon (1949), I do not know of a 16mm source. Another early Magoo film is *Bungled Bungalow* (1950, 7 min.: AB or CF). In the same year, the same company, UPA, founded by Stephen Bosustow, produced *Gerald McBoing Boing* (8 min.: AB or CF), co-designed by John Hubley, a master animator who is also represented in this program by two other films: *Adventures of An* * (1956, 12 min.: AB, CF, CT or G) and *Moonbird* (1960, AB, CT or G). In 1953 UPA turned a short story by James Thurber into a bittersweet film, *Unicorn in the Garden* (9 min.: AB or CF). Meanwhile the Warner Bros. studio introduced the shrewdest of all cartoon characters in the *Road Runner* (created by Chuck Jones), *Beep Beep* (1952, 7 min.: AB or UA). Ernest Pintoff, who once worked at UPA and who has since turned to the making of live-action feature films, completed

275

The Violinist (7 min.: AB or CT) in 1960, and *The Critic* (4 min.: AB or CT) three years later. Although Carmen D'Avino does not make cartoons (he animates furniture, mannequins and whatever else that does not usually move), his films have an infectious good naturedness that is like the cartoon spirit: *Pianissimo* (1963, 10 min.: G). Fred Mogubgub's four-minute *Enter Hamlet* (1967) is being released by PY. MT distributes a 20-minute program of eighteen animated television commercials made between 1963 and 1966.

91. AVANT-GARDE PROGRAM NUMBER 3 (Rather long, this program should be divided.)

A Movie (1958, 12 min.: AB, CC, FM, G or MT), *Prelude: Dog Star Man* (1961, 25 min.: AB, FM or G), *Scorpio Rising* (1962–64, 31 min.: CF or FM), *Kiss* (excerpt) (1964, 14 min.: FM), *Circus Notebook* (excerpt from Mekas's *Diaries, Notes & Sketches*) (1966, 12 min.: FM), *Castro Street* (1966, 10 min.: AB, CC, FM or MT), *Ming Green* (1966, 15 min.: FM), *Bardo Follies* (1967, 18-minute version: FM), *Billabong* (1968, 9 min.: CC, CF or MT). Both *Billabong* and *Scorpio Rising* are recommended for older audiences only.

92. *2001: A Space Odyssey*

This film is still in theatrical release. FI will probably distribute it when it is available in 16mm. The *New York Times* lists the original running time at 160 minutes. It was subsequently cut by the filmmaker himself (141 min.).

93. AVANT-GARDE PROGRAM NUMBER 4 (Extensions of Animation)

Douglass Crockwell's *The Long Bodies* (1947, 4 min.: MT), John Whitney's *Celery Stalks at Midnight* (1951, 4 min.: PY), *A Man and His Dog Out for Air* (1957, 3 min.: FM, G or MT), *Horse over Teakettle* (1962, 6 min.: FM, G or MT), *Breathdeath* (1964, 10 min.: FM, G or PY), *Off/On* (1967, 10 min.: CC, CF, FM or MT), *Permutations* (1969, 10 min.: MT or PY), *Samadhi* (1966–67, 6 min.: U16), *Moon 69* (1969, 10 min.: CC or MT), *69* (1969, 5 min.: FM or MT), *Our Lady of the Spheres* (1969, 10 min.: CC). It is not recommended that an audience see this program as a whole. It should either be broken up into several shorter experiences, or some of the short films could accompany a feature.

122. *Alone on his cycle, the director, Dennis Hopper, watches Peter Fonda and novice cyclist Jack Nicholson in* Easy Rider. (Courtesy Columbia Pictures)

94. *Easy Rider*

This film is still in theatrical release. CQ will probably distribute it when it becomes available in 16mm (see Figure 122). (94 min.)

95. *In the Year of the Pig* (101 min.: CT)

96. Two Films of Rebellion

Ira, You'll Get into Trouble (85 min.: SS); *Wreck of the New York Subways* (16 min.: NR)

97. *Tom, Tom the Piper's Son* (90 min.: FM or MT)

98. *Little Big Man*

This title is still in theatrical release. A picaresque, poetic Western

277

that questions some of the romance that has previously been associated with the winning of the West. As in *Dr. Strangelove,* black and often absurd humor is indicative of the uneasy laughter of the sixties. However, the film is mellowed by scenes of tenderness and love that are as moving as any of the folk songs of the same decade. Since in its scenes of savagery, it is fairly gruesome, this title is recommended for older audiences only. (147 min.)

99. *Watermelon Man*

This title is still in theatrical release. CQ will probably distribute the film when it becomes available in 16mm. Recommended for older audiences only. (102 min.)

100. *Zorn's Lemma* (60 min.: FM)

and the films you yourself make and those made by your family and friends (folk art?).

Distributors of 16mm Films

Main offices only are listed. Those marked with an asterisk maintain branches or exchanges in major cities across the country. Please note that not only do titles frequently change distributors, but running times are often listed differently from catalogue to catalogue. Company addresses may also change from year to year.

*AB: Audio/Brandon Films, 34 MacQueston Parkway South, Mount Vernon, New York 10550.

*CT: Contemporary/McGraw-Hill Films, 330 West 42nd Street, New York, New York 10036.

CF: Creative Film Society, 8435 Geyser Avenue, Northridge, California 91324.

CC: Canyon Cinema Cooperative, Room 220, Industrial Center Building, Sausalito, California 94965.

CQ: Columbia Cinematheque, 711 Fifth Avenue, New York, New York 10019.

*FI: Films Incorporated, 1144 Wilmette Avenue, Wilmette, Illinois 60091.

*FG: Film Images, 17 West 60th Street, New York, New York 10023.

FM: Filmmakers' Cooperative, 175 Lexington Avenue, New York, New York 10016.

GR: Grove Press/Evergreen Films, 85 Bleecker Street, New York, New York 10013.

HW: Hurlock Cine World, 13 Arcadia Road, Old Greenwich, Connecticut 06870

IV: Ivy Films, 165 West 46th Street, New York, New York 10036.

*JA: Janus Films, 745 Fifth Avenue, New York, New York 10022.

MT: Museum of Modern Art, Department of Film, Circulating Library, 21 West 53rd Street, New York, New York 10019.

*NR: Newsreel, 322 Seventh Avenue, New York, New York 10022.

PY: Pyramid Films, Box 1048, Santa Monica, California 90406.

SS: Stephen Sbarge, Old Chelsea Station, Drawer E, New York, New York 10011.

TL: TIME/LIFE Films, 43 West 16th Street, New York, New York 10011.

*UA: United Artists, 16mm Division, 729 Seventh Avenue, New York, New York 10036.

*U16: Universal 16, 630 Ninth Avenue, New York, New York 10036.

WB: Warner Brothers, 16mm, 4000 Warner Boulevard, Burbank, California 91503.

ZP: Zipporah Films, 54 Lewis Wharf, Boston, Massachusetts 02110.

New Yorker Films (2409 Broadway, New York, New York 10024), New Line Cinema (121 University Place, New York, New York 10003), EYR (78 East Fifty-Sixth Street, New York, New York 10022), Genesis Films (40 West Fiftieth Street, New York, New York 10019), and Cinema 5 (595 Madison Avenue, New York, New York 10022) also include interesting independent American films in their catalogues.

Index of Titles

$\longleftrightarrow$ (1969), 234, 237
Abbott and Costello Meet Dr. Jekyll and Mr. Hyde (1953), 128
Abbott and Costello Meet Frankenstein (1948), 128
Abbott and Costello Meet the Mummy (1955), 128
Abraham Lincoln (1930), 79
Adventures of An ° (1956), 275
Adventures of Dollie, The (1908), 58, 264
Adventures of Kathlyn, The (1913), 87
African Queen, The (1951), 111
After Many Years (1908), 56–57
All About Eve (1950), 111
All Quiet on the Western Front (1930), 153, 261, 267
American in Paris, An (1951), 207
American Madness (1932), 153, 270
American Tragedy, The, see *Place in the Sun, A*
America's in Real Trouble (1967), 219, 274
Anastasia (1956), 112
Applause (1929), 148
Artful Husband in Distress, The, 34 (*illus.*)
Astray from Steerage (1920), 264
At Land (1944), 224, 237
Avenging Conscience, The (1914), 67

Bank, The, 264
Bardo Follies (1967), 234, 237, 276
Batman (1943), 87
Battle of Russia, The (1944), 272
Beau James (1957), 126
Becky Sharp (1935), 148
Bedford Incident, The (1965), 175
Beep Beep (1952), 275
Behind the Great Wall (1959), 188

Behind the Screen, 120
Bells of St. Mary, The (1945), 112
Ben Hur (1908 and 1959), 47
Beware My Husband Comes, 52
Big Business (1929), 126, 267
Big Heat, The (1953), 144
Big Parade, The (1925), 150, 183, 260, 266
Big Sleep, The (1946), 138
Billabong (1968), 235, 276
Birth of a Nation, The (1915), 67, 68 (*illus.*), 69 (*illus.*), 70–74, 72 (*illus.*), 75, 85, 171, 218, 249, 260, 264
Birth of a Race, The (1919), 171
Black King, The (1932), 172
Blackmail (1929), 139
Blind Husbands (1919), 163
Blonde Venus (1932), 111
Blue Dahlia, The (1946), 114
Bonnie and Clyde (1967), 209
Boys' Town (1938), 115
Brandy in the Wilderness (1969), 236–237
Brats (1930), 126 (*illus.*), 268
Breathdeath (1964), 232, 276
Bridges-Go-Round (1958), 226, 274
Brig, The (1964), 230 (*illus.*)
Bringing Up Baby (1938), 111, 138, 261, 271
Broadway (1929), 220
Broken Blossoms (1919), 79, 110, 141, 260, 265
Broken Earth, 173
Broncho Billy's Capture (1913), 264
Bronze Buckaroo, The (1938), 172 (*illus.*), 173
Bronze Venus (1948), 173
Buccaneer, The (1938), 134
Buck Rogers (1939), 87
Bullfight (1955), 226
Bungled Bungalow (1950), 275

281

Bus Stop (1956), 198, 199 (*illus.*)
Butterfly Dance, The (1894), 20
Bwana Devil (1953), 186

Cameraman, The (1928), 123
Camille (1937), 109 (*illus.*), 153, 261, 270
Carrots and Peas (1969), 235
Casablanca (1942), 114
Castro Street (1966), 219, 276
Celery Stalks at Midnight (1951), 276
Champion (1949), 167
Chang (1927), 161, 183
Chelsea Girls, The (1966), 245
Chimes at Midnight (1967), 170
Cinderella, 52
Circus Notebook (1966), 276
Citizen Kane (1941), 166–167, 168 (*illus.*), 187, 261, 271
City, The (1939), 261, 270
City Lights (1931), 121
City Streets (1931), 148
Civilization (1916), 85, 86 (*illus.*), 260, 265
Clansman, The (1915), 67–70
Cleopatra (1934), 133
Clever Dummy, The (1917), 264
College Boy's First Love, 52
Computer Art #1 (1966), 233
Comrades (1911), 264
Cool World, The (1964), 241 (*illus.*), 242, 261, 274
Coon Town Suffragette, 71
Corner in Wheat, A (1909), 263
Count of Monte Cristo, The (1907), 29
Countess from Hong Kong (1966), 122
Cover Girl (1944), 111
Covered Wagon, The (1923), 85, 104, 260, 265
Critic, The (1963), 276
Crowd, The (1928), 149 (*illus.*), 150, 260, 267
Cure, The (1917), 263, 265

Dance Chromatic (1959), 226, 274
Dance in the Sun (1953), 226, 274
Dark Town Jubilee (1914), 173
Day the Earth Stood Still, The (1951), 206 (*illus.*), 207, 261, 272
Defiant Ones, The (1958), 175

Destination: Moon (1950), 205 (*illus.*), 206, 261, 272
Devil Is a Woman, The (1935), 111, 151 (*illus.*), 152
Dial M for Murder (1954), 187
Diaries, Notes & Sketches, 1965–69, (1969), 231, 276
Dinner at Eight (1933), 111, 153
Divide and Conquer (1943), 272
Docks of New York, The (1927), 152
Dr. Jekyll and Mr. Hyde (1932), 148
Dr. Strangelove (1964), 208, 261, 274, 278
Dog's Life, A (1918), 120
Don Juan (1926), 103
Don't Change Your Husband (1919), 133
Double Whoopee (1929), 126, 268
Dream of a Rarebit Fiend, The (1906), 46, 157, 263
Dream Street (1921), 71
Duck Soup (1933), 127, 261, 268
Duo Concertantes (1964), 232

East of Eden (1955), 200
Easy Living (1937), 150, 261, 271
Easy Rider (1969), 232, 262, 277 (*illus.*)
Easy Street (1917), 120, 265
Eat (1963), 245
Emperor Jones, The (1933), 174
Empire, 245
Enoch Arden (1908 and 1911), 56, 65, 264
Enter Hamlet (1967), 276
Ex-Convict, The (1905), 45, 46, 62
Exploits of Elaine, The (1915), 87

Faces (1968), 245
Fall of Babylon, The (1916), 74 (*illus.*)
Fall of the House of Usher, The (1928), 221 (*illus.*), 272
Falstaff (1967), 170
Fantasia (1940), 155 (*illus.*), 156, 222
Fantasia Will Amazia (1940), 157
Fatal Glass of Beer, The (1933), 125
Felix the Cat (1924), 269
Fiddler on the Roof (1971), 248
Film in Which There Appear Edge Lettering, Sprocket Holes, Dirt Particles, Etc. (1966), 234

Index of Titles

Film That Rises to the Surface of Clarified Butter (1968), 234
Finian's Rainbow (1968), 116
Fireworks (1947), 236, 237, 273
Five (1951), 206
Flash Gordon (1936), 87
Flesh (1968), 245
Flower Fairy, The (pre-1902), 37
Flying Down to Rio (1933), 269
Fool There Was, A (1915), 111
Forbidden Planet (1956), 207
42nd Street (1933), 115, 269
Four Horsemen of the Apocalypse, The (1921), 112
French Connection, The (1971), 273
Frenzy (1972), 140
Freshman, The (1925), 125
Fugitive, The (1915), 264
Fun in a Chinese Laundry (1894), 21
Fury (1936), 144

Gaieties of Divorce, The, 52
Gaslight (1944), 112
General, The (1927), 122 (*illus.*), 123, 125, 260, 266
Gentlemen Prefer Blondes (1953), 138
Georg (1964), 236
Gerald McBoing Boing (1950), 158, 275
Gertie the Dinosaur (1909), 268 (*illus.*), 269
Giant (1956), 200
Gilda (1946), 111
Gimme Shelter (1970), 240
Gold Diggers of 1933, 269
Gold Diggers of 1935, 269
Gold Rush, The (1925), 121, 260, 266
Gone with the Wind (1939), 70, 114, 166, 194
Grapes of Wrath, The (1940), 114, 136, 137 (*illus.*), 167, 261, 271
Grass (1925), 161
Great Dictator, The (1940), 121
Great McGinty, The (1940), 150
Great Train Robbery, The (1903), 41, 42 (*illus.*), 44 (*illus.*), 45, 61, 85, 263
Greatest Show on Earth, The (1952), 134
Greed (1924), 164 (*illus.*), 165, 260, 265
Gun Moll (1933), 173

Gunfighter, The (1950), 115, 153, 261, 272

H_2O (1929), 222 (*illus.*)
Haircut (1965), 245
Hallelujah (1929), 148–149, 174
Hallelujah the Hills (1963), 230, 231 (*illus.*), 261, 274
Hands Up! (1926), 126, 260, 265
Hatari! (1962), 137
Hazards of Helen, The (1916), 87
He Who Gets Slapped (1924), 141
Hearts in Dixie (1929), 173 (*illus.*), 174
Hell's Hinges (1916), 85, 264
High and Dizzy (1920), 125, 260, 265
High Noon (1952), 114, 208, 261, 273
High School (1968), 243
His Bread and Butter (1916), 264
His Girl Friday (1940), 138
His Trust (1911), 263
His Trust Fulfilled (1911), 263
History (1970), 233
Home of the Brave (1949), 167, 174
Home, Sweet Home (1914), 67
Homesteader, The (1918), 171
Horse over Teakettle (1962), 276
Hospital (1970), 243
How Green Was My Valley (1941), 136, 257
Hunchback of Notre Dame, The (1923), 118
Husbands (1970), 245
Hustler, The (1961), 261, 274, 275, (*illus.*)

I Wake Up Screaming (1941), 111
Immigrant, The (1917), 120, 265
Impossible Voyage, An (1905), 39 (*illus.*)
In Caliente (1935), 269
In the Street (1952), 238, 239 (*illus.*), 261, 273
In the Year of the Pig (1969), 246, 247 (*illus.*), 262, 277
Incredible Shrinking Man, The (1957), 207, 261, 273
Informer, The (1935), 136
Inspector General, The (1949), 125
Institutional Quality (1969), 234

Index of Titles

Intolerance (1916), 67, 73–75, 74 (*illus.*), 76–77 (*illus.*), 79, 85, 145, 163, 183, 218, 260, 265
Intruder in the Dust (1949), 175
Invasion of the Body Snatchers (1956), 207, 261, 273
Invocation of My Demon Brother (1969), 236
Ira, You'll Get Into Trouble (1969), 243, 262, 277
Iron Horse, The (1924), 135, 136, 183, 260, 265
Iron Mask, The (1929), 108
It Happened One Night (1934), 114 (*illus.*), 153, 261, 269
It's a Gift (1934), 125
It's Love I'm After (1937), 111

Jackknife Man, The (1919), 150
Jamestown Baloos (1957), 232
Jazz Singer, The (1927), 103, 260, 266
Jezebel (1938), 111
Judith of Bethulia (1913), 65–66

Kaiser Wilhelm Reviewing His Troops (1896), 26
Kid, The (1921), 116, 120 (*illus.*), 121
Kid Auto Races at Venice (1914), 118 (*illus.*), 119, 264
King in New York, A (1957), 122
King Kong (1933), 161
King of Jazz (1930), 220
King of Kings, The (1927), 133
Kiss (1963), 245, 276
Kiss, The (1896), 36, 51 (*illus.*)
Kiss Me, Deadly (1955), 207
Kleptomaniac, The (1905), 45, 62, 263

Lady from Shanghai, The (1948), 170 (*illus.*)
Lady Vanishes, The (1938), 139
Language of Love, 203
Last Command, The (1928), 152, 260, 267
Last Laugh, The (1924), 144
Last Moment, The (1927), 219 (*illus.*), 220
Laughing Gas (1914), 119
Learning Tree, The (1969), 175

Left Handed Gun, The (1958), 209, 261, 273
Lemon (1916), 235
Letter from an Unknown Woman (1948), 140
Life and Death of a Hollywood Extra, The (1928), 220, 272
Life of an American Fireman, The (1903), 41, 43, 44, 263
Lights of New York (1928), 266
Limelight (1952), 121
Lineup, The (1958), 273
Little Big Man (1970), 45, 249, 250 (*illus.*), 262, 277–278
Little Caesar (1930), 98
Living Desert, The (1953), 153
London after Midnight (1927), 116
Lonedale Operator, The (1911), 62, 65, 263
Lonely Villa, The (1909), 24 (*illus.*), 60, 61–62, 263
Lonesome (1928), 220
Lonesome Cowboys (1969), 245
Long Bodies, The (1947), 276
Looney Tom — The Happy Lover (1951), 235, 273
Lot in Sodom (1934), 221
Louisiana Story (1948), 162, 261, 272
Love Me Tonight (1932), 115, 148, 261, 267
Love Parade, The (1929), 143
Love Story (1970), 70
Lucifer Rising, 236

Mabel's Dramatic Career (1913), 264
Macbeth (1950), 170
McTeague, see *Greed*
Mad Dog (1932), 269
Magnificent Ambersons, The (1942), 166, 169, 261, 271
Male and Female (1919), 133, 260, 265
Maltese Falcon, The (1941), 114, 273
Man and His Dog Out for Air, A (1957), 232, 276
Man with the Golden Arm, The (1955), 197, 198 (*illus.*)
Manhandled (1924), 110 (*illus.*)
Manhatta (1921), 218, 222, 272
Man's Castle, A (1933), 153
Marriage Circle, The (1924), 143
Meditation on Violence (1948), 224

Index of Titles

Meshes of the Afternoon (1943), 224, 272

Millhouse: A White Comedy (1971), 246

Ming Green (1966), 235, 276

Miracle, The (1948), 201, 202 (*illus.*)

Miracle Man, The (1919), 116, 117 (*illus.*)

Mr. Deeds Goes to Town (1936), 153, 261, 270

Mr. Magoo, 157 (*illus.*), 158

Mr. Smith Goes to Washington (1939), 115

Moana of the South Seas (1926), 162

Modern Times (1936), 121, 261, 270

Monsieur Verdoux (1947), 121

Monte Carlo (1930), 143

Moon Is Blue, The (1953), 197

Moon 69 (1969), 235, 276

Moonbird (1960), 275

Morning Glory (1933), 111

Morocco (1930), 152, 261, 267

Mother and the Law, The (1916), 75, 77 (*illus.*)

Mother's Day (1948), 235

Motion Painting No. 1 (1949), 222, 223 (*illus.*)

Movie, A (1958), 233, 276

Murder (1930), 139

Murphy's Wake (1907), 52

Music Box, The (1932), 126, 268

Music in the Air (1934), 269

Musketeers of Pig Alley, The (1912), 263

Mutt and Jeff (1918), 269

My Darling Clementine (1946), 135, 261, 272

My Friend Irma (1949), 126

Mystery of the Leaping Fish, The (1916), 108, 260, 265

Naked City, The (1948), 273

Naked Spur, The (1953), 208

Nanook of the North (1922), 159 (*illus.*), 160–161, 260, 265

National Velvet (1944), 116

Navigator, The (1924), 123

Neptune's Daughter (1914 and 1949), 111

Never Give a Sucker an Even Break (1941), 125

New York Hat, The (1912), 106, 263, 264

Newman's Laugh-O-Gram (1920), 269

Night at the Opera, A (1935), 127, 261, 269

Ninotchka (1939), 109, 142 (*illus.*), 143, 261, 271

No Way Out (1950), 175 (*illus.*)

North by Northwest (1959), 114, 139–140, 261, 274

North West Mounted Police (1940), 134, 261, 271

Northwest Passage (1940), 115

Now, Voyager (1942), 261, 271

Nuptiae (1969), 236

N.Y., N.Y. (1957), 218 (*illus.*), 274

O (1967), 219

Off/On (1967), 235, 276

Old Wives for New (1918), 133

On the Bowery (1956), 239, 261, 273

On the Waterfront (1954), 198, 208 (*illus.*), 261, 273

One A.M. (1917), 120

One Hundred Men and a Girl (1937), 116

One Week (1920), 123, 260, 266

Only Angels Have Wings (1939), 114

Optical Poem (1938), 222

Origins of the Motion Picture, The (1955), 263

Orphans of the Storm (1922), 79, 110

Othello (1955), 170

Our Daily Bread (1934), 150, 261, 269

Our Lady of the Spheres (1918), 232, 276

Outlaw, The (1943), 111

Outlaw and His Wife, The (1917), 141

Palestine of Christ, The (1916), 74 (*illus.*)

Paris Slums, 52

Paths of Glory (1957), 209 (*illus.*), 261, 273

Penalty, The (1920), 118

Perils of Pauline, The (1914), 87

Permutations (1969), 233, 276

Phantom Chariot, The (1920), 141

Phantom of the Opera, The (1925), 117 (*illus.*), 118

Pianissimo (1963), 276

285

Index of Titles

Pickup on South Street (1953), 207, 261, 273
Pigeon Lady (1968), 219
Pinky (1949), 174
Pinocchio (1939), 156
Pippa Passes, 264
Place in the Sun, A (1951), 198, 208
Plainsman, The (1937), 134
Playhouse, The (1921), 124, 260, 265
Plow That Broke the Plains, The (1936), 261, 270
Point of Order (1963), 246
Pollyanna (1920), 106
Poor Little Rich Girl, A (1917), 106
Postman Always Rings Twice, The (1946), 111
Prelude: Dog Star Man (1961), 276
Prelude to War (1943), 261, 271–272
President Vanishes, The (1934), 153
Pride of the Clan, The (1917), 140
Primary (1960), 240–241, 261, 274
Psycho (1960), 139
Public Enemy, The (1931), 98, 153, 261, 267, 273
Pumpkin Race, The (1907), 38, 269

Quaint Holland, 52
Queen Christina (1933), 109
Queen Elizabeth (1912), 66
Queen Kelly (1928), 166
Quiet One, The (1948), 238 (*illus.*), 261, 272
Quixote (1964–1965), 232
Quo Vadis? (1912), 66

Ragtime Bear (1949), 275
Ramona (1910), 55–56
Ray Gun Virus (1966), 233
Reap the Wild Wind (1942), 115
Rear Window (1954), 115, 139 (*illus.*), 261, 273
Rebel without a Cause (1955), 198, 200 (*illus.*)
Red Badge of Courage, The (1951), 130, 256
Red River (1948), 115, 137, 261, 272
Re-Entry (1964), 233
Relativity (1966), 226
Report (1965), 233
Rescued from an Eagle's Nest (1907), 46, 53, 263
Rio Bravo (1959), 137, 138 (*illus.*), 261, 274

Rio Lobo (1970), 138
Rio Rita (1929), 269
Ritual in Transfigured Time (1946), 224
River's Edge (1957), 153
Road Runner, see *Beep Beep*
Robe, The (1953), 187
Robin Hood (1922), 108, 153
Roman Scandals (1933), 125
Rosita (1923), 142
Royal Wedding (1951), 116

Saboteur (1942), 140, 261, 271
Safety Last! (1923), 124 (*illus.*)
Saint Bartholomew's Massacre of the Huguenots in France, 1572, The (1916), 74 (*illus.*)
St. Louis Blues (1928), 260, 266
Salvation Hunters, The (1925), 152
Samadhi (1967), 233, 276
Sands of Iwo Jima (1949), 115
Sausalito (1948), 219, 274
Scar of Shame, The (1927), 172
Scarface (1932), 98
Scarlet Empress, The (1934), 152
Scarlet Letter, The (1927), 141
Scent of Mystery (1959), 188
Science Friction (1959), 232
Scorpio Rising (1963), 236, 276
Sea Waves (1896), 26
Secrets (1933), 106
Serene Velocity (1970), 274
Sergeant York (1941), 113
Set-up, The (1949), 167
Seven Chances (1925), 123
Seven Men from Now (1956), 208
Seventh Heaven (1927), 153, 260, 266
70 (1970), 232
Sex Life of the Polyp, The (1928), 266
Shadows (1960), 244 (*illus.*), 261, 274
Shaft (1971), 175
Shall We Dance (1937), 116
Shane (1953), 115, 208
Shanghai Express (1932), 152
Shaw Talks for Movietone News (1927), 266
She Done Him Wrong (1933), 111
She Wore a Yellow Ribbon (1949), 135
Sheik, The (1921), 112, 113 (*illus.*)

286

Index of Titles

Sherlock, Jr. (1924), 123, 260, 265
Shootin' Mad (1918), 264
Shoulder Arms (1918), 120
Sign of the Cross, The (1932), 133, 134 (*illus.*), 261, 267
Silly Symphonies, 155
Singin' in the Rain (1952), 207, 261, 273
69 (1969), 232
66 (1966), 232
Sky High (1922), 264
Sky Pilot (1921), 150
Slavery Days, 71
Sleep (1963), 245
Slippery Jim (1905), 38
Smiling Lieutenant, The (1931), 143
Snow White and the Seven Dwarfs (1937), 155 (*illus.*), 261, 271
So This Is Paris (1926), 143, 260, 266
Soldier Blue (1970), 45
Some Like It Hot (1959), 209
Sound of Music, The (1965), 70, 167
Southerner, The (1945), 140, 261, 272
Spellbound (1945), 115
Spyin' the Spy (1917?), 171
Squaw Man, The (1913), 134
Stage Struck (1925), 110
Stagecoach (1939), 135
Steamboat 'Round the Bend (1935), 135
Steamboat Willie (1928), 154 (*illus.*), 266, 269
Stella Maris (1918), 106
Story of a Three-Day Pass, The (1968), 176
Strangers in a Train (1951), 139
Street Scenes (1970), 243
Strong Man, The (1926), 125, 260, 266
Struggle, The (1931), 79
Study in Choreography for Camera, A (1945), 224, 225 (*illus.*), 274
Sullivan's Travels (1942), 150, 261, 271
Sun Valley Serenade (1941), 111
Sunrise (1927), 143 (*illus.*), 144 (*illus.*), 145, 260, 267
Sunset Boulevard (1950), 166, 210 (*illus.*), 211, 261, 272
Superman (1948), 87
Surf and Seaweed (1931), 222
Surf Girl, The (1916), 264

Sweet Sweetback's Baadasssss Song, 176

Taking of Luke McVane, The (1915), 264
Teddy at the Throttle (1917), 264
Tempest, The, see *Forbidden Planet*
Ten Commandments, The (1923 and 1956), 133
Tess of the Storm Country (1914 and 1922), 106
They Died with Their Boots On (1941), 153
Thief of Bagdad, The (1924), 108 (*illus.*), 153, 260, 266
39 Steps, The (1935), 139
This Is Cinerama (1952), 185
This Island Earth (1955), 207
Thread of Destiny, The (1910), 59-60
Three Caballeros, The (1944), 157
Three Musketeers, The (1920), 108
Tillie's Punctured Romance (1914), 119
Titicut Follies (1967), 242
To Be or Not to Be (1942), 143
Tol'able David (1921), 153, 260, 265
Tom, Tom the Piper's Son (1905 and 1969), 234, 262, 277
Touch of Evil (1958), 170
Tramp, The (1915), 119 (*illus.*), 264
Trash (1970), 245
Treasure of the Sierra Madre (1938), 115
Trilby (1915), 140
Trip to the Moon, A (1902), 38
Trouble in Paradise (1932), 143
Trouble with Harry, The (1956), 139
Troublemakers (1966), 242, 262, 274
20th Century (1934), 138
Twenty-Four-Dollar Island (1925), 219
Two Rode Together (1961), 135
Two Tars (1928), 126, 267
2001: A Space Odyssey (1968), 208, 262, 276

Uncle Tom's Cabin (1903), 40 (*illus.*), 263
Underworld (1927), 152, 260, 267, 273
Unicorn in the Garden (1953), 275
Union Pacific (1939), 134
Unknown, The (1927), 118

287

Index of Titles

Up in Arms (1944), 125
Uptight (1969), 136

Vanishing Prairie, The (1954), 158
Venice—Showing Gondolas (1896), 26
Violinist, The (1960), 276
Virginian, The (1914 and 1929), 113, 115 (*illus.*), 134

Walden, 231
Watermelon Man (1970), 176 (*illus.*), 262, 278
Watersmith (1969), 235
Wavelength (1967), 234
Way Down East (1920), 79
Wee Willie Winkie (1937), 116
What Happened to Mary (1912), 87
What Price Glory (1926), 153
When the Clouds Roll By (1919), 108

White Rose, The (1923), 56 (*illus.*)
Whoopee! (1930), 125, 249
Wild and Woolly (1917), 260, 265
Wild Strawberries (1957), 142
Wind, The (1928), 141, 260, 267
Wishing Ring, The (1914), 140
Wizard of Oz, The (1939), 116
Wonders of Canada, 52
Wrath of the Gods, The (1914), 180
Wreck of the New York Subways (1970), 242, 262, 277

You Only Live Once (1937), 114, 144, 261, 271
Young Mr. Lincoln (1939), 135
Your Astronaut (1970), 219

Zaza (1923), 110
Zorn's Lemma (1970), 235, 236 (*illus.*), 262, 278

General Index

Abbott, Bud, 128
"absolute" films, 215
abstract films, 215, 222–223, 233–234, 249
Academy Award, 93, 112, 222, 268
actors and acting, 20, 54–55, 88, 95–96, 106–128; under Griffith, 57–58; child, 116; comic, 118–128; black, 173–175, 266
advertising films, 41, 269
afterimage, 4
Agee, James, 238
Aldrich, Robert, 207
amateur films, 215
American Film Institute Collection, 171, 191
American Mutascope and Biograph Company, 26, 263; see also Biograph, Mutascope
American Telephone and Telegraph Company, 104
Anderson, Gilbert M. (Max Aronson), 84; see also Broncho Billy
Anger, Kenneth, 236
animated films, 38, 46, 153–158, 223, 233, 260, 261, 268–269, 275–276
Anthology Film archives, 229
Antonio, Emile de, 246
Aristotle, 3, 22
Armat, Thomas, 25–26
Arnold, Jack, 207
Arnold, John, 142
AromaRama, 188
Aronson, Max, 84
art, film as an, 67, 82
Art in Film Series, 226
artists, film, 216–218, 222, 224, 227
Arvidson, Linda (Mrs. D. W. Griffith), 254
Astaire, Fred, 116, 269
athletes, women, 111
audiences, 26, 31, 32–33, 45, 193, 237

auteur theory, 132, 151
avant-garde films, 213–214, 215, 216, 218, 219–220, 223, 225, 229, 256; Griffith and, 79; first American sound, 221; kinds of, 232–237; programs of, 260, 261, 272–273, 274, 276
Ayres, Agnes, 113 (illus.)

Bacon, Lloyd, 269
Badger, Clarence, 265
Bagley, Richard, 239
Baillie, Bruce, 219, 232
Balshofer, Fred J., 257
Bancroft, George, 267
Bara, Theda, 111
Barry, Iris, 255
Bartlett, Scott, 235
base, 8, 13, 14, 15, 180
Bathing Beauties, 61, 110
Beatty, Talley, 224
Beavers, Louise, 174
Belson, Jordan, 233
Benchley, Robert, 266
Benny, Jack, 143
Bergman, Ingmar, 142
Bergman, Ingrid, 111–112
Bergsten, Bebe, 257
Berkeley, Busby, 269
Bernhardt, Sarah, 66
Biograph, 26, 27, 28, 30, 49, 60, 64, 234; see also Griffith at Biograph
Biograph Girl, the, 88–89
Bitzer, Gottfried Wilhelm ("Billy"), 58, 59 (illus.), 255
Black Maria, 19 (illus.), 20, 26
blacks in films, 171–176, 206, 266
"blind selling," 191
"block booking," 191
Boetticher, Budd, 207–208
Bogart, Humphrey, 114, 115
Borzage, Frank, 153

Bosustow, Stephen, 275
Bowger, Eileen, 255
box-office receipts, 192, 196
Brakhage, Stan, 237
Brando, Marlon, 122, 198, 208 (*illus.*)
Breer, Robert, 232
Britain, 26, 162, 272
Broncho Billy, 84 (*illus.*), 85, 106, 264
Broughton, James, 235–236
Burstyn, Joseph, 202
Bute, Mary Ellen, 223

Cagney, James, 267
California, 29–30, 219
Cambridge, Godfrey, 175 (*illus.*)
camera: "atomic," 8; early types of, 13, 14, 19–20; mobilized, 57, 62–63; battle, 179–180; portable, 241–242; EVR, 251; *see also* lens, sound camera
camera obscura, 8, 10 (*illus.*), 22
camera techniques, 246, 269; Griffith's, 55–56; dolly, 62; tracking or trucking, 62, 63 (*illus.*); tilting or panning, 63; Welles's 169
"candid" films, 200
Cantor, Eddie, 125
Canyon Cinema, 228
Capra, Frank, 153, 270, 271
Carradine, John, 137 (*illus.*)
cartoons, 38; sound, 154, 155; UPA, 158; characters in, 268–269, 275; *see also* animated films
Casler, Herman, 26
Cassavetes, John, 244–245
cassettes or cartridges, 237
censorship, 47, 51–53, 99–101, 177–179, 197, 201–205, 213, 227; and *The Birth of a Nation*, 72–73; by the Catholic Church, 98–99, 201–202; and foreign films, 200–201; for children, 204
Chandler, Raymond, 138
Chaney, Lon, 116, 117 (*illus.*), 118, 141
Chaplin, Charlie, 61, 92, 107, 118–122, 118 (*illus.*), 119 (*illus.*), 120 (*illus.*), 126, 260, 264–265, 270
Chevalier, Maurice, 148
Chicago, 29, 51, 52, 219
children in films, 116

Chrétien, Henri, 187
cinema, 9, 23, 30, 34, 71; artists', 217, 226; "floating," 228–229; "Invisible," 229
Cinema 16 Film Society, 226
cinéma vérité, 240, 243–246, 274
CinemaScope, 187, 274
Cinématographe, 23, 26, 32
Cinéorama, 183
Cinerama, 185–186, 188
circus and parades, 219
Clarke, Shirley, 226, 241
close-ups, 44 (*illus.*), 56, 57, 62
Coconuts, The, 127
Cohl, Emile, 269
Cohn, Harry, 94
Colbert, Claudette, 114 (*illus.*), 134 (*illus.*)
collage films, 233
Columbia Pictures, 94, 189, 192, 194
comedy, 60–61, 118–128, 138, 143, 150; Golden Age of, 118; effect of sound on, 125; programs, 264–265
computer films, 215, 233
"concrete" films, 215
Conner, Bruce, 233
contracts, 95–96, 194–195
Coogan, Jackie, 116, 120 (*illus.*), 121
Cooper, Gary, 113, 115 (*illus.*)
Cooper, Merian C., 161
copyright, 47–48, 64
Costello, Lou, 128
Cotten, Joseph, 168
court decisions, 48, 192, 193, 203; *see also* United States Supreme Court
Crane, Stephen, 256
Crockwell, Douglass, 276
Crosland, Alan, 266
cross-cutting, 62, 75
Cruze, James, 85
Cukor, George, 153
Curtis, Tony, 209
czars, 81, 82, 90, 93–94, 96, 104–105

Daguerre, Louis Jacques Mandé, 7–8
dance films, 224–226, 269, 274
"Dance of the Hours" (Ponchielli), 156 (*illus.*)
dancers, 115–116, 224, 269
Darwell, Jane, 137 (*illus.*)
Dassin, Jules, 136
D'Avino, Carmen, 276
Davis, Bette, 111, 271

General Index

Dean, James, 198, 200 (*illus.*)
de Forest, Lee, 104, 266
DeMille, Cecil B., 133–135, 210
depth, illusion of, 185, 186–187
Deren, Maya, 224–225
diaries, film, 231–232
Dickson, William Kennedy Laurie, 14–15, 18, 21, 22, 25, 26
Dietrich, Marlene, 111, 151 (*illus.*), 170
directors, 129–130, 131–132, 140–141, 175–176, 256
Disney, Walt, 100, 153–158, 222, 269
distributors, 90–91, 92, 195, 197, 227–228, 229, 279–280
Dixon, Thomas, Jr., 67, 70
documentary films, 137, 158–159, 240, 243–246, 273
Donen, Stanley, 116, 207
double exposure, 40 (*illus.*)
double features, 86
Douglas, Melvyn, 143
Dracula, 116
Dreiser, Theodore, 208
Durbin, Deanna, 116
Dwan, Allan, 110, 153

earphones, 15
Eastman, George, 13–14, 191
Ebony Players, 171
"Edison, Mr. Thomas, Jr.," *see* Porter, Edwin S.
Edison, Thomas Alva, 14, 15, 17 (*illus.*), 25–26, 48, 49, 91, 185, 254; and the Kinetoscope, 18–20, 28; fighting his competitors, 27–28
Edison studio, 37 (*illus.*)
editing, 41, 43, 45, 62, 130
effects, special, 37–38, 40, 83, 169
Electronic Video Recording (EVR), 251, 252 (*illus.*)
Emerson, John, 265
Emshwiller, Ed, 226
emulsion, 8, 9
England, *see* Britain
Epoch Film Company, 70
Essanay, 119, 264–265
Europe, 140–141, 198–201; *see also* names of countries
"exact" films, 235
exchanges, 90–91; *see also* distributors

exhibitors, 33–34, 90–91, 192, 196, 228–229
experimental films, 214–215

Fairbanks, Douglas, Sr., 92, 107, 108 (*illus.*), 112, 265
Faulkner, William, 138
Federal Council of Churches of Christ, 141
Federal Theatre Project, 166
Fejos, Paul, 219–220
Fields, W. C., 125
film (material): early, 3, 9, 13–16, 23, 24 (*illus.*); materials used for, 13–14, 31 (*illus.*), 32; projection of, 22–23, 25–26 (*see also* projectors); combustibility of, 32; length of, 36; widths of, 179–180, 186, 188, 237, 238, 244, 248, 258, 279–280; 3–D, 186–187; to be used on a personal basis, 249–251
Film Culture, 226–227, 228, 229
Film Forum, 229
"film truth," 240
filmmakers and filmmaking, 37, 79, 132, 192, 217, 224, 253; *see also* producers, independent filmmakers
Film-Makers' Cinematheque, 229, 230
Film-Makers' Cooperative, 227–228, 229
films (motion picture productions): early, 26, 27, 33–37; length of, 36, 41, 64–65, 193; social aspect of, 45, 67, 200, 201, 238–239, 270; as an art, 67, 82, 224; as an industry, 82, 216; style in, 128–129; blacks in, 171–176; a "spectacle," 201, 218; *see also* motion pictures
Fischinger, Oskar, 222
Flaherty, Robert J., 159–163, 219, 240
Fleming, Victor, 147
Florey, Robert, 220
Fonda, Henry, 114, 137 (*illus.*)
Fonda, Peter, 277 (*illus.*)
Ford, John, 135–137, 140
foreign films, 65, 198–203
Forman, Henry J., 98
Foster, Lewis, 268
Fox, William, 92–93, 94, 102
Fox-Case Movietone, 104
Fox Film Corporation, 92, 102
Fox Studio, 102, 103, 104
Foy, Bryan, 266

General Index

frames, 15, 23, 24 (*illus.*), 78 (*illus.*), 185, 188
Frampton, Hollis, 235
France, 23, 32, 37, 38, 81, 132, 175–176, 183, 209, 213–214
Frankenstein, 116
freedom of speech and the press, 201, 202–203
Freeland, Thornton, 269
Fruchter, Norman, 242
Fuller, Samuel, 207

Gable, Clark, 113, 114 (*illus.*)
gangster films, 98, 152, 207, 273
Garbo, Greta (Gustafsson), 109 (*illus.*), 140 (*illus.*), 143
Garland, Judy, 116
Gehr, Ernie, 233, 274
Germany, 81, 144, 154, 180, 272
Gilbert, John, 112–113
Gish, Dorothy, 59 (*illus.*)
Gish, Lillian, 59 (*illus.*), 72 (*illus.*), 109–110, 141, 263
Gleason, Jackie, 274, 275 (*illus.*)
Goldmark, Peter, 251
Grable, Betty, 111
Grant, Cary, 114
Greenberg, Joel, 255
Greenwich Village, 212, 228–229
Griffith, D. W., 46–47, 53–80, 56 (*illus.*), 59 (*illus.*); "Lawrence," 53; early years, 53–54; at Biograph, 53, 55, 57, 63, 65–67, 89, 254–255, 260, 263–264; camera techniques, 55–57, 62–63; film acting under, 57–58; experiments in lighting, 58–59; and Mary Pickford, 60, 106; and length of films, 64–65; and film as an art, 67, 82; and *The Birth of a Nation*, 67–73, 218; and *Intolerance*, 67, 73–79, 183, 218; and Epoch Film Company, 70; use of thematic approach, 75; death of, 79; his objective, 80; and Triangle Productions, 86; and United Artists, 92, 107; America's first film artist, 217, 218
Griffith, Raymond, 125, 265
grotesque roles, 116
guerrilla screenings, 215, 228
Gulf and Western Corporation, 197

Hale, George C., 27

Hardy, Oliver, 126 (*illus.*), 260, 267
Harlow, Jean, 111
Harris, John P., 34–36
Hart, William S., 84, 85, 264
Harvard University, 73
Hawks, Howard, 135, 137–138, 140
Hawthorne, Nathaniel, 141
Hays, Will (Office), 97–98, 99
Hayworth, Rita, 111, 170 (*illus.*)
Hearst, William Randolph, 167
Hemingway, Ernest, 129
Henie, Sonja, 111
Hepburn, Katharine, 111
Hermann, Bernard, 167
Heston, Charlton, 170
Higham, Charles, 255
Hindle, Will, 234–235
Hitchcock, Alfred, 138–140, 187
Hitler, Adolf, 154, 224
Hoffman, Dustin, 250 (*illus.*)
Hollywood, 29, 96–98
home movies, 215, 248
Hope, Bob, 125–126
Hopper, Dennis, 232, 277 (*illus.*)
Horne, J. Wesley, 267
Horne, Lena, 173
House Committee on Un-Amercian Activities, 178
Hubley, John, 275
Humphrey, Hubert, 241
Huston, John, 130, 256

IMP production company, 91
improvisations, film, 244–245
Ince, Thomas A., 82–87, 128, 180
Inceville, 82–85
independent filmmakers and filmmaking, 192, 214, 217, 218–247, 256; *see also* filmmakers
independent producers, 28–29, 49–50, 65, 66, 195, 214; *see also* producers
India, 196
industry, film as an, 82
International Film Guide Series, 255
"Invisible Cinema," 229
Irwin, May, 51 (*illus.*)
Italy, 45, 65, 154, 201–202
Iwerks, Ub, 157

Jacobs, Ken, 234
Jacobs, Lewis, 255
Jagger, Mick, 236
Japan, 154

Jeffrey, Herbert, 173
Jenkins, C. Francis, 25
Johnson, Arthur, 58
Johnson, Noble, 171
Jolson, Al, 103
Jones, Chuck, 275
Jordan, Larry, 232–233

Kalem production company, 47–48, 49
Karloff, Boris, 116
Kaufman, George S., 128
Kaye, Danny, 125
Kaye, Stanton, 237–238
Kazan, Elia, 174, 208
Keaton, Buster, 122–125, 122 (*illus.*), 210, 265, 266
Keeler, Ruby, 115, 269
Kellerman, Annette, 111
Kelly, Grace, 139 (*illus.*)
Kennedy, John F., 233, 241
Keystone Cops, 60, 61 (*illus.*)
Keystone studio, 60–61, 119, 257, 264
Kinematoscope, 9
Kinescope, 246
Kinetoscope, 15, 16 (*illus.*), 18–22, 25, 28, 48, 185, 246
Kinetoscope parlors, 15, 20 (*illus.*), 22, 27, 30, 33, 44, 93
King, Henry, 153
Kircher, Athanasius, 22
Kodak snapshot camera, 14
Koster & Bial's Music Hall, 26
Kreuger, Miles, 257
Kubrick, Stanley, 208
Ku Klux Klan, 171

Ladd, Alan, 114, 208
Laemmle, Carl, 88–89, 91, 92, 163
Landow, George, 234
Lang, Fritz, 143–144
Langdon, Harry, 125
Laurel, Stan, 126 (*illus.*), 260, 267
Laurents, Arthur, 174
Lawrence, Florence, 88 (*illus.*), 89, 106
Leacock, Richard, 240
learning techniques, motion pictures for, 249
Legion of Decency, 99, 201
Lemmon, Jack, 209
Lenin, Nikolai, 75
lens, anamorphic, 187, 188
Lerner, Carl, 239

LeRoy, Mervyn, 269
Levitt, Helen, 238
Lewis, Jerry, 126, 195
Liberty Theatre, 70
Library of Congress, 171, 191
lighting, experiments in, 59
Lincoln Motion Picture Company, 171
Liszt, Franz, 222
Living Theatre, 230
Lloyd, Harold, 124 (*illus.*), 125, 265
"location" shooting, 29, 196, 241
Loeb, Janice, 238
Loew, Marcus, 92
loop, 234
Loren, Sophia, 122
Lorentz, Pare, 270
Los Angeles, 29–30, 194
"love goddess," 111
Lubitsch, Ernst, 142–143
Lugosi, Bela, 116
Lumière, Auguste and Louis, 23

McCarthy, Joseph, 178, 246
McCay, Winsor ("Little Nemo"), 268–269
McClellan, George, 50–51
McDaniel, Hattie, 174
MacDonald, Jeanette, 115
Macgowan, Kenneth, 254
Machover, Robert, 242
McQueen, Butterfly, 174
Magic Lantern, 22
Magnani, Anna, 202 (*illus.*)
Magnascope, 183
Magoo cartoons, 275
Maltin, Leonard, 257
Mamoulian, Rouben, 147, 148
Mankiewicz, Herman J., 167, 168
Mankiewicz, Joseph, 175
Mann, Anthony, 207
"Mannahatta" (Whitman), 218
March, Fredric, 134 (*illus.*)
Marey, E. J., 13
Markopoulos, Gregory, 235
Marsh, Mae, 56 (*illus.*), 74 (*illus.*)
Martin, Dean, 126
Marvin, Arthur, 58
Marx Brothers, 127–128
May, Joe, 269
Mayer, Louis B., 94
Maysles, Al, 240
Maysles, David, 240
Mekas, Adolfas, 231

Mekas, Jonas, 229–231, 230 (*illus.*), 276
Méliès, Georges, 37, 39 (*illus.*), 46, 49, 64, 157
Mercury Players, The, 166
Metro-Goldwyn-Mayer (MGM), 92, 94, 106, 142, 163, 192, 194, 222
Metro Studio, 92
Meyers, Sidney, 238
Mickey Mouse, 153–155, 154 (*illus.*), 156, 269
microphone, 145, 147
Milennium Film Workshop, 229
Milestone, Lewis, 153
Miller, Arthur C., 257
Minelli, Vincente, 207
Mischeaux, Oscar, 171
Mix, Tom, 85, 264
Mogubgub, Fred, 276
Mohr, Hal, 220
Monogram studio, 192
monopolies, 91, 93, 191, 197
Monroe, Marilyn, 198, 199 (*illus.*), 209
mood, 58, 234–235
Moore, Annabelle, 20
Moorehead, Agnes, 168
Morrissey, Paul, 245
Moscow, film archive in, 219
Motion Picture Association of America (MPAA), 97, 99–100
Motion Picture Patents Company, 48–50, 53, 64–65, 88, 89, 91, 92–93, 257
Motion Picture Producers and Distributors Association (M.P.P.D.A.), 97
Motion Picture Story Magazine, 89
motion pictures, 3–7, 9–13, 15, 233, 249, 251, 253; first commercial screening of, 23
Movietone, 104, 266
Murnau, F. W., 144
Murphy, Dudley, 174, 266
Muse, Clarence, 173 (*illus.*), 174
Museum of Modern Art, 191, 226, 229, 255
music, film, 131–132
Music Corporation of America (MCA), 197
musicals, 143, 173, 207, 261, 269
Mutascope, 21 (*illus.*), 22, 26
Mutual Film Corporation, 120, 265

Muybridge, Eadweard (Edward James Muggeridge), 12 (*illus.*), 13

National Association of Colored People, 73
National Association of Theatre Owners (NATO), 204
National Board of Censorship, 253
National Board of Review, 53, 97
National Catholic Office for Motion Pictures, 99
National Legion of Decency, 99, 201
Nelson, Ricky, 138 (*illus.*)
New American Cinema Group, 227, 229, 246
New York City, 28, 192, 196, 218, 219, 226
New York State censorship board, 53, 213
New York *Times,* 276
New York University, 243
Newman, Joseph, 207
Newman, Paul, 274, 275 (*illus.*)
Newsreel, 242
newsreels, 160, 193
Nicholas II of Russia, 81
Nicholson, Jack, 277 (*illus.*)
Nickelette, 34
Nickelodeon, 34 (*illus.*), 35 (*illus.*), 36, 44, 45, 49, 50, 90, 92, 93, 101
Niepce, Joseph Nicéphore, 7
Nixon, Richard, 246
Norris, Frank, 164

Oboler, Arch, 186, 206
O'Brien, George, 144 (*illus.*)
Olympics, original, 4
O'Neill, Eugene, 174
Ophuls, Max, 140
Ott, Fred, 20

"package," 195
Pal, George, 205–206
Palazzolo, Tom, 219
parallel editing, 41, 43, 45
parallel shots, 61–62
Paramount Pictures, 92, 135, 152, 161, 192, 197
Paris, 32, 183; *see also* France
Parks, Gordon, 175
Parrott, James, 267, 268
Patents Company, *see* Motion Picture Patents Company
Paul, Robert, 26

General Index

Peck, Gregory, 115
peep shows, 15, 22, 27, 31, 263
Penn, Arthur, 208, 209, 249
Pennebaker, Don, 240
Perelman, S. J., 128
peripheral vision, 183, 185
personal films, 132, 214, 217, 224, 233, 237, 240, 246–247
Philadelphia Symphony Orchestra, 156
Phonofilm, 104, 266
Phonograph, 14
"photogenic drawings," 8
Photophone, RCA, 104
Photoplay Magazine, 89
Pichel, Irving, 205
Pickford, Mary (Gladys Smith), 60, 92, 106–109, 107 (*illus.*), 263
Picture (Ross), 256
Pintoff, Ernest, 275
Pitts, ZaSu, 164 (*illus.*)
Poe, Edgar Allan, 221
poems, film, 56–57, 173, 233, 237
Poitier, Sidney, 175 (*illus.*)
political films, 242–243
Porter, Edwin S. ("Mr. Thomas Edison, Jr."), 40 (*illus.*), 41, 44–46, 156, 263
Powdermaker, Hortense, 256
Powell, Dick, 269
Preminger, Otto, 197
previews, "sneak," 130
Prickett, James R., 257
producers, 28, 47, 91, 129; *see also* filmmakers, independent producers
Production Code, 99–101, 177, 197, 200
projectors, 11 (*illus.*), 15–16, 22–23, 25–26, 30, 92
propaganda, 178–179, 199, 271–272
publicity stunts, 89

Quigley, Martin, Jr., 263

Radio City Music Hall, 101, 102 (*illus.*)
Radio-Keith-Orpheum (RKO), 192
Ramsaye, Terry, 254
Rapper, Irving, 271
RCA Photophone, 104
reel, 36, 186
Reid, Wallace, 97
religious films, 59, 65–66, 133
Renan, Sheldon, 256

Renoir, Jean, 140
Republic studio, 192
revolver, photographic, 13
Reynolds, Lynn, 264
Rice, John C., 51 (*illus.*)
"Rite of Spring" (Stravinsky), 156
Roach, Hal, 126, 265, 267
Robeson, Paul, 174
Robson, Mark, 167
Rockefeller Center, 102
Rogers, Ginger, 116, 269
Rogosin, Lionel, 239
Rolling Stones, 240
Roosevelt, Franklin D., 270
Rosher, Charles, 144
Ross, Lillian, 256
Rossellini, Robert, 201
Rossen, Robert, 274
Roxy theatre, 101–102, 219
Russell, Jane, 111
Russia, 219

Sack Amusements, 266
Saint, Eva Marie, 208 (*illus.*)
St. Louis Exposition, 27
San Francisco, 30, 226
San Gabriel Mission, 59–60
Sarris, Andrew, 256
Sbarge, Stephen, 243
Scandinavia, 248
scenarios, 84
scenes, 43
Schoedsack, Ernest, 161
Schwartz, Michael, 256
science fiction films, 205–207, 226
Scott, George C., 274
screen, shape of, 183, 185, 186, 187, 188–189
Screen Gems, 189
screenwriters, 131
scripts, shooting, 69–70, 84
Seastrom (Sjöström), Victor, 140–142
Selig, William N. (Colonel), 29
Selig studio, 49
Sellers, Coleman, 9
Selznick, Lewis J., 81, 152
Sennett, Mack, 60, 61 (*illus.*), 86, 260, 264
serials, 87
Shakespeare, William, 129, 170, 207
Sharits, Paul, 233
Shaw, George Bernard, 266

Sheeler, Charles, 218
Shell Oil Company, 162
shots, 36, 43, 57, 58, 61–62, 63 (*illus.*)
Siegel, Don, 207
silent film programs, 258–259
Simon, S. Sylvan, 269
Sinatra, Frank, 195, 198 (*illus.*)
singer/comediennes, 115
singer/dancers, 116
Sloane, Everett, 168
Sloane, Paul, 174
Smell-O-Vision, 188
Smith, Bessie, 266
Snow, Michael, 234
social aspect of films, 45, 67, 200, 201, 238–239, 270
"Sorcerer's Apprentice" (Dukas), 156
sound, 79, 96, 103–105, 139, 145–148, 168, 180, 188; and comedy, 125; and animated films, 154, 222
sound camera, 145–148, 147 (*illus.*)
sound films, 103–104, 260, 266; first American avant-garde, 221
sound track, 146 (*illus.*), 147, 149
speed of films, 38–40
spool, 36
stage plays, 36, 43, 66
Stalin, Joseph, 178
Stanford, Leland, 9, 12
star system, 54, 60, 88, 96, 118, 198; and TV, 182, 189
Stauffacher, Frank, 219, 226
Steinbeck, John, 136
Steiner, Ralph, 221, 270
stereophonic sound, 188
stereoscopic vision, 186
Sternberg, Josef von, 151–152
Stevens, George, 208
Stewart, James, 115, 139 (*illus.*)
Stiller, Mauritz, 109
stills, production, 42 (*illus.*)
Stokowski, Leopold, 156
"stop-motion" photography, 38
Strand, Paul, 218
Strand theatre, 101
strikes, 181
Stroheim, Erich von, 163–166, 210
Struss, Karl, 144
studios: early, 19–20, 37 (*illus.*); growth of, 89–92; power of, 93–96; and morality, 96–98; and sound, 96, 103–105; in the '20's and later,

129–132; after World War II, 177–179; and TV, 181–183, 189–191, 193–194; and the courts, 191–192; decline of, 194–197, 256
Sturges, Preston, 150
style, 128–129, 152
Sullivan, Pat, 269
supernatural films, 232
Swanson, Gloria, 110 (*illus.*), 166, 210 (*illus.*), 264, 269
Sweden, 81, 141, 142, 203

Talbot, William Henry Fox, 8
"talkies," 103, 125, 183; *see also* sound film
talking machine, 14, 18
tape recorders, 180
Tarkington, Booth, 169
Taylor, Deems, 156
Taylor, Elizabeth, 116, 198
Technicolor, 148, 198
television, 25, 181, 182–183; films for, 189–191, 197, 239–240, 249–251, 257; commercials on, 246, 276
Temple, Shirley, 116
Tennyson, Alfred, Lord, 56
Thalberg, Irving, 165
Thaumatrope, 5 (*illus.*)
theatres, motion picture: vaudeville, 26, 27, 30, 44; storefront, 33, 34, 36; "palaces," 101; flagship, 102; open-air, 180–181; drive-in, 180–181; and TV, 184 (*illus.*); floating, 228–229; future of, 253
Thompson, Francis, 218
3-D film, 186–187
Thurber, James, 275
Toland, Gregg, 167, 169, 220
Tourneur, Maurice, 140
Tracy, Spencer, 115
Triangle Productions, 86–87
"trick" films, 38–40; *see also* effects
Turner, Lana, 111
Twentieth Century–Fox, 92, 187, 192, 194
Twentieth Century Pictures, 92

"underground" films, 79, 212–213, 215–216, 256
unions, 175
United Artists (UA), 92, 107, 192
United States Supreme Court, 48, 201–203, 218

United States War Department, 271
Universal City, 197
Universal Film Manufacturing Company, 91
Universal-International, 192
Universal MCA, 91
Universal Pictures, 163, 197
UPA, 158, 275

Valentino, Rudolph, 112, 113 (*illus.*)
Vanderbeek, Stan, 232–233
Van Dyke, Willard, 270
Van Peebles, Melvin, 175–176
vaudeville theatres, 26, 27, 30, 44
Verne, Jules, 205
videotape, 189, 251
Vidor, King, 147, 148–150
Village Voice, The, 229, 230
Vinci, Leonardo da, 4, 8, 22
vision, 4, 183, 185, 186
Vitagraph, 30, 89
Vitaphone, 103, 104, 266
Vitascope, 25–26, 30
Vogel, Amos, 226
voice-over, 241
Vorkapich, Slavko, 220

Walker, Billy, 209
Wallace, Lew, 47
Walsh, Raoul, 153
Warhol, Andy, 245
Warner brothers, Jack and Harry, 92, 94
Warner Brothers Pictures, Inc., 103–104, 192, 194, 275
Warwick, Ruth, 168
Watson, James S., 221
Wayne, John, 115, 138 (*illus.*)

Webber, Melville, 221
Welles, Orson, 166–170, 168 (*illus.*), 170 (*illus.*), 187
Wellman, William, 153
Wells, H. G., 166, 205
West, Mae, 111
Western Electric Company, 104
Westerns, 45, 82, 85, 135, 153, 208, 249, 260, 264, 277–278; black, 172 (*illus.*), 173
"Wheel of Life," 5 (*illus.*)
White, Pearl, 87
White Rats (union), 30
Whitman, Walt, 218
Whitney, John, Sr., 233, 276
Widmark, Richard, 175 (*illus.*)
Wilcox, Fred, 207
Wilder, Billy, 210
Williams, Esther, 111
Wilson, Woodrow, 71, 85
Wise, Robert, 167, 206
Wiseman, Frederick, 242–243
Wister, Owen, 115
"woman's film," 271
Wonder Disc, 5 (*illus.*)
"Wonder Wheel," 5
World Fairs, 27, 183, 270
World War I, 75, 81, 85, 171
World War II, 79, 137, 174, 177, 179 (*illus.*), 180, 224
writers, *see* screenwriters
Wyler, William, 47

Young, Robert, 109 (*illus.*)

Zecca, Ferdinand, 37
Zinnemann, Fred, 208
Zoëtrope, 5 (*illus.*)
Zukor, Adolph, 66, 91–92